For any sports fan, QUARTERBACKS HAVE ALL THE FUN is just the ticket to enjoy the breathtaking action, drama and madcap humor of the game.

You'll read great quarterback stories by Dan Jenkins, Peter Gent, George Plimpton and Jimmy Breslin. And you'll get to know Joe Namath, football's ultimate playboy, and Bart Starr, the game's ultimate boy scout; Bobby Layne, who may have sipped whiskey in the huddle, and John Brodie, who may have had psychic experiences in the huddle; Johnny Unitas, who was cheered even by his opponents' fans, and Don Meredith, who was booed off the field into the announcing booth, and then was cheered.

Ranging from the quarterback with a Ph.D. in mathematics to the former asparagus picker, from hitting the seams of a zone to hitting the bars on the road, this book is as absorbing to read as its heroes are exciting to watch.

**WE HOPE YOU
ENJOY THIS BOOK.**

IF YOU'D LIKE A
FREE LIST
OF OTHER PAPERBACKS
AVAILABLE FROM
PLAYBOY PRESS,
JUST SEND
YOUR REQUEST TO
MARILYN ADAMS,
PLAYBOY PRESS,
919 NORTH
MICHIGAN AVENUE,
CHICAGO, ILLINOIS
60611.

THE GOOD LIFE AND HARD TIMES OF BART, JOHNNY, JOE, FRANCIS

AND OTHER GREAT QUARTERBACKS

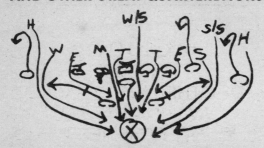

QUARTERBACKS HAVE ALL THE FUN

—WRITTEN AND EDITED BY—
DICK SCHAAP

PLAYBOY PRESS

QUARTERBACKS HAVE ALL THE FUN

Cover photo by Martin Blumenthal/*Sport* magazine.

Published simultaneously in the United States and Canada by Playboy Press, Chicago, Illinois. Printed in the United States of America. Revised edition.

PLAYBOY and Rabbit Head design are trademarks of Playboy, 919 North Michigan Avenue, Chicago, Illinois 60611 (U.S.A.), Reg. U.S. Pat. Off., marca registrada, marque déposée.

This book is available at discounts in quantity lots for industrial or sales-promotional use. For details, write our Special Projects Agency: The Benjamin Company, Inc., 485 Madison Avenue, New York, New York 10022.

Acknowledgments

ACKNOWLEDGMENTS *vi*

DEDICATED TO
MY FAVORITE
QUARTERBACKS
FRAN NAMATH
AND
JOE TARKENTON

I ALWAYS GET THEM MIXED UP

Contents

FOREWORD *Is* *Forearmed*

By Joe Namath

Dick Schaap brings a certain amount of knowledge to an anthology about quarterbacks. After all, he has spent a lot of time with me, and a little of my knowledge must have rubbed off.

Very little.

This puts Schaap even with most experts, who know as much about playing quarterback as I know about performing brain surgery.

Actually, orthopedic surgery is my specialty. The title of this book is perfectly accurate, provided you consider knee operations fun. Based on my own experience with sportswriters, the contents of this book are probably equally accurate. I really enjoy reading sportswriters. I also enjoy being hit by 280-pound defensive linemen. It's a toss-up as to which is more fun.

I suppose that Dick Schaap's reason for putting this book together is the same reason most professional football players play football, and I hope he makes a lot of it. Otherwise, why collect quarterbacks? I have asked that question several times, of police officers in Alabama and Florida, and they have never given me a good answer.

If Schaap has any class, he will give a share of his earnings off this book to the offensive linemen who make quarterbacks possible. (I did not write the preceding sentence. Give me back the typewriter, Winston. Give it back, Mr. Hill. Gently, please.)

If this book does not tell you enough about quarterbacks, I suggest you read *A Matter of Style,* my favorite book. Modesty prevents me from revealing the name of the author.

Modesty also prevents me from telling you the name of my favorite quarterback, but I'm sure that if you go through this book carefully, you'll find plenty of words about him. Some of them will probably even be true.

INTRODUCTION
What Is a Quarterback?

The question of intelligence is one that is often raised with quarterbacks. I raised it myself once with a quarterback named Namath. "Does a quarterback have to be very smart?" I asked.

Joe understood the question immediately. "[Blank] is so dumb," he said, filling in the blank with the name of a prominent and successful National Football League quarterback, "he can't cross the street by himself."

Namath was overstating. He admitted he was overstating shortly after I helped him across Madison Avenue. But Namath was also being serious. His point was that you don't have to be dumb to play quarterback in the NFL, but it probably doesn't hurt, at least not as much as the analytical experts, the ones who hype football as a complex art, would have you think.

As a case in point, I was sitting with Namath one Sunday afternoon watching the Pittsburgh Steelers play the Detroit Lions on television. The quarterback for the Steelers was Terry Bradshaw, who, despite his youth, has earned a reputation as the least cerebral of the current crop of quarterbacks. (Bradshaw is also one of the most successful, if victories and defeats count, which they do in the standings.) Late in the game, with Pittsburgh nursing a narrow lead, Bradshaw called a rather risky pass play.

When Namath saw Bradshaw drop back to pass, Joe almost fell off the couch, he was so stunned by the downright stupidity of the call. Bradshaw's dumb pass went for a touchdown, and Pittsburgh won the game.

The following night, facing the Green Bay Packers, Namath called a reasonably smart game and failed to put a single point on the scoreboard. His team, the New York Jets, lost.

Obviously, this book is not dedicated to the proposition that all quarterbacks are created brilliant. Frank Ryan, who labored for the Cleveland Browns in the 1960s, was probably the most intellectual quarterback ever; he owned a doctorate in mathematics, which means at least that he could do more tricks with Xs and Os than anyone else. But with his splendid I.Q. and a splendid collection of teammates, Ryan never quite soared into superstardom, and except among true fans of advanced algebra, his name will fade long before Terry Bradshaw's. The second smartest quarterback ever was probably Eddie LeBaron, now a lawyer, once a Redskin and a Cowboy. As articulate as he was, LeBaron was never able to persuade his body to grow to more than five-foot-seven.

The truth is that among the attributes essential to a successful quarterback, general intelligence is not paramount. (If it were, Henry Kissinger might have been an All-American, and Richard Nixon would have been too much in awe of him to make him secretary of state, and the whole course of history might have changed.) But football intelligence, an entirely different thing, is important. Important, not infallible.

Namath, who admits he has rarely read a book and who rarely wasted any of his time thinking until, at 30, he took up transcendental meditation, is generally conceded to have a sound football mind. In his finest moment, the 1969 Super Bowl, he did a near-perfect job of reading, decoding and cutting up the Baltimore Colts' defense.

To watch Namath watching football films is to observe the most intense concentration and perception. One night during the 1972 season, I sat in Namath's apartment as he did his homework. His projector faced the living-room wall. One of his hands cradled the switch that could make the projector go, stop or reverse. He flicked on the machine, and the Baltimore defense spread out on the wall.

Namath ran a few plays. Suddenly, he spotted something. He noticed that when the Jets lined up in a certain offensive formation, and the Colts lined up in a certain defensive formation, Baltimore's strong-side linebacker would try to slow down the Jets' tight end. That left John Riggins, the Jets' running back, free to head downfield, catch a quick pass and gain 10 or 15 yards before a Colt defender could get to him.

Namath reran the play half a dozen times to be sure he had seen what he thought he had seen. He studied the first step of each defender. He studied the second step of each defender. He looked for the same pair of formations in other plays, and when he found them, he replayed *them* half a dozen times. Finally, Namath was convinced. He had found something that neither he nor the Jets' coaches had detected in earlier films—a play that would definitely work against the Baltimore defense. Namath expertly diagrammed the play on a piece of scrap paper.

The following day, the day before the game, Namath showed the diagram to Kenny Meyer, the Jets' receiver coach. Meyer, and then Riggins, agreed: The play couldn't miss.

On Sunday, during the first half, Namath spotted the Colts in the vulnerable defensive alignment. Smartly, he called the new play. He told John Schmitt to center the ball "on two." When Namath calls signals, he barks out a series of colors, then a series of numbers. John Schmitt is very intelligent, but he is not perfect. He made a slight mistake. Instead of centering the ball on "two," he centered it on the second color. This maneuver so stunned the rest of the Jets' offensive linemen that they, too, made slight mistakes. They forgot to block. Namath had the ball in his hands and saw several very large Colts charging toward him. He threw the ball ten yards over Riggins's head. He did not call the play again.

The game, however, was not a total loss. With little more than a minute to play and the Colts leading, 20–17, the Jets had the ball on their own 17-yard line. Namath figured out a smart play. He turned to a wide receiver named Eddie Bell. "Eddie Bell," said Namath, "run your ass off."

As the ball was snapped, Eddie Bell took off straight downfield. Namath stepped back, reared back and lofted the ball more than 50 yards in the air. The trouble was that he threw it straight at two Baltimore defenders, Jerry Logan and Charlie Stukes. The ball hit Charlie Stukes in the hand, bounced off Stukes's hand, and fell into the lap of Eddie Bell. Eddie Bell ran to the end zone, and the Jets won, 24–20. Brilliant call.

Several weeks later, Terry Bradshaw threw the most brilliant pass of the year, a bold variation on the Namath-to-Bell play. Bradshaw's pass ricocheted off several hands and maybe a few shoulders and landed in the paws of Franco Harris, who was not Bradshaw's primary, secondary or even tertiary receiver. Harris wisely carried the ball to the end zone for a last-second victory over Oakland in the American Football Conference playoffs.

Which carries us back to the question: What is a quarterback?

During the 1972 NFL season, *Sport* magazine, of which I am editor, decided to take a mini-survey to determine which quarterbacks best personified the individual qualities needed by a successful quarterback. Bobby Layne, Y. A. Tittle, Babe Parilli and Bart Starr, championship quarterbacks all, served as consulting experts. They voted on several categories: best arm, best legs, best physique, best brain, best heart and best leadership. The winners were Sonny Jurgensen (arm), Greg Landry (legs), Roman Gabriel (physique), Johnny Unitas (brain), Bob Berry (heart) and Joe Namath (leadership). Terrific selections: The Super Bowl game that season was played between Bob Griese, who got little mention, and Billy Kilmer, who got none. By the following fall, three of the six winners—Gabriel, Unitas and Berry—had been traded, and only one, Gabriel, played much for his new team; the other three were in varying degrees of agony, from injury or from defeat or, in Namath's case, from both. So much for the expert view of what a quarterback is.

I have my own view, based on observation. The first pro quarterback I ever met was an ex-quarterback named Paul Hornung. He was also an ex-altar boy. By the time I met Hornung, the late Vince Lombardi had converted him to halfback. Lombardi's personal hero, Saint Paul, never made a better conversion. The second quarterback I met was Bart Starr, or "Saint Bart," as his close friends were permitted to call him. If there were any similarities between Hornung and Starr, beyond the fact that both wore uniforms on Sunday, they escaped me.

What a quarterback is, I think, is *different,* different from other pro-football players and different from each other. The difference between quarterbacks and their teammates is apparent to any Internal Revenue agent; the quarterbacks are in the top tax brackets. They are also the most publicized, most praised, most maligned, most loved and most booed of all football players.

Yet despite these common rewards and common hazards, quarterbacks cannot neatly be typed. They can be as short as LeBaron or as tall as Gabriel, as slim as Fran Tarkenton or as paunchy as Jurgensen, as brittle as Namath or as durable as George Blanda. They can enjoy night life as much as Layne did or as little as Griese does. They can be as hirsute as Terry Hanratty or as crew cut as Earl Morrall. Historically, pro quarterbacks have had only one trait in common, the whiteness of their skins, and Pittsburgh's Joe Gilliam is the current hope to change that.

If I have detected one common denominator beyond the shortage of common traits, it is that quarterbacks are *interesting.* Since the culture shock of meeting Hornung and Starr in quick succession, I have spent varying amounts of time with many other present and ex-quarterbacks, including Tarkenton, Namath, Zeke Bratkowski, Unitas, John Hadl, Don Meredith, Griese, Roger Staubach, Norm Snead, Randy Johnson, Jim Finks, Al Woodall, Bob Davis, Layne, Kilmer, a remarkably tall midwestern farm boy who was Minnesota's third-string quarterback in 1973 and, presumably, several others whose names, like the farm boy's, do not spring immediately to mind. All of them, in one way or another, were interesting, with the possible exception of Griese, whose character reflects his play: No visible flaws. Perfection tends to bore and may explain why, in this book, there is no story on Griese.

But there are stories about more than a dozen other past and present quarterbacks, and I hope that the stories, like the men, are both different and interesting. My friend, Jerry Kramer, the former Green Bay All-Pro, assures me that a collection of stories about offensive guards would be even more interesting, and it would certainly be different: It would be a book about nine pages long. Settle for quarterbacks—and settle for some brilliant writing.

The writers represented in this book are a very smart bunch. Some of them earn as much money as a quarterback. They are, like their subjects, different and interesting. The list includes the authors of the two bestselling sports novels in recent years, Dan Jenkins *(Semi-Tough)* and Peter Gent *(North Dallas Forty);* the author of a bestselling nonsports novel, Jimmy Breslin *(World Without End, Amen);* the author of a bestselling political book, Joe McGinniss *(The Selling of the President);* the ghostwriter of a book that turned into a hit movie and television series, W. C. Heinz *(M.A.S.H.);* plus, to name a few, George Plimpton *(Paper Lion),* Leonard Shecter (collaborator with Jim Bouton on *Ball Four*) and the man who collaborated with Jerry Kramer on *Instant Replay* and with Joe Namath on *I Can't Wait Until Tomorrow . . . 'Cause I Get Better Looking Every Day.*

False humility prevents me from naming the last man.

QUARTERBACKS HAVE ALL THE FUN

1 / UNITAS

"Sure It Hurts When I Throw, It Hurts All the Time"

By Larry L. King

John Unitas is the first quarterback in this book for one simple reason: He is the first quarterback in just about everything else. Going into the 1974 season, after 17 years with the Baltimore Colts and one with the San Diego Chargers, Unitas had attempted more passes (5,186), completed more passes (2,830), gained more yards passing (40,239) and thrown for more touchdowns (290) than any other man in the history of pro football. Artistically as well as statistically, Unitas is, almost beyond argument, the greatest quarterback ever. As recently as 1972, when he was 39 years old, he passed for 376 yards in one game against the New York Jets and directed his team's offense so expertly, so efficiently that his rival quarterback, Joe Namath, who himself threw for 496 yards that day, was genuinely more impressed by Unitas's performance than by his own.

"Did you see the way he directed their offense in the last quarter?" Namath said to me after the game. "When they had to score, he was perfect, absolutely perfect. Good passes. Smart passes. He didn't waste any effort or any time. I can't imagine any quarterback playing a better game." Namath had long been a Unitas fan; in high school, Joe wore No. 19, Unitas's number, and one of his nicknames, which delighted him, was "Joey U."

*As a fellow Pennsylvanian, fellow quarterback, fellow Weeb Ew-
bank protégé and fellow survivor of painful injuries, Namath
could appreciate better than anyone Unitas's brilliance that autumn day in 1972.*

*Yet four years earlier, in 1968, when Larry L. King wrote the
following article, Unitas's arm was practically given up for dead.
King, once a reasonably skilled high-school guard in Texas, later
a dreadful quarterback in the U.S. Army Signal Corps, has
profiled with wit and perception men as diverse as Lyndon Johnson and Louis Armstrong, Bill Buckley and Buck Owens. In his
Unitas profile, King captures the twin agonies of pain and aging,
the agonies that, inevitably, attack every quarterback.*

He grunted when he threw the football—a short peg, covering perhaps only a dozen yards, a pass so off-target that the
receiver pulled up short, permitting the ball to tumble to earth,
aimless and heavy as some wounded mallard.

"Uuunnhh!" is the way the sound of the grunt looks on
paper, but to hear it—involuntary, explosive, a sound conceived
in pain and born of a sudden convulsion of ripped muscles—
was to hear sandpaper grating across the brain. Johnny Unitas
bent over, clutching his right arm, his helmeted head tucked
almost between his legs. "Oh, hell!" he said. "God*damn!*"

Unitas's Baltimore teammates inspected their big feet or
monitored the empty sky. Coach Don Shula stared at invisible
objects at some distant point on the practice field. Even the
small herd of reporters had enough decency not to gawk. For,
as everyone knew, Johnny Unitas is not given to emotional
outbursts or to easy surrenders to pain. He has suffered frac-
tured ribs, a broken back, a shattered collarbone, multiple
bruises, bloody lacerations, countless bumps and knocks (the
bridge of his nose is pocked from the times his face guard has
been pushed in or clawing hands got through it), and he has
played uncomplainingly despite his hurts. "He spits ice water,"
they say of him around the N.F.L.—a not ineloquent tribute to

his coolness under pressure. So there was something in Johnny Unitas's moment of agonized failure that reminded one of the night they carried out a paunchy, balding old Joe Louis; some sense of things all wrong and out of place.

Unitas straightened. He spoke a little hoarsely, a bit gruffly: "OK, let's go." He walked back and again awaited his throwing turn behind Earl Morrall and behind young Jim Ward from Gettysburg College, a second-year quarterback so anonymous that all he must do to keep out of the newspapers is stay out of jail.

Unitas threw twice more. Though he seemed to throw with his classic motion, following through until the damaged right arm crisscrossed his body in a neat and natural dissection, Unitas threw only for shallow distances, and his passes had a soft, balloonlike look. After a brief, low-keyed confrontation with Coach Shula he walked off the field with his head down, his shoulders sagging.

An hour later Unitas toweled himself in front of the small cubicle marked with his name and the famous No. 19. He looked much pudgier, whiter, less formidable than in football gear. With his cropped butch haircut and sloped shoulders, he seemed not so much the Marine D.I. he appears in uniform but more one of the middle-aging workmen who drink to their heroes in Baltimore bars—to George Wallace, Hoss Cartwright, and Johnny Unitas. To a visiting writer who said he would probably stay with Unitas "until you play again," the quarterback said wryly, "Well, you may be with me until training camp next summer."

"We doubt that surgery will do it," Unitas went on. "With a torn muscle on top of 'tennis elbow' it's pretty complicated. Now, three or four weeks of complete rest might cure it. If we were out of the race I'd rest it. But I have to keep working in case they need me. You only get about fourteen weeks up here to take your shots." Asked whether the arm ached, pained or throbbed, he said, "It's like a toothache. You know it's there all the time. Sure, it hurts when I throw. It hurts all the time."

It is late in the season, and the precious little football that Johnny Unitas has played has been a disaster. There was one brief, encouraging moment near the end at San Francisco when Unitas tossed his 253rd touchdown pass as a pro (more than anyone else in the game's history), but it was only a six-yard lob that even George Plimpton might have thrown against the thoroughly beaten 49ers. In Unitas's only other appearance, against Cleveland, only one of his 11 passes connected and three were intercepted; twice he grabbed his arm after throwing. When he came off, muttering and kicking the turf, his Colts trailing 13–30 in a game they were long-odds favorites to win, Johnny Unitas heard the unfamiliar, hostile roll of boos.

"I threw well in the warm-up before Cleveland," Unitas said. "So I told Shula I was ready. The ball seemed to take off on me —to sail. I couldn't control it. . . . Since then . . . it seems I'm getting worse. I can't seem to put anything on the ball—no zip."

Last year Johnny Unitas was good enough to win his second N.F.L. Most Valuable Player Award, be named All-Pro for the sixth time, and play in his 10th Pro Bowl in 12 seasons. His 255 completed passes gained 3,428 yards and 20 touchdowns; his percentage of completions (58.5) made Unitas 3.7% more accurate than Green Bay's Bart Starr, 4.4% better than the Giants' Fran Tarkenton, almost 6% better than the L.A. Rams' Roman Gabriel, about 10% more effective than Cleveland's Frank Ryan and a staggering 16.7% more productive than Detroit's Karl Sweetan. With Unitas at the throttle, Baltimore lost but one game in 14 and established new club records for offensive production. At 34, Unitas seemed to be aging with the grace of good wine.

At the start of this season, taking note of Unitas's half-dozen individual records and the fact that he had twice led his team to world championships in three title games, a sports publication's poll named him the "All-Time Quarterback." Then, on September 7 of this year, in the final preseason game against Dallas, Unitas let go a snap pass and "felt something pop—a ripping or tearing sound." There followed long hours in the training room: whirlpool baths, heat lamps, ice packs, massages, X rays, and God or the Baltimore officials only know what else. Baltimore sources played down the Unitas condition. Behind the scenes, however, they were frantically hunting a quarterback. From the New York Giants they got a much-traveled old pro, Earl Morrall, in exchange for one Butch Wilson, an end—a trade that may rank with the Indians' unloading of Manhattan. For though in 13 seasons Earl Morrall had known many more bench splinters than Sundays of glory, and though he arrived too late to be even mentioned in Baltimore's *Press Handbook,* before you could say Whatever Happened to Johnny Unitas? they were calling Earl Morrall "Super Sub."

Morrall, throwing 12 touchdown passes, marched Baltimore to five consecutive victories—over San Francisco (27–10), Atlanta (28–20), Pittsburgh (41–7), Chicago (28–7) and San Francisco again (42–14). When Cleveland's Browns led Baltimore, 14–7, at halftime in the sixth game, Coach Shula substituted Unitas. That was the day Unitas fell apart, the Colts lost, their fans booed, and several jokers in a Baltimore tavern hung Johnny Unitas in effigy. A sign on the dummy read: THIS BUM IS DEAD.

On the day after the lynching, his arm puffy and discolored, Johnny Unitas sat in the Baltimore locker room saying the randy incidents did not bother him. "You're a hero when you win and a bum when you lose," he said. "That's the game. They pay their money and they can boo if they feel like it." Yet, straddling a small white stool while ripping into a pile of letters, he was obviously pleased that fans had written in apology. "This is typical," he said in handing over a letter. "Read all of them if you want." The letters proclaimed "Johnny U." to be the greatest, urged him to keep his chin up, thanked him for several miracles of the past and predicted future ones. Barefoot, Unitas began to scoop the letters up and return them to a cardboard box before suiting up for practice. Does he answer all fan mail? "Well, yeah. I always answer the kids. Most of 'em just want autographed pictures. Somebody else helps me answer the rest." He paused over some unopened letters. "I better open this one," he said, grinning. "That handwriting's too pretty to be from a man." Tim Brown, the flashy running back who came to the Colts from Philadelphia this season, called out, "Is it really from a fox, John?" "Naw," Unitas said, still grinning. "It's from some little kid's mother." The day would offer John Unitas no more smiles.

No, there is nothing wrong with Johnny Unitas's arm that tomorrow or the day after won't cure; No, he is not finished, he is not washed up, he has not reached the end of his career; No, there is no fluid on the golden arm; No, you cannot go in the training room to watch Unitas's treatments.

When Unitas emerged from the training room after two hours of mysterious cures, there was something on him of damp spirits. He sat on his stool, doing nothing, and to all who inquired after his health he gave the same response: "About the same." Someone asked when he might play again. "A month," Unitas guessed. Then, quickly, as if to correct an error: "Aw, honestly, I don't know. I just don't know."

At noon, before yet another meticulous study of films of their upcoming opponents, the L.A. Rams (who had beaten to humiliation both Baltimore and Unitas for the Coastal Division title last December), the Colts gathered in their dining hall. Pro football players are big men and they eat to size. Hungry titans could choose among crab cakes, fried oysters, clam chowder, beef stew, cold cuts and cheese, banana pudding, apples, coffee, tea or milk.

Bubba Smith, the 23-year-old former All-American from Michigan State and now left defensive end for the Colts, loomed before the serving table: his six-foot-seven-inch, 275-pound frame threatened to eclipse the sun. "What's for lunch?" the goateed giant demanded. Willie Richardson, a happy soul who drives opponents crazy with his pass grabs, exotic moves and constant chatter, said, "What you care, Bubba? You gonna eat it anyway." "I never ate me a snake yet," Bubba reported. "You would if they'd fricassee it," Richardson said.

Johnny Unitas, sitting several chairs away from his nearest companion at a table far removed, paid little or no attention to the banter that had everybody else grinning. Sneaking glances at him as he ate without much interest in his food, an observer thought of lines Unitas had written and wondered if they had lately passed through the quarterback's mind:

"When you're twenty-five and a big star, and the coach sends for you, it doesn't mean a thing. When you're thirty-five and the coach sends for you, you tighten up inside. And when he tells you you're through, it doesn't matter what words he uses or how much he tries to soften the blow. Your life can't ever be the same again."

One remembered the Unitas history: a little-remarked record as a quarterback in three losing seasons out of four at the little University of Louisville; the briefest of training-camp looks before being cut by the Pittsburgh Steelers; a return home to Pittsburgh to quarterback the sandlot Bloomfield Rams for six dollars per game until one star-kissed day in 1955 when a Baltimore assistant coach telephoned to offer a tryout and thereby got Mr. Quarterback for an 80-cent toll call.

Young Bubba Smith carted six apples off from the dining room and sang all the way. Johnny Unitas departed silently, alone, carrying a single apple.

The only fault to be found with Colt trainer Eddie Block as a source of information is his tendency to tell you one thing now and something else later. Conversation with him is like Ping-Pong with three balls. In one moment he says, "When I treat a ballplayer, I explain the reasons for certain therapy. Knowing something of their injury and treatments helps them heal. Some won't listen—but Johnny does. And he'll heal in three weeks with an injury where others might take six." Then he immediately disagrees with Unitas's contention that complete rest might cure the ailing arm—"Johnny doesn't really know what will help. He's not medically trained to know."

"It is a matter of overusage," Block ultimately volunteers, and one is startled. "Mechanical parts wear out. So do human parts." Now the layman pounces: Then Unitas's arm *is* worn out? And how can you replace that "human part"? "Your statement is an oversimplification," Block insists. No, the visitor reminds, it was your statement. Block talks faster, saying that he will doubtless be misquoted. There is a long pause when Block is asked how much fluid has been removed from the Unitas arm, how often has it been removed, and what its appearance and texture are. "We can dispel small amounts of liquid by massage," he finally answers. Well, has he *ever* tapped fluid from Unitas's arm, or removed fluid in any way other than by massage? The visitor might have completed a beginner's course in brain surgery during the time it takes Block to answer. "No," he finally says. "Never." Then he advises that any additional comments must come from team physicians—he, after all, is only the trainer. One discovers that as a club policy team physicians make no public statements on the treatment of injuries—and one suspects Block of knowing a safe harbor when he reaches one.

On some teams a Super Star is only minimally approachable to ordinary ballplayers and not at all to rookies; such men are deferred to as royally as they demand to be. One learns, however, that Super Star Unitas comes on pure Boy Scout. He regularly brings in cases of Nehi Red, a soft drink he picks up at cut-rate prices somewhere, to a young and relatively obscure Colt who thirsts after them. When Notre Dame's Terry Hanratty, then a callow junior, wrote his idol asking how to avoid the horrors of pass interceptions, he promptly received a helpful essay on how to spot secondary receivers and the importance of standing firm and cool under fire ("Learn to eat the ball or scramble when a receiver is in trouble"). Unitas never hazes rookies; he drinks only beer, and that in moderation; he smokes not at all; and if there is any of the philanderer in him it is well concealed. He is a sucker for kids, rarely able to resist their pleas for autographs, pictures, helmet chin straps, an occasional football. He takes pains to quietly thank and encourage those ditch-digging linemen whose work wins football games but rarely lands them in the headlines.

Everything about the man seems admirable, and people are quick to praise him. "Nobody loafs on this team," says Alex Hawkins, the free spirit who captains the Colt specialty teams, "because for one thing Johnny U. wouldn't stand for it. He's in charge out there, and if somebody dogs it he'll get chewed on. Johnny's a helluva leader. A helluva man." End Jimmy Orr says simply, "He's the best that ever was. He can read defenses like you can read a book."

Dressing at his cubicle next to the one used by Unitas—who at the moment is in the training room—Earl Morrall echoes a question: "How has Johnny reacted to 'Super Sub'? Great. He's been nothing but helpful. He's practically lived with me to teach me the Colts' system." Morrall is a big-boned, open-faced man of 34; in street clothes he might be taken for a young executive or president of the Jaycees. He has the Unitas country-boy sinc:.ity, touched up by traces of Dale Carnegie.

By Saturday, 24 hours before the Colts were to seek revenge upon the Los Angeles Rams, sportswriters all over America—and some editorial writers—were reviling Colt fans for their hooting of Unitas and for the hanging-in-effigy; letters to the editor in Baltimore newspapers treated of little else. As Johnny U. dressed for the brief kicking drill, a Baltimore newsman led forward two nervous tavern-keepers. The lynching was a gag, they confessed—their gag, and it got out of hand. "We did it to needle one of our best customers because he's such an unreasonable Unitas fan," one of the barkeeps gulped. "Somebody thought it would make a good gag picture, so we telephoned the newspapers. We explained it was a gag. We were kidding, ya know? Fooling around. It made us sick when that picture was played straight, Johnny! It told a lie! Look, we admire you. God

bless you. We're sorry as we can be." Unitas had listened silently to the stammered but fervent apology. Quietly, he said
that he understood, don't worry about it, everything's OK. He
smiled and shook hands with the relieved barkeeps before trotting out to practice, but he didn't seem to care one way or
another.

Though he knew he would play no football against the Rams,
Unitas was early to the locker room on Sunday. He talked
quietly with Morrall about the game plan and the Rams' personnel. Along with Morrall and Jim Ward he had a meeting
with Coach Shula.

Controlled violence was evident in the Baltimore locker
room at least three hours before the showdown; for months the
Colts had remembered how Los Angeles had laid it on them last
December, ruining a fine season and keeping them from a shot
at Super Bowl gold. Bubba Smith (who would later confess to
being so nervous he "couldn't even eat from Friday morning
on") was as grouchy as a hungry bear. Fun-loving Willie Richardson snapped at somebody.

The capacity 60,000-plus made a hellish din the instant they
spotted No. 19 leading the Baltimore team on-field. Unitas did
nothing to acknowledge the clamor, any more than he had
noted the boos; nor did he appear to study signs directed at him:
JOHNNY U. WE LOVE YOU, HANG 'EM ALL, JOHNNY! and
UNITED FOR UNITAS.

Once the game started, Unitas studied the Ram defenders as
if they were bugs. When Morrall came off the field after each
offensive series, he headed straight for Unitas. Now and then
Unitas conferred with Shula or spoke on the phone to coaches
in their press-box observer points.

One wondered how so fine a team as the Rams could look
so hapless. Angry Mike Curtis would make 10 unassisted tackles this day, force a key fumble and earn defensive Player of the
Week honors in the N.F.L.; Defensive Tackle Fred Miller
scooped up a Ram fumble and bulldozed 30-odd yards to the
L.A. four; Bubba Smith went at Roman Gabriel like soul food,

once cracking him down so fiercely that the unfortunate quarterback's head literally bounced.

Morrall set up the first Baltimore score with a swing pass to Tom Matte who, ulcer and all, went 50 yards; shortly thereafter Morrall scored the second Colt touchdown on a one-yard sneak. With the score 13–3 and rowdy Colt fans shrieking like the Democrats in Chicago, Jimmy Orr sought out Unitas with the information that he could beat his defender when cutting to the inside. Unitas walked over to suggest that Morrall call a certain slant-in pattern at the next opportunity. Four plays after the Colts reclaimed the ball Morrall did exactly that—and found Orr wide open for a 44-yard touchdown. In the second half Morrall passed for a second touchdown (his 15th of the season) on a 41-yard shot to tight end Tom Mitchell. Baltimore coasted in, 27–10.

The working press swarmed into Morrall's dressing room for the postgame autopsy. Though he had performed well in key situations, Morrall had been a bit erratic—11 of 27 passes completed, three intercepted. "I'm still having a little trouble reading," he said. "A couple of times my receivers cut one direction and I threw in another direction. Somebody had to correct an incorrect call I made in the huddle, once. My protection out there was fantastic—I should have hit more. And John Unitas called the touchdown pass to Jimmy Orr."

As the happy crush closed in around Morrall, Unitas quietly withdrew to other quarters to dress—possibly to escape the confusion, possibly so as not to intimidate Morrall or steal any of his new glory. When the newsmen dispersed, he reappeared. The two quarterbacks stood talking for a few minutes, replaying key plays, discussing certain failures, wondering if this or that might have worked against the Rams. A visitor asked Unitas when he thought he might play again. "I dunno," he said. "I don't think they really need me, do you?"

Through the next week Unitas threw ineffectively, briefly, painfully. Coach Shula publicly doubted that his ailing star would play against the Giants. On Saturday night Eddie Block, sipping a libation before the II P.M. bedcheck, guessed that "Unitas could play about a quarter if he *had* to. He might throw two or three minutes without hurting—adrenaline would take him that far. After that, he'd be hurting."

The Colts didn't need Unitas even for two or three minutes against New York. Morrall had a dream day—16 of 24 passes completed for two touchdowns in an easy 26-to-0 victory that boosted Baltimore's record to 7–1. In a 14-play, 84-yard drive culminating in a plunge by Tom Matte for the final Baltimore touchdown, Morrall truly was "Super Sub"—with third and 18 deep in his own country, he completed a 29-yard shot to Ray Perkins; with third and 10 near midfield, he hit John Mackey for exactly that; with fourth and one on the New York 43, he confidently called on Matte to gouge it out; with third and nine at the Giant 40, Morrall passed to Orr good to the two-yard line. It was his most settled, polished performance; his passes were on target and he called most of the plays himself.

Earl Morrall was obviously happy in the locker room, seeming not to mind when newsmen pinned him in a corner, delayed his shower for almost an hour. He avoided boasting and did not claim special vengeance on his former team. Meanwhile, Coach Shula was telling the press in clipped, executive tones that Earl had helped the ball club greatly. Yes, he had come through in very difficult circumstances; no, he hadn't given up on Unitas —his arm was a day-to-day thing, seemingly better and then flaring up; no, he wasn't worried about having to choose between Morrall and a healthy Unitas, but it was the kind of problem any coach might enjoy.

Few reporters bothered with Unitas though he chatted briefly with well-wishers and graciously shook hands with a seven-year-old named Douglas who was more than moderately awed. To a reporter who had been shadowing him for two weeks he said, "No news. It's about the same. I can't throw more than twenty yards."

Pro football can take a Johnny Unitas, a poor Lithuanian kid from the steelier parts of Pittsburgh, and in time set him up as a $250,000-a-year man (salary plus endorsements) enjoying an $80,000 home in a green Maryland suburb. It can give him business opportunities (including a posh restaurant, The Golden Arm, a name that carries a bit of irony now), gold Pontiacs, color television, boats, travel, excitement, fame. Pro football can do these marvelous things, provided the Johnny Unitases are willing to pay the price—and so long as they produce.

The price is not easily met. There is the frequent pain; the presence of danger; the pressures to win; the Spartan training camps with their harsh rules. August nights are sweated away in ragged exhibition games in places like Norfolk and Louisville and Hershey, Pennsylvania. There are the 10- to 14-hour days from September through mid-January if things go well (and a longer season in the heart if they don't): days of running, throwing, drilling, films, tedious blackboard exercises. There are promotional lunches or dinners, interviews, personal appearances, radio and TV shows, odd or exotic demands from the paying customers—all taking Johnny Unitas away from his wife, his five children, his home and his restaurant. Given his private personality, the multiple dangers and the inconveniences, you wonder why Unitas or other middle-aging men tolerate the life even for the good money in it. Perhaps the answer is best summed up by Johnny U. in speaking of the six dollars per game he drew for quarterbacking the Bloomfield Rams back in the dark days: "I don't think any of them have ever understood that what mattered the most . . . was not the six dollars but the fact that there was a football team that wanted me."

They still want John Unitas in Baltimore, for there are the fearsome Rams waiting for their revenge in Los Angeles in mid-December, and there is a shot at the Super Bowl money. (When Johnny U. was photographed throwing *left*-handed in practice, Coach Shula formally denied rumors that Unitas would be placed on the injured-reserve list. "We just hope he'll

be ready when we need him," Shula said.) With Unitas's reputation and record, Baltimore will not easily give up on him: He
is their Institution, a phenomenal drawing card and public-
relations asset, a living legend. They will carry him on a silk
pillow for greater distances than pro football players are generally so transported. But that is not enough; Johnny Unitas
wants to play, to be needed.

He still leads the Baltimore Colts onto the field, evidence that
he remains the official Main Man even if the program shows a
stranger in his shoes, but sometimes he must wonder about
those footsteps behind him—are they really those of his teammates, or are they the relentless steps of time? He is a cool cat,
one who will not say much from the soul, a loner who politely
turns down all outsider invitations to socialize; very much the
private man. Only his head knows what goes on inside it in this,
the longest season of Johnny Unitas, but there must be moments when he wonders if he's really needed by a football team
anymore—or if he ever will be again.

2/JURGENSEN

"I Suppose You Could Say I've Learned a Little About the Passing Game"

By Joe McGinniss

One of the saddest sights in football history was Sonny Jurgensen at the 1973 Super Bowl game, standing on the sidelines, supported by crutches, watching his Washington Redskins lose to the Miami Dolphins. For most of his professional career, Jurgensen's enormous talent had been wasted on losing teams, and now, finally, he was with a winner but his body had betrayed him before the championship game. Like Moses, Jurgensen had made it only to the edge of the Promised Land.

Sonny Jurgensen, most football people agree, is the finest pure passer the game has ever produced. There is a story, perhaps apochryphal, that when John Unitas opened a restaurant called The Golden Arm, Jurgensen thanked Unitas for naming the place after him. If it didn't happen, it should have. Under a complicated rating system, based on percentage of completions, percentage of touchdowns, percentage of interceptions and average gain, Jurgensen ranks second in pro history, behind only Len Dawson, who compiled his best statistics in the AFL before the AFL gained parity with the NFL.

There is one side to Jurgensen that puzzles me. People like myself, people whose favorite athletes are the ones who refuse to be conventional, have always liked Jurgensen, liked what he represents and cheered for him to succeed. Outwardly, Jurgensen seems the sort of man who does his job, does it right and doesn't give a damn what people think about him. Yet, for some reason, Jurgensen is strangely wary of the press. During the 1973 season, as editor of Sport, *I asked a couple of writers to attempt articles about Sonny. Each time the assignment fell through because Sonny refused to cooperate. He simply didn't want anything written about him, and it's hard to understand why. He appeals to writers. Joe McGinniss, who wrote the following story, enjoyed Jurgensen's company and enjoyed doing the story. But when the article came out, Jurgensen went out of his way to denounce it. He didn't deny saying or doing the things McGinniss reported, but he insisted his remarks were taken out of context. The funny thing is that Jurgensen came through the prose as a likeable guy, but he didn't like the way he came through.*

Joe McGinniss's story was written in 1968, the year after Jurgensen enjoyed the busiest season any quarterback ever produced. In 1967, Sonny threw 508 passes, a record, and completed 288, a record, for 3,747 yards, an NFL record—all for a Washington team that couldn't win half its games.

Incidentally, McGinniss's article appeared in The Saturday Evening Post *only three weeks after Richard Nixon became president, which means McGinniss researched the article while he researched his bestseller,* The Selling of the President. *McGinniss has to be the only man ever to turn out a primer in politics and a primer in passing at the same time.*

Cutty and water with a twist.

It had been Cutty and water with a twist for an hour and a half.

"Would you like another, Sonny?" one of the automobile men asked.

The dim, Maryland-suburban motel bar was almost empty on a Monday afternoon. "All right. Thank you."

Earlier it had been Bloody Marys. Made with Mr. and Mrs. "T" Bloody Mary Mix, which, Sonny Jurgensen had said, was "absolutely the best Bloody Mary mix in the world." He had spoken with the authority he reserves for those areas in which he is particularly expert: Bloody Mary mixes, Scotch, wine, calcium deposits, women, sex, marriage, divorce, antiques and football.

"So what we want to know, basically, is whether you'd be able to do some work for us in the off-season," the automobile man said. "Showroom appearances, TV spots, things like that."

The man paused and stared across the table. This was the critical moment. He could see Jurgensen sitting there now, with those clear blue eyes, that orange hair dipping down over the forehead, the sideburns roaming down across the broad, Scandinavian face; and in his mind's eye he could see this—*Quarterback*—in sportcoat and turtleneck, leaning casually against a brand-new car in a showroom window, while hundreds of kids —and their parents—lined up waiting for an autograph and a smile. And Sonny Jurgensen, almost as an afterthought, tapping the roof of the car and grinning his warm, natural grin and saying, "Nice automobile."

The automobile man slowly moved his tongue across his lips.

"Yes," Sonny Jurgensen said. "I think I'd be available."

"Well that's just wonderful, Sonny, that's just grand. Hey, how about another drink."

"This is just locally, of course," the other automobile man was saying. "We're only talking about using you in the Washington area."

"I see."

"Our plan now is to build our national campaign around Fran Tarkenton."

"I see," Sonny Jurgensen said. "Fran Tarkenton."

Tarkenton plays football for the New York Giants. A good quarterback. He is smart, he can run and he can throw the ball well. But there has never been a day when Fran Tarkenton could throw a football as well as Sonny Jurgensen.

Being best in the world at what you do, however, is not enough. To make it pay, you must either do it with a winner or do it in New York.

Give Sonny Jurgensen one year in New York City, and the East Side bartenders would be asking Joe Namath for proof of age. But Sonny has never had that year. Eleven seasons in the provinces—most of them with losing teams. It is as if Barbra Streisand were held captive in New Haven with a road show.

He throws the ball farther, faster and more accurately—under the most intense sort of physical and psychological pressure—than anyone else who is paid to play the game. And it does no good. He throws 50 yards to the end zone and a receiver drops the ball. Coming from behind, he completes his seventh pass in a row—and a rookie tackle is penalized for holding. No matter how many touchdowns he manages to direct, his defense always seems to give up more.

Last year, despite all this, and with the calcium so heavy in his elbow that he needed drugs to kill the pain, Sonny Jurgensen set new National Football League records for most passes thrown, most passes completed and most yards gained by passing. He also led all quarterbacks in passes thrown for touchdowns and in lowest percentage of interceptions.

He is the only quarterback in history to pass for more than 400 yards in a single game more than twice. He has done it five separate times.

Now, in the motel bar, he was finishing his drink, and the automobile men were saying they were sure glad he was interested.

The afternoon was warm when Sonny got outside. He walked through the sunlight to his dark green Mercedes. The license plate said SJ-9—his initials and uniform number.

"Let's put the top down," he said, and drove back to Washington very fast.

Twelve years ago he played for a Duke University coach who did not like the forward pass. Sonny Jurgensen threw the ball 59 times all season. Still, his size and strength and brains drew attention. The Philadelphia Eagles decided that he was worth a look. But the Eagles also had a line on a kid named Harris from Oklahoma, and before they went for Jurgensen they wanted to be sure he could pass. They dispatched an assistant coach, a man named Charlie Gauer, now a sports broadcaster in Philadelphia, to Durham, N.C., to see. Gauer brought Sonny Jurgensen onto a field one day and watched him warm up. Just tossing to a couple of kids for 10 minutes. Then Gauer went inside and called Philadelphia. "Jurgensen can pass," he said.

Sonny Jurgensen parked the Mercedes behind The Goalpost and went inside. The Goalpost is a dark little pocket near the northwest end of Wisconsin Avenue. Not many people unknown to Maggie, the owner, ever go inside. Maggie, who is a man, knows Sonny Jurgensen very well.

The Goalpost was not crowded. Stan was there, drinking beer. Stan is a friend of Sonny Jurgensen. Together they are planning to open a carry-out taco stand in Washington. It will be called Sonny's Sock-A-Taco-To-Me.

"How's the arm feel?" Stan asked.

"Terrible. Hurts so much I'm even drinking left-handed."

"How's Otto?"

This brought a laugh. Jurgensen and Otto Graham, the Redskin coach, are not exactly the best of friends.

"There's only one difference between Otto and me," Sonny says. "He likes candy bars and milkshakes and I like women and Scotch."

Sonny is 34 years old now, with a surgeon's scar on his elbow, and he is growing impatient with a team that has gone nowhere in the three years since Graham took over.

The day before, Jurgensen had lost to the Giants, 48 to 21, as mental errors by his linemen and receivers and a total collapse by the defense overcame his own early brilliance. The loss had been the Redskins' second in three games.

"I thought at the beginning of the year that we'd be lucky to win five," he was saying, sitting now at one end of the bar. "That's a hell of a way to go into a season. Thinking you'll be lucky to win five games."

He looked into his drink.

"I'd say my arm is eighty, maybe eighty-five percent of what it was before the operation. It's not as strong, so I can't throw a lot in practice during the week. That's what hurts. When they suddenly put the clamps on during a game and I've got to throw long, I've got no feel for it. I haven't done it for seven days, because I'm trying to rest the arm during the week, so I can't be sure of my touch."

He looked at his watch. "Hey, we'd better get going," he said. "It's six-thirty." He picked up his drink and walked out to the Mercedes.

In Philadelphia it is possible to acquire a checkered reputation simply by taking one's mother out to dinner after dark. Sonny Jurgensen occasionally did take his mother out to dinner. He also took out other ladies. He liked a few drinks before his meal, wine with it, and a few drinks after. Sometimes more than a few.

"Sonny never did anything that everybody else doesn't do," says a friend and former coach. But Sonny did it in the open. Philadelphia is too small a town to hide in, but Sonny didn't even try. He was big and red-headed and he loved to laugh and he came rolling north out of Duke in the Eisenhower years and he bought drinks for half the population while the other half crawled into spiteful little corners and called him names.

It was not the drinking or the girls. It was that he was so obviously enjoying himself. It is perfectly permissible, under our current moral code, to run around with girls or have a few extra drinks in public, as long as it makes you unhappy. What other people cannot stand is the thought of your having fun at it. And Sonny Jurgensen was obviously having fun.

He was separated from his wife and two children and living with a bachelor named Jack Edelstein. Jack Edelstein is this kind of man: He and Sonny Jurgensen visited Arlington National Cemetery one day and found a big line at the Tomb of the Unknown Soldier. Sonny wanted to see the tomb but did not want to wait in line. "OK," Jack Edelstein said, "just follow

me and keep a straight face." And he began to edge his way
through the crowd, pointing at Sonny and saying, in funeral
director tones, "Pardon us, please, could you excuse us please,
this man is a relative."

The Philadelphia team was sold in 1964. The first thing the
new coach did was get rid of Sonny Jurgensen, shipping him to
Washington in return for a young man named Norman Snead
who liked to stay home at night and read.

Sonny Jurgensen finished the drink he had carried home
from The Goalpost and poured another. Then he put a new
King Curtis tape on his stereo.

"Getting out of Philadelphia was the best thing that ever
happened to me," he was saying. "I got divorced when I left and
I came down here all alone and out from under a lot of things."

Then his second wife walked out of the bedroom carrying
their 10-week-old son, and joined us.

"I met Margo by the swimming pool right outside," he said,
smiling up at her. "I never thought I'd get married again, but
this was different. Margo had been married before, too, so we
both knew what it was all about.

"You know, the first time you go into it you think it's all that
love-and-sex stuff. We had both learned kind of painfully that
it wasn't. We knew that it was sharing things and working hard
to build a life together. I said, 'Margo, we don't have to do this
and there's no sense in our doing it unless we're going to do it
right.'

"See, the first time I got married I was only twenty-three and
hardly out of school. It was too soon. I finally decided I had
to get out because to go on would have been to live a lie. And
that's one thing I've never been able to do.

"You can say, well what about the kids? How can you walk
out on two kids? And that's a point. I still think about how this
will affect them. I know they're growing up differently than
they would if I was still around, but whether it's better or worse
I can't say. Besides, in the end it's your own life you have to

live. You stay married for twenty years just because of the kids, and then one day you're forty-five and your oldest comes walking in and says, 'Hey, Dad, guess what: I'm getting married.' And then where are you, and what purpose has it all served? You've got to make your own life."

There was steak and wine and salad, and Hubert Humphrey making a speech on television, and the *Laugh-In,* and stereophonic King Curtis after dinner and Sonny dancing in the middle of the living-room floor, on the thick, wall-to-wall carpet. Dancing and smiling on Monday night.

Tuesday was a bad day. Sonny had arranged a meeting between Edward Bennett Williams, the Redskins' president, and the players. No coaches allowed. All year Sonny had been listening to the players griping about the coaching, and he thought there were some points of which Williams should be made aware. So the owner came and said, "All right, fellows, what are the problems?" and everybody sat there in silence. All these kids who had been complaining to Sonny Jurgensen about the coaching and how it was going to ruin their careers sat there staring at the floor now, not saying anything, and then one of them said, "We'll be all right, we've just got to pull together," and another said, "Yeah, that's right, we've just got to pull together," and they all nodded, and Edward Bennett Williams looked at Sonny Jurgensen with this look in his eye that said, "What the hell, Sonny?" and the meeting was over.

This week's opponent was to be the Philadelphia Eagles, a team even more forlorn than the Redskins. The Eagles had lost their first three games; their owner was staving off creditors week to week; their coach was an object of ridicule in his own town; their quarterback, Snead, would be playing for the first time since breaking an ankle eight weeks before, and besides, it would be the Redskins' first home game.

Certain things stood out from the scouting reports and the movies of Eagle games that Sonny Jurgensen watched. Pettigrew, an end the year before, had been removed to tackle. He appeared overeager and susceptible to trap plays. There was a glaring weakness at corner linebacker, where Medved, a safety-man, had been brought up to play. "He'll probably cover passes as if he were still a safety," Sonny Jurgensen said. "That means he'll be dropping back and it might be possible to throw in front of him." Then there was Scarpati, the free safety, who always was a problem. "Joe watches to see which way I look, and then he goes in that direction, figuring he'll be able to intercept. What I have to do is look one way and come back real quick in another."

These insights, and a dozen or so others, of varying degrees of obscurity, were distilled, through a series of meetings with the coaches, into what is called a game plan.

"The game plan is nothing more than what we think we're going to do, based on what we anticipate from the defense," Jurgensen said. "But the key word is anticipate. They're spending all week trying to figure out ways to surprise us, too, so once you get in the game it's basically a question of outguessing them."

After 11 years of playing with teams that, for lack of talent, have been forced to use the forward pass as the basic offensive weapon—the way most teams use the running play—Sonny Jurgensen has become a pretty good guesser.

"I suppose you could say I've learned a little about the passing game," he said, grinning. "I suppose you could say that."

He came in with one great natural gift that none of the others could match—the ability to get rid of the ball in a hurry. Quick release, it is called; it is considered essential, and it is Sonny Jurgensen's strongest point. Because it takes him less time to let go of the ball once he decides to throw, he can afford to wait longer—as the linemen close in—giving his receivers more chance to get free.

Besides that, he throws the ball a number of different ways. Like a baseball pitcher, with fast ball, curve, slider and change-up, Jurgensen has a variety of speeds and styles. There are times when a receiver is clear only for an instant; when the alley open to him is being shut by a linebacker's arms. There are other times, when a receiver is taller than a defender, when the ball should be simply hung in the air.

"Another thing I can do," he explained, "is throw off balance. Some quarterbacks have to go back and set up and stay there. I have control even from the weirdest positions. I slide around a lot, from side to side, because the linemen are so tall today that I can't get the ball over them a lot of times. I've got to find an alley. This means that I'm frequently leaning sideways when I get rid of the ball.

"And then, like I said, I've learned some things about the throwing game. For instance, a standard pattern is for a receiver to go straight down and then cut across the field. There are three linebackers he is cutting behind, which means two gaps: between the first and second and between the second and third. A young quarterback, who is anxious to get rid of the ball when he sees an open receiver, is likely to throw through the first gap. I'm more likely to wait now, for the second, because I've learned that it's usually bigger. When a corner linebacker drops back on pass coverage, he doesn't go straight back, he sort of naturally angles toward the sideline. It's a small thing, but there's such a small margin of error in the throwing game anyway that it's significant."

It was Thursday night, and Sonny Jurgensen had just finished taping his weekly television show, which is shown Sundays before the Redskin games. Jerry Smith, a kid from California, who was the league's No. 2 pass receiver last year, had been a guest on the show. Now he was back at The Goalpost for a drink with Sonny.

"Gee, this is really a thrill for me," he was saying. "I've looked up to Sonny for so long. This is the first time I've ever associated with him socially." It also was the first time that Jerry Smith had ever drunk five Cutty-and-waters in one night.

"A great kid," Sonny Jurgensen was saying. "And a great

football player. Big, strong, smart, fast. At the end of the season last year he wrote me a letter that started off: Dear Mr. Jurgensen. He said he just wanted to thank me for throwing to him so much that he had a good year. Thank me, hell. I was throwing to him because he was open and he could catch."

Sonny Jurgensen made a face. "That's what I mean about this team. There's talent here, good talent, and it's a frustrating thing to see it go to waste. Look at Smith. He was tight end last year, and suddenly this year they make him a flanker. Messing with the Number Two receiver in the league."

On Saturday afternoon Sonny Jurgensen, wearing a white T-shirt and cowboy boots, lay sprawled across his king-sized bed, watching the third game of the World Series on television.

"Margo? Are there any Pepsis or anything?"

"No, but I'll go up to the machine and get some."

"Would you?"

"Yes."

"That's nice, Margo. You're a nice person."

"Regular Pepsi or diet?"

"Diet, naturally."

Sonny Jurgensen weighs 210 pounds, five more than he did a year ago. In uniform his stomach is visible, even from the cheaper seats.

"Wait'll you see what happens if we lose tomorrow," Sonny said. "Then the talk will really start. 'Jurgensen looks heavy. He must be out of shape. His arm is gone. He was out late Thursday night.'

"People are amazing. Why do they boo? If Ed Williams loses a case in court they don't stand outside and boo him when he leaves. You don't read in the paper, 'Williams's lousy cross-examination blows case.' You don't read that about surgeons: 'Dr. Barnard lost his third consecutive patient today as he moved to the right ventricle when he should have gone left. And he was out late drinking the night before.' But sports is different. For a six-dollar ticket they think they can run your life."

A lady who predicts football scores for newspapers had

picked the Redskins over the Eagles, 42–7. The gambling cards favored Washington by 10. Sonny Jurgensen, for about the 400th time in his life, was wondering why time passed so slowly on the day before a game.

"In the end," he was saying, as the Detroit Tigers batted in the eighth inning, "it's the defense that dictates your game. The defense tells you when to throw, where to throw and how to throw. The most important thing a quarterback has to learn is how to react to the defense."

The Series game was over. It was followed by a West Coast college football game. "Come on," Sonny Jurgensen said. "I have to drive out to my in-laws."

The weather had turned cool the day before. Now, late on this first Saturday of October, Washington was into autumn. The sun was bright and the air was clear. Sonny Jurgensen drove toward Bethesda.

"You know, in all that stuff we were talking about before— marriage and running around and everything—I'd like to make one point. I think the most important thing a man has is his character. I think that comes before anything else. People got upset because I was flaunting these women in front of them, but these same people were sneaking it on the side.

"Now, character is what you think of yourself. Reputation is what other people think. I think my character came through intact, but my reputation was something else."

He was driving now through neat, quiet streets. Kids were playing on well-trimmed lawns, and he was driving slowly enough to be recognized.

"Hi, Sonny." . . . "Hey, Sonny, good luck tomorrow." Sonny Jurgensen grinned and waved.

"I'd never do it again, though. It really got to be awful. You're out every night with someone different and you wake up in the morning and you can't even remember where you were or who you were with the night before. Nothing has any meaning. The people don't care about you as a person—they just think it's a big deal to go out with the quarterback.

"Look, I still like broads, I still like to drink, I still like to have a good time. But most nights now I'm happy just to sit at home with Margo. I'm happier than I've ever been in my life, and it's all because of her and what we're building together. I have the feeling I'm going someplace. I have the feeling there's some purpose to my life."

Sonny Jurgensen's father-in-law, who was supporting George Wallace for President, offered him a drink.

Sonny, who leaned toward Humphrey, said no, thanks. "Not on Saturday, Arnold, not tonight."

Sunday was windy, cloudy and cool—a better day for playing than for watching. Margo Jurgensen was there, but she was not happy. "I don't like to watch Sonny play. I don't know why, I just don't."

It was apparent from the start that the Eagles, indeed, were even a worse team than the Redskins. Snead looked as if he were throwing a medicine ball, and the line seemed to be staging a sit-down strike.

The Redskins were competent but lacking in dash. The play-calling was routine, the execution adequate; nothing more. It was as if Jurgensen were a boxer who, knowing he was in no danger, had decided to forgo the knockout and win on points.

"How about the bomb, Sonny?" a man sitting behind Margo Jurgensen yelled.

"I don't think he can throw it anymore," the man next to him said. "I think there's something wrong with his arm."

The Redskins kicked a field goal in the second quarter, and toward the end of the half, Jurgensen, intending to pass from the Eagle four-yard line, could find no one open to receive, and instead ran for a touchdown. For the first time the crowd reacted.

"I can just hear them if he hadn't made it," Margo Jurgensen said. " 'Jellybelly.' That's one of their favorites."

Later there was one moment, one brief moment, when Sonny

Jurgensen saw a receiver get behind a defender, and with explosive grace he lofted the ball on an arc that brought it six feet from the ground at the precise point where the receiver's hands were waiting. The play went for 34 yards. Touchdown. After the conversion Washington led 17-0.

Near the end of the game the Eagles scored, making it 17-7, and, following the kickoff, their defense stiffened, forcing Jurgensen to pass long on third down. He was close to his own goal at the time, a dangerous place to be passing late in a game.

Again a receiver—the same one who had caught the touchdown, Charley Taylor—shot past a defender and was clear at midfield. Jurgensen saw him and threw. The ball fell short. An Eagle defender knocked it to the ground. The Redskins had to punt.

On the return, Haymond, the cornerback, scored a touchdown, reducing the Redskin advantage to 17-14. Fortunately there were only 40 seconds left, and Washington was able to hold the ball until the final gun.

The Redskins had won, and Sonny Jurgensen had run for a touchdown, passed for a touchdown and completed 21 of the 29 passes he tried. But the feeling that something had been missing was heavy in the air.

As the gun sounded to end the game, Sonny Jurgensen raced toward the Redskin locker room. He was running faster than he had when he scored. He had half his uniform off by the time he reached his locker, and three minutes later, already through with his shower, was throwing clothes over a still damp body, combing his still dripping hair. Eight minutes after the end of the game, he was starting the white Chrysler that is his second car. Margo was sitting beside him. They were heading for the airport and the five-o'clock shuttle to New York.

"I would've been here sooner, but a couple of writers caught me in the hall," he said. "The least that Otto could do would be hold them for ten minutes to give me a chance to get out. He knows how I feel about that."

Sonny Jurgensen does not like to talk about a game right after it has been played. He prefers to wait a day or so and sort things out in his mind. It is a sensible approach, and undoubtedly leads to more intelligent conversation, but sportswriters want quotes for their stories, and want them right away.

"It all went just as we had planned," he said, as he overpowered the traffic. But he knew there had been something missing. That, uncharacteristically, it had all been done without flair. That only the one pass to Taylor could be remembered for its style. That on this afternoon he had been a workman who had done his job, nothing more. He had thrown the ball more than 40 yards only once in the whole game—on the final somewhat desperate attempt to Taylor.

"That was just like I was telling you. If you don't throw all week, you don't have the touch on Sunday." He shook his head. "But the funny thing about that one was that I thought I overthrew it. And then it came up short."

And you thought back to the closet in his apartment, in which Sonny Jurgensen was saving, in a plastic container full of preservative, the dime-sized, gray-brown piece of calcium that had been removed from his elbow before the season.

"Funny," he repeated, "I thought I overthrew it and then it came up short."

He parked the Chrysler. He and Margo walked toward the terminal.

"We're in good shape for the five-o'clock," he said. "Anyway I've got a special agent working here who takes care of me."

"Yeah, you used to date her," Margo said.

"Oh, I took her out once or twice," Sonny Jurgensen said.

They were going to have to stay at The Barclay Hotel in New York that night because the places they usually stayed were filled, and, no, Mr. Jurgensen's name was not on the special lists of people who are never refused. The next day he would make an appearance at a hardware convention. Then they would take a shuttle home. And on Tuesday he would be back at The

Goalpost, sipping a Mr. and Mrs. "T" Bloody Mary and being grateful for the fact that at The Goalpost nobody got too pushy about his arm. The arm would be all right. It was getting stronger every week. By November he would be throwing long again. He was sure of it. He had been able to throw long all his life.

"Sonny, we'll be in New York so early we won't know what to do with ourselves," Margo said.

"You mean we'll just have to keep each other company?"

"That's right."

"I guess I can stand it. For one night, at least." And he laughed and reached out and took her hand.

3 / TARKENTON

The Second Coming of Saint Francis

By Dick Schaap

Fran Tarkenton does not throw the world's prettiest passes. Fran himself seems amazed each time he throws a spiral. His amazement is feigned. Tarkenton takes tremendous pride in his skills, and his record amply justifies his pride. If Tarkenton continues to play football through the 1976 season (which he intends to), through the age of 36 (which is young by quarterbacking standards), and if he manages to avoid serious injury (which he has managed through his first 13 seasons), and if in 1974, 1975 and 1976 he matches his career average in pass attempts (342 a year), pass completions (189), passing yardage (2,558) and touchdown passes (18.5), then by New Year's Day, 1977, he will be the leading passer, statistically, in pro-football history. He will have thrown almost 5,500 passes, completed more than 3,000, gained more than 40,000 yards and thrown more than 300 touchdown passes, surpassing all of John Unitas's records in those four departments. Even if Tarkenton slips below his averages, he will surely break the records in four seasons, by New Year's Day, 1978.

Tarkenton has already broken the records for time spent talking to reporters. Of all quarterbacks, he is the most accessible, the most articulate, the most conscious of his role as a public figure. He enjoys conversation, almost compulsively, a trait which separates him from most of his peers and one which enabled him to host a weekly television show, covering a wide variety of subjects, when he played for the New York Giants. On his TV show, he was even able to hold his own conversationally with author Jacqueline Susann, no easy feat, but once, at a dinner party, I saw Tarkenton meet his match: Erich Segal, the author of Love Story. *Against Segal, Tarkenton could barely get a word in, no matter how skillfully he scrambled.*

I wrote the following story one year too soon. I wrote it during the 1972 season, when Tarkenton's mission—to lead the Minnesota Vikings to the Super Bowl—failed. The next year, 1973, Tarkenton succeeded. The story would have looked better if he had made it in 1972, but I can't be too harsh on Tarkenton. After all, two years isn't much time for the prophecies of a Second Coming to be fulfilled.

Fran Tarkenton had flat run out of plays to call. He had already gone through every play on his ready list—the three dozen or so considered most likely to succeed against the Washington Redskins' defense. Tarkenton had called most of the plays at least twice, some three and four times. Now the Minnesota Vikings were getting ready for their 79th offensive play of the game—fourth down on the Washington four-yard line, three and a half yards to go for a first down. Tarkenton wanted to try something the Redskins hadn't seen. He leaned into the Viking huddle and called, "Sixty-four . . . three . . . screen right . . . on two. . . ."

In the year 1972, the Minnesota Vikings cheerfully gave up quarterback Norm Snead, wide receiver Bob Grim, running back Vinnie Clements and two high draft choices to get Fran Tarkenton from the New York Giants. The Vikings brought Tarkenton back to the Twin Cities, the place where he had begun his pro football career 11 years earlier, for one reason: To put power in their offense—or, more precisely, to put points on the scoreboard.

For four straight years, from 1968 through 1971, the Vikings —without Tarkenton—had won their divisional championship. For three straight years, from 1969 through 1971, the Vikings— without Tarkenton—had led all 26 pro football teams in fewest points allowed. But only once had the Vikings traveled to the Super Bowl, and that one time, to face Kansas City in January, 1970, the trip was a waste. The Vikings were outclassed to the brink of embarrassment. The Chiefs beat them, 23–7.

The trouble with the Vikings—particularly in the 1970 and 1971 seasons, after Joe Kapp elected to carry his *machismo* to a ridiculous extreme—was that they had a champagne defense and a waterlogged offense. The futility of the offense became so evident, during the 1971 season, Minnesota fans began to suspect, quite seriously, that their team's best chances for scoring came when the other team had the ball. Alan Page might scoop up a fumble. Carl Eller might toss the enemy quarterback for a safety. Paul Krause might pick off a pass. Faced with Minnesota's Purple Gang of defenders, an opposing quarterback— out of sheer fright, like a prisoner of war inventing and revealing military secrets to escape inhuman torture—might give the Vikings anything they wanted: The ball, six points, anything, just to get off the field alive.

The Minnesota offense was frightening, too—but only to its supporters. In 1971, Gary Cuozzo, Norm Snead and Bob Lee took turns at directing the Viking attack, each with some degree of failure. Raquel Welch could have been as effective, and a lot more fun to watch. Not once, in 14 games, did the Vikings score as many as 30 points. Not once, in 14 games, did the Vikings accumulate as many as 25 first downs. Not once, in 14 games, did the Vikings score as many as four touchdowns. And not once, in 14 games, did the Vikings gain as many as 350 yards, running *and* passing. Minnesota's frustration reached a peak in the play-off game against Dallas, the winner favored to go all

the way to the Super Bowl title. Dallas won, 20–12, but the
game wasn't that close; Dallas led, 20–3, entering the final
quarter.

Then Dallas went on to the championship—and Minnesota
went on to get Tarkenton. In the first exhibition game of 1972,
on the opening kickoff, Clint Jones of the Vikings caught the
ball on his own one-yard line and raced 99 yards for a touchdown. As Jones reached the end zone, Tarkenton turned on the
sidelines to Viking coach Bud Grant. "See," said Tarkenton, "I
told you I'd help your offense."

When the season began, with the official opener against
Washington, Tarkenton stopped joking—and started proving
his point. By the time Minnesota huddled before its fourth-
down play on the four-yard line, the Vikings had already col-
lected 26 first downs and 378 yards against the Redskin defense,
one of the finest in football. The Vikings had already run off 78
offensive plays, about 20 above the average. No one could recall
the Vikings ever running that many plays; Tarkenton could not
recall any team he ever quarterbacked running so many plays.
It was an incredible display of offensive strength, of offensive
domination.

*"Sixty-four . . . three . . . screen right . . . on two. . . ." A screen
pass. On fourth down. On the four-yard line. Tarkenton had
never in his 12-year career called a screen pass inside the five-yard
line. None of the Vikings could remember any quarterback ever
calling a screen pass inside the five-yard line. Even the ABC trio
up in the television booth—armed with the trio's collective memory and collective vocabulary—could draw no parallel. But nobody argued with Tarkenton in the huddle. No one said a word.*

The beauty of Francis Asbury Tarkenton as a quarterback,
beyond his natural gifts, is his unpredictability. No quarterback, not even the ones with far stronger arms, not even the one
with far weaker knees, has ever done so much to drive opponents to the edge of psychoanalysis. When the Green Bay Packers were the greatest team in football, and Henry Jordan one

of the greatest defensive tackles, Jordan used to have night-mares about Tarkenton. The nightmares were endless: Jordan endlessly chasing Tarkenton, endlessly trying to grab him, to punish him, endlessly failing.

When the Vikings regained Tarkenton in 1972, they brought to the drabbest offense in football the most imaginative quarter-back. Tarkenton will do anything short of a felony to gain yardage. He loves the short pass; he enjoys using his backs and tight ends as receivers. He doesn't mind the long pass, either; he is capable, by his own measurement, of throwing a football 61½ yards. Tarkenton's passes don't always look pretty—he fluctuates between the spiral and the lob—but they are effective, so effective that he now ranks fifth among all the passers in pro football history. Only Jurgensen, Dawson, Unitas and Starr—all of whom have put in at least 16 seasons—rate higher.

But his passing is not the quality that makes Fran Tarkenton special. It is his running, his scrambling, his logic-defying abil-ity to avoid tacklers that separates Tarkenton from other professional quarterbacks, that gives him his unique crowd appeal. Tarkenton does not have the piston-power of a Greg Landry or even of a Roger Staubach. He does not run hard; he runs slippery. He squirms, he ducks, he darts, he escapes.

A 190-pound six-footer who looks smaller, Tarkenton is about as far from a picture runner as possible. He will never be asked to pose for the Heisman Trophy, yet, in at least one measurable sense, he is the greatest runner in the history of pro football. Of all the thousands who have played the game in the past half a century, Tarkenton is the only man who has aver-aged six yards or better per rushing attempt for more than 500 carries. And that puts Tarkenton ahead of Jimmy Brown, ahead of Gale Sayers, ahead of everybody.

If Tarkenton's rushing record is improbable, his health record is impossible. In 20 years of playing organized football —four years in high school, four in college and 12 as a pro— Tarkenton has never missed a game because of an injury. He has never even pulled a muscle.

"That," says Tarkenton, "is because I don't have one."

"Sixty-four . . . three . . . screen right . . . on two. . . ." The Vikings broke from their huddle and moved to the line of scrimmage. Tarkenton positioned himself behind the center and scanned the Washington defense. Mick Tinglehoff, the Minnesota center, leaned over the ball. Milt Sunde and Ed White, the guards, flanked Tinglehoff. Ron Yary and Grady Alderman were at the tackles, John Beasley at tight end. Gene Washington and John Gilliam were the wide receivers, Bill Brown and Dave Osborn the running backs. Tarkenton barked the signals, "Hut . . . hut. . . ." On the second "hut," Tinglehoff slapped the ball into Tarkenton's hands.

In the year 1972, Fran Tarkenton cheerfully gave up a reasonably secure job as quarterback of the New York Giants, the fringe financial and publicity benefits New York City offers a talented athlete and a comfortable rented suburban home—complete with private waterfall and natural pool—to return to the playing fields of Minnesota, a state he had fled five years earlier. Tarkenton was delighted with the trade; more than anything else in the world, he wanted to play—for the first time in his career—on a team that stood a chance of winning a Super Bowl.

It didn't require a quarterback of Tarkenton's intelligence to realize that the Giants were not that team—and were not likely to become that team before Tarkenton became eligible for Medicaid. Even a defensive lineman could figure that out. (As a matter of fact, one did. His name was Fred Dryer, and mostly because he thought—sometimes out loud—that the Giant lineup was miserable, he got his wish and was traded, eventually landing with the Los Angeles Rams.)

Tarkenton was on better than speaking terms with adversity by the time he joined the Giants in 1967. He had already served six seasons in Minnesota, starting with the year the team was born. In Tarkenton's six seasons, the team won more than half its games only once. In Tarkenton's six seasons, the team was never seriously in contention after the first month of official competition.

When Tarkenton became a Giant in 1967, he took over the leadership of a team that had won only one game in 1966, a team that had plummeted from first place to last in three seasons. Under Tarkenton, the Giants improved 700 percent; they won seven games in 1967. But still, in Fran's five years in New York, the Giants won more than half their games only once, in 1970, when they went into their final regular-season game, against Los Angeles, fighting for a playoff berth. The Rams won the game, and in 1971, the Giants fell apart. They won only four games and lost ten.

Tarkenton, like Dryer, made no secret of his unhappiness with the 1971 Giants. In fact, he made a poll. Each time he bumped into an old friend, who happened to be playing against the Giants, Fran asked the old friend which pro team was the worst he had seen all year. Invariably, the answer was the same, confirming Tarkenton's fears.

He had nothing personal against his Giant teammates (although he did wonder what in the world made the team's management think that Rocky Thompson, as good as any kick-off-return man alive, would ever become a skilled receiver). He lavished praise on Dryer, on tight end Bob Tucker and on running back Ron Johnson, who missed the 1971 season with an injury. Frequently, he invited the Giant offensive line to dinner at his home, partly to promote team spirit, partly to review strategy and partly in the hope that his wife's cooking would make the linemen strong enough to protect his outwardly frail body. (Tarkenton was sacked more often than any other passer in his conference in 1971; the fault, presumably, lay with Fran's blockers, Fran's scrambling and Fran's wife's cooking.)

Tarkenton did have something personal against defeat. He was no longer in football for the money, if he ever was; he was a walking business conglomerate and, more important, a successful one. But at the age of 32, he wanted a championship, and when the Giants dealt him to Minnesota, a team that seemed to lack only a quarterback for a championship mix, naturally Tarkenton was ecstatic.

No one doubted the worth of the Minnesota defense, and

Tarkenton himself had no complaints with the offense. "As far as having people around me," said Tarkenton, "I couldn't ask for more."

He ticked off the Viking lineup with enthusiasm. "Ron Yary. Awesome. He manhandles people. Milt Sunde. A nine-year veteran. A Dave Herman-type. Mick Tinglehoff. None better. Ed White. Very likely the strongest man in pro football. Before our exhibition game in Miami, he tore the Yellow Pages book of Miami *in half. Miami.* That's a big city. During training camp, we were coming out of a parking lot and there was a big pillar blocking the driveway. Bill Brown, Paul Krause and I tried to move it, and we couldn't. All together. White lifted it himself. Nobody'll arm-wrestle him. Grady Alderman. Probably better than any offensive tackle in the game."

Tarkenton felt equally pleased with his receivers. "Gene Washington. Enormous talent. Holds the Big Ten hurdles record. Learning something new every day. John Gilliam. A polished receiver. Quick-footed. Great patterns. John Beasley. A good blocker, rough and tough. Not great speed, but he'll catch anything."

The Minnesota running backs, too, left nothing for Tarkenton to desire. "Clint Jones. Not Ron Johnson yet, but he has Ron Johnson-type of ability. Oscar Reed. The quickest fullback I've ever played with. Dave Osborn. Solid. The best No. 4 running back in football. Bill Brown. He's 34, and he doesn't know it."

Tarkenton smiled. "If we don't win," he said, "there's only one place to lay the blame—and that's with me."

As soon as he took the snap from center, Tarkenton moved straight back, drawing the defensive linemen toward him. Tinglehoff, Sunde and White pulled out, sliding to the right, setting up a wall of blockers. Bill Brown, the 12-year veteran with the rookie body, feigned a blocking stance, then moved to his right, four, maybe five yards behind the line of scrimmage. Tarkenton drifted back beyond the ten-yard line and as Ron McDole, the

Redskin end, lunged toward him, Fran lobbed the ball over
McDole. Bill Brown grabbed it, his fifth reception of the game.

Tarkenton and Brown entered the NFL the same year. After
one season in Chicago, Brown went to Minnesota, and for five
years the two men were teammates and friends. Brown hadn't
been used much in 1971, either as a runner or a pass receiver.
He had caught only ten passes all season, his lowest total since
his first year with the Vikings. But Tarkenton intended to use
Brown fully. In 1964, a year when Brown caught 48 passes,
Tarkenton hit him nine times for touchdowns—a record for
running backs.

The Tarkenton who teamed with Brown in 1972 bore only a
passing resemblance to the Tarkenton who had teamed with
Brown in 1964. During his first tour in Minnesota, Tarkenton
looked—and acted—the All-American boy. He was, as everyone said, the son of a preacher man from Georgia—the fact that
he spent most of his pre-teen childhood in Washington, D.C.,
was immaterial—and he lived the role. He was very active in
the Fellowship of Christian Athletes, and he was not above
implying that when he danced away from a tackler, he wasn't
doing it by himself; he was being helped by the Great Blocker
in the Sky. Tarkenton wore his hair short, not crew-cut, but
definitely collegiate, and he wore his clothes to match. He wore
white shirts and rep ties, and suits so square they would have
embarrassed Lawrence Welk. "When I left Minnesota," Tarkenton now recalls, "I didn't even know what Gucci shoes
were."

Then he came to New York, arriving a year after a rookie
quarterback named Joe Namath assaulted the town, and the
contrast between the hell-raising son of a mill worker and the
God-fearing son of a preacher man was just too tempting for
the press and public to pass up. The two quarterbacks were
billed as the saint and the sinner, and it made no difference that
neither label fit snug. Broadway Joe, it was assumed, divided his
evenings between bar stools and bed; St. Francis split his nights,

reportedly, between Bible reading and milk shakes. Actually, without any disrespect to either, Namath and Tarkenton probably would have enjoyed each other's company.

In New York, Tarkenton discovered Gucci shoes with their dazzling patent-leather shine. He discovered Cardin suits, and Bill Blass slacks, and he learned that a hair stylist was a lot more than just a barber. Tarkenton discovered discotheques, and "21," where two could eat for the price of 20 in Minneapolis, and he found out that Coke wasn't the only good-tasting drink on the market. Tarkenton didn't challenge Namath's hours, appetites and habits, but his chances for beatification dimmed. He drifted away from the Fellowship of Christian Athletes, closer to the fellowship of P. J. Clarke's, a celebrity saloon. In Minnesota, Tarkenton was called Francis; in New York, Fran.

For the Second Coming of St. Francis to Minnesota, Tarkenton's clothes were New York sharp—and his hair, sideburns and all, was modishly long. At 34, Bill Brown still had a crewcut. And he wore pink sports jackets which he paired with blue slacks. "Godawful," laughed Tarkenton.

Bill Brown tucked the ball under his arm and followed his blockers inside the five-yard line. Then he veered to the inside— he would have had a clear field to the outside—and just short of the goal line, ran into a tribe of Redskins. Brown powered, drove and burrowed his way into the end zone. The Vikings had a touchdown, and after Fred Cox kicked the extra point, the score was Minnesota 21, Washington 24. With only 70 seconds to play.

From the day the Giants traded him, Fran Tarkenton had been waiting for Minnesota's opening game of the 1972 season. For more than seven months, he had been looking forward to showing what he could do with a real football team. "I never worked harder getting ready for a season," Tarkenton said.

The night before and the day of the game, Tarkenton and all the Vikings stayed in the Holiday Inn near the Minneapolis-St. Paul airport, not far from Metropolitan Stadium. "It was," said

Tarkenton, "the longest day of my life." He wandered from room to room, restless, impatient. "Sure, I felt scared," he said. "I had a fear of losing. I wanted to win so badly."

In the first quarter, Bill Malinchak, a member of the Redskins' specialty teams, promoted from the taxi squad only a few days earlier, burst in on the Viking punter Mike Eischeid, threw himself through the air and blocked a kick. Malinchak scooped up the ball and ran for a touchdown. It was the first time a Minnesota punt had been blocked since the year the team was founded. Since 1961, the Vikings had punted 681 times without once being blocked.

Still, with Tarkenton in command, the Vikings struck back and took a 14–10 lead into the final period. Then, the Redskins scored two touchdowns in a minute and a half, and even after the Tarkenton-to-Brown screen pass, Minnesota trailed by three points.

But the Vikings' fans were not quite ready to surrender, to quit on Tarkenton. Most of them remembered the heroics he had provided the first time the Minnesota Vikings played an official football game. The game was played in Minnesota, against the Chicago Bears, and no one expected the Vikings, who had lost five straight exhibitions, to threaten the Bears. But Fran Tarkenton, a 21-year-old rookie, a third-round draft choice from the University of Georgia, came off the bench, threw four touchdown passes, ran for a fifth and beat the Bears, 37–13.

Minnesota lined up for the kickoff, and everyone in Metropolitan Stadium knew that the Vikings were going to attempt an on-sides kick. Fred Cox moved up to the ball and toed it gently over the midfield stripe. Eleven Vikings raced toward the ball. A Redskin fell on it.

"Right then," said Tarkenton, "I knew we had lost. Up until the moment the on-sides kick failed, I thought we had a chance to pull it out."

Tarkenton walked off the field, each step showing his disappointment. He entered the dressing room and flopped down in front of his locker. Only a couple of Minnesota sportswriters interrupted his thoughts, and they quickly left him alone.

"It's funny," Tarkenton said afterward. "In New York, there would've been 20 or 30 writers around me, all of them wanting to know what I did wrong, how I felt, what happened. Out here, the writers stay away. It's like they're suffering with you."

Tarkenton showered and dressed, and as he emerged from the dressing room, Phyllis Tinglehoff, the center's wife, walked up to him. "Francis," she said, "I feel so sorry for you."

Tarkenton, personally, needed no pity. He had turned in a glittering performance. He had completed 18 of 31 passes for 233 yards. He had passed for two touchdowns. He had not surrendered a single interception. He had run with the ball three times and he had gained 35 yards, an average of almost 12 yards a carry. Nobody could blame him for the defeat.

Almost nobody.

In the press box, two Minnesota writers were working on their stories for the next day's papers. One pointed out to the other how Minnesota had dominated Washington statistically. The Vikings earned 26 first downs, Washington 11. The Vikings gained 382 yards, Washington 203. The Vikings ran 79 plays, Washington 48.

The other writer nodded. "It's just like I figured," he said. "Last year, we used to lose the statistics and win the ballgame. Now, we'll win the statistics and lose the ballgame. I told you that's what Tarkenton does for you."

After 12 years in professional football, Fran Tarkenton remains a target for critical assaults upon his manhood and his winning zeal, upon his ability and his leadership. The anti-Tarkenton party line can be traced directly to the man who coached Tarkenton during his first Minnesota stay, Norm Van Brocklin. The gospel, according to Van Brocklin, was this: "Fran Tarkenton will win games he should lose, and he'll lose games he should win, but he'll never win games he has to win."

That theory explains, quite clearly, why Tarkenton concluded after Minnesota's 1966 season that either he or Van Brocklin had to go. (Ironically, both went.)

Tarkenton wrote letters to each of the Vikings' directors, telling them of his desire to be traded, to be shipped as far as possible from Norm Van Brocklin. Tarkenton said he would never play for Van Brocklin; he would sooner retire from football.

Faced with that ultimatum, Jim Finks, the Vikings' general manager, traded Tarkenton to the New York Giants for four draft choices. (The four draft choices turned out to be Clint Jones, Bob Grim, Ron Yary and Ed White. Because of Jones' promise, the Vikings then dealt Tommy Mason to Los Angeles for a draft choice, who turned out to be Alan Page, and for Marlin McKeever, who was traded to Washington for Paul Krause. Because the Vikings had so many high draft choices, they traded one to New Orleans for Gary Cuozzo, who was later sent to St. Louis for John Gilliam. In other words, as a direct or indirect result of that 1967 Tarkenton trade, the Vikings picked up six current starters—Jones, Yary, White, Page, Krause and Gilliam—plus Bob Grim, the key man in the 1972 trade that brought Tarkenton back to Minnesota.)

Tarkenton scrambled away from Van Brocklin—who lost the Viking job to Bud Grant in 1967—but he did not escape Van Brocklin's label. The knock on Tarkenton was modified slightly; what it came down to, essentially, was that Fran Tarkenton was a fine quarterback for a losing team, colorful and exciting, great as a gate attraction, but that he couldn't quarterback a winning team, he wasn't a winner himself, he wouldn't win the big games. It didn't seem a terribly fair judgment—considering the quality of the Minnesota and Giant teams Tarkenton guided in his first 11 seasons—but still it stuck.

The anti-Tarkenton line altered perceptibly as a result of his final season in New York. During the exhibition season, Tarkenton quit the team before a game in Texas, arguing that he would not play without a signed contract and that the Giants were unwilling to negotiate a fair contract with him. Tarkenton said he would rather retire than accept an unfair offer.

Wellington Mara, the Giant owner, did not bend one inch. He did not say, "Come back, Francis." He said, "Lots of luck in your new career." After a brief holdout in his Atlanta home —he did about as well as the Confederates did against Sherman —Tarkenton came back to New York and accepted essentially the same contract he had labeled unfair a few days earlier. Tarkenton not only lost his demands; he lost face. This did not make Wellington Mara his favorite person.

And then when the season began, and the Giants staggered, and Tarkenton hardly bothered to disguise his unhappiness, Wellington Mara decided that Fran Tarkenton, despite his fine moral upbringing, was not his hero, either.

Tarkenton was shipped back to Minnesota—coach Bud Grant definitely wanted him; general manager Jim Finks, who had felt slighted when Tarkenton wrote to the board of directors instead of turning to him in 1967, went along with Grant —and the Giant organization immediately began to bad-mouth Tarkenton. The new party line was that Tarkenton was a divisive force on the Giants, that he drove a wedge between head coach Alex Webster and the players, that he tried to assume Webster's job, that his ego and his mouth were far larger than his talents. Besides, his passes were hard to catch. Judging from reports filtering out of the Giant office, Tarkenton was being blamed for about eight of the team's defeats in 1971 and Fred Dryer for the other two.

Tarkenton, who is as self-controlled as he is self-confident, accepts the criticism without outward bitterness. The charge that he is not a winner, that he can't win big games, he dismisses as ridiculous. "I've won a lot of games," he says. "In high school. In college. In the NFL. Some of them had to be big ones."

The charge that Tarkenton hurt the Giants, with his attitude and with his play, he accepts as ill-founded but understandable.

"Maybe it's the best thing," he says. "When you make a trade, you have to rationalize. You can't make a trade and say it's for the bad of the club. If I were a general manager and I made a trade, I wouldn't praise the guy I was giving away. How could I? How could anyone? You have to say the trade is going to improve your team, and you hope that if you keep saying it enough, maybe the rest of the players will believe it and benefit from it. Don't take it too seriously when people say how bad you are—or how good you are. Only you know."

Tarkenton is very serious, very sincere when he says these things. He knows he sounds mature, and Tarkenton is proud of his maturity.

The morning after the Washington game, the Minneapolis Tribune *came out with a headline :* TARKENTON CRUSHED BY LOSS TO REDSKINS. *The story underneath began, "Fran Tarkenton probably never has taken a defeat harder. . . ."*

Fran Tarkenton was in a perfectly amiable mood the day after Washington beat the Vikings. If some deep depression was gnawing at him, Tarkenton was a terrific actor. In the afternoon, he went shopping for a motorcycle, he viewed the movies of the Redskin game and he turned down an offer from Sargent Shriver to appear with Shriver at a rally at the Twin Cities airport. Tarkenton and Shriver are friends; they socialize together. But Tarkenton's main business interest—Behavioral Systems, Inc., a company that trains the disadvantaged to enter the working force—has a multi-million dollar contract with the Nixon Administration. Tarkenton did not feel compelled to take a strong stand in the 1972 election.

In the evening, Tarkenton went to dinner at a restaurant called The Jolly Green Giant, a family-type place, large and busy. No one in the restaurant said, "Hello, Francis," no one asked him how he felt, no one asked him about the game, no one asked for an autograph. In P. J. Clarke's, he wouldn't have escaped so easily.

Tarkenton talked about the defeat, and about its impact on

him. "I wanted to win," he said. "I wanted to win very much. But not any more than anyone else. This team expects to win. This team should win."

Tarkenton sipped a gin-and-tonic. "You know, I feel funny playing a children's game in my 30s, but I do it for one reason. I love it. Nothing in my life compares to the ecstasies I get from this game. And nothing compares to the horrible things. But everybody has enormous setbacks in every field. People want to put finality into sports, and it's ridiculous. Look at Jerry West. He went through all those years without winning a championship, and everybody worried about how he suffered, and now he's finally won one, and what has it done to him? Nothing. It hasn't affected him. He's still the same man.

"If I can win a championship, it won't change me one way or the other. I want to win a championship. I want to win one desperately. It's probably what I want right now more than anything else in the world. But if I don't, I'm not going to kill myself. And if I do win a championship, it will probably make me happier than anything else could—right now. But in a few years, it won't make much difference."

Tarkenton finished dinner and left the restaurant. If anyone recognized him, they didn't show it. "In a few years," he said, "I'll be out of football, and not that many people will really care whether I ever won a championship or not. I'll be thinking about other things myself—other goals, other challenges." Tarkenton paused. "I feel bad about losing last night," he said. "But it ain't gonna shake the world."

4 / BONUS

Caught With Our Pants Down:
A Super Bowl Diary

By Fran Tarkenton

In 1973, Fran Tarkenton and his Minnesota Vikings won five straight exhibition games and the first nine games of the regular season. Then, after clinching the division title and coasting till the playoffs, Tarkenton and the Vikings beat Washington and Dallas to win the National Football Conference championship. The Vikings lost in the Super Bowl, but Tarkenton glittered. He completed 18 of 28 passes, breaking Joe Namath's Super Bowl record for completions, and he ran for Minnesota's only touchdown.

It was a pity that Miami dominated the game so decisively in the first quarter, because if there had been any degree of doubt about the outcome, Tarkenton's singular style of play would have made SB VIII the first exciting Super Bowl game since SB III, the one in which Joe Namath guaranteed and sparked a victory. But even in one-sided defeat, Tarkenton's skills saved the Super Bowl audience from falling asleep.

His diary is a unique record of what it is like to be the most spotlighted player in the most spotlighted game of the year. To put it together, Tarkenton and I sat down each day and reviewed the previous 24 hours. He talked and I typed, and on Super Bowl Sunday we both suffered.

Saturday, January 5

After we beat Dallas last Sunday for the NFC championship, Harry Peter Grant, our emotional coach, gave us a locker-room talk. Harry Peter said, "Practice tomorrow at noon." That was his whole speech. Harry Peter doesn't believe in wasting words.

He also doesn't believe in wasting energy. When we showed up for practice Monday, Harry Peter told us we could have the rest of the week off. He told us to report back at noon today. The assistant coaches spent the week studying Miami films. I think Harry Peter went hunting.

It took a lot of guts for him to give us four days off. I don't think any Super Bowl coach had ever done that before. But I think that, like most of Harry Peter's moves, it was a smart one. The build-up to the Super Bowl is so tremendous that, in recent years, teams seem to have gotten tight and then not played the way they were capable of playing.

I know the rest was good for me. I went home to Atlanta, and by Tuesday, I was already impatient. I kept telling myself I didn't belong in Atlanta. I couldn't wait to start playing football again. It's a pretty good coach who can make you feel that way after five exhibitions, 14 regular-season games and two playoffs.

From a physical standpoint, I needed the time off. Midway through the season, against Los Angeles, I got a rib injury, and the following week I wasn't able to throw until Friday. When I did start throwing, I had to change my motion, to avoid pain and strain in my ribs. As a result, I hurt my arm. For the rest of the season, I never did throw quite right. (Yet in the playoffs, against Dallas, I threw the longest pass of my life, a touchdown pass to John Gilliam, so maybe the new motion wasn't so bad. Maybe the critics were right: Maybe I had been throwing wrong all my life.)

Now, after four days of rest, the pain's gone from my arm for the first time in a couple of months. The only question is whether, after the layoff, I'll be able to throw.

I didn't get a chance to find out today. The temperature was 20 degrees below zero, so we stayed inside. Harry Peter gave us a little talk, putting the Super Bowl game in perspective. He doesn't believe in painting any picture other than a real one. He told us we were going to a showcase, to an extravaganza. He said it was going to be one big festive happening—for everybody but us and the Dolphins. We're the ones who have to work. We're the gladiators.

Sunday, January 6

We flew to Houston today, and I spent the flight playing bridge with Bill Brown, Grady Alderman and Mick Tingelhoff. We've kept the game going all season long, and I have to play with a handicap: Bill Brown is my partner. You can tell from the way Bill plays bridge that he has spent too many years playing on the special teams. All that contact has gotten to his mind.

We had plenty of room for our card game because all four of us were sitting in first class. On our team, seating in the airplane is based strictly on seniority. You need at least ten years in the NFL to qualify for the good seats. We've got about a dozen guys with that much seniority. Bill, Grady, Mick and I have 51 years of NFL experience among us.

The trip was uneventful—except for Brown's weird bidding —until we got to the Houston airport. First, our bus driver got lost. Then the bus broke down. We made it faster from Minneapolis to Houston than we did from the airport to the Sheraton Inn.

Monday, January 7

Today, we got our first look at our training quarters for the Super Bowl. We'd heard that the NFL was spending about $100,000 to take care of the press at the Super Bowl; it looked like they were spending about $10 to take care of us.

The building didn't look too bad from the outside. Unfortunately, we had to go inside. We were set up in a junior-high gymnasium. It looked like the kind of gym I used to play boys' club basketball in in Washington, D.C. Around the perimeter of the room, somebody had plastered all our names on the wall, and in front of the names, there were tables, plain rectangular tables, for us to lay our clothes on. In the middle of the room there was one table for all the coaches to share. Harry Peter had one corner of the table, an area about two feet by two feet. Obviously, the place was never meant to be a locker room.

The shower room was worse. We counted ten showerheads, and only three of them worked—for 50 men. Jim Marshall insisted he spotted sparrows on some of the showerheads. There was no soap. None at all. It's going to be a big week for deodorant.

We went outside to loosen up, our first workout in eight days, and we looked like clowns. My legs were wobbling, and my arm felt like spaghetti. I got a little nervous, wondering if I'd be able to throw hard by Sunday.

After our workout, we met the press. Harry Peter had warned us that we'd have press conferences Monday, Tuesday, Wednesday and Thursday, and that we had better be ready to hear the same questions over and over. I enjoy talking with the press, but I did get a little upset today. One newspaperman kept asking me how badly I'd feel if we lost the Super Bowl. I told him that no matter what happens, I'll wake up happy Monday morning. He wouldn't accept that. He kept pressing, wanting to know how deeply I'd be hurt.

I won't be hurt. I want to win. I want to win very badly. I want us to prove we're the best football team in the world. We're good enough to be that. But if we lose, it's not the end of the world. It's not the end of my life. If I thought this were the climax of my life, that from here on it's all anti-climax, then I'd really be unhappy.

Tuesday, January 8

We've been watching films of the Miami Dolphins, and we know what they can do. We have a game plan ready, but game plans are overrated. Against Dallas, for instance, everybody said we had a terrific game plan because I threw 19 times on first down. I hadn't planned to throw 19 times on first down. I did it because that's what was working.

The most important part of our game plan is right on the front of it. It tells me the names of the Miami defensive players, their sizes and their uniform numbers. That's to make sure I'll recognize them Sunday.

Actually, the defense has a much more complex game plan than the offense. Our defensive coaches have studied the Miami offense very carefully, and they have calculated very precisely the Miami *tendencies.* That's the key thing—tendencies, meaning the plays Miami tends to use on a given down, with a given distance to go, in a given field position. Our defensive coach has these tendencies charted—I don't think we used a computer to make up the chart, but some teams do—and he'll have the chart with him on the field Sunday. On every defensive play, depending on the down, the yardage and the line of scrimmage, he'll signal our defense what to do. The idea is to make the offense go against its tendencies, go against what it tends to do best.

Our offensive game plan isn't anything special—*except* that we make adjustments to the *uniqueness* of the defense. The Cowboys, for instance, flexed their line, so we adjusted to that. Miami's uniqueness is its 53 defense, its use of an extra linebacker, Bob Matheson, No. 53. A lot of teams'll do something like that in special situations, but Miami will do it first down, second down, anytime. We're gearing ourselves for that.

We've put in a couple of special plays for this game—two running plays for me. I'm afraid the theory behind using these plays has nothing to do with the Miami defense. The theory, I suspect, is that we can use these plays now because, no matter what happens, I'll have seven months to heal.

Wednesday, January 9

We had an excellent workout today, one of our best all year. We were crisp, we were concentrating, we were catching the ball, nobody was missing assignments. The rest had done my arm a lot of good, and I'm throwing as well now as I did early in the season.

I'll have to be throwing my best to have success against the Dolphins. They have the two best safeties in the NFL—Dick Anderson and Jake Scott. They disguise their coverage well. They're like two extra linebackers.

Each time I look at the films and watch Scott at free safety, I kind of wonder, "What's that little kid doing out there?" I've known Jake since he was a little kid. I was his coach in Pony League baseball, and around that time, his mother, Mary Scott, was teaching me educational psychology at the University of Georgia. I used to kid Jake about getting me copies of the tests in advance. He never did, but I've got to give him credit. I think he tried.

The Dolphins do use a zone defense, but that's mostly just a play on words. At some point, all zones become man-to-man. I don't mind facing a zone; it doesn't have much of an effect on me.

The funny thing is, the other day Weeb Ewbank of the Jets said something like, "Tarkenton likes to beat the zone on the outside seam, and the Dolphins play the outside seam very well."

That's an interesting theory, with only one flaw: I really don't know what a seam in a zone is.

Thursday, January 10

For the second straight day, we had a super workout. It doesn't necessarily mean anything—I've gone from great workouts into terrible games and vice-versa—but still it's one touch of sanity in an insane week. I've gone to two Super Bowls as a spectator, and I've talked to Super Bowl players, and Harry Peter warned us this would be an extravaganza, but nothing quite prepares you for the reality of the unreality of this week.

It's a make-believe world. For this week, at least, we're national celebrities. The press wants to talk to us every day. (I've run out of honest answers, so today, when someone asked if we're going to do anything different Sunday, I said we were experimenting with a shotgun offense. I said it with a straight face, as much as I could, but no one seemed to take me seriously.)

The phone in my motel room never stops ringing, and every hour of the day, there are kids and adults running all around, looking for autographs and looking for chances to take our pictures and just looking at us. I've always wondered what it's like to be a Johnny Carson or a Joe Namath, and this week I'm getting a taste of it. It's not fun. I can understand now why Mrs. Onassis loses her temper with photographers.

Friday, January 11

We had a light workout today—short-yardage situations—and we watched the film of last year's Super Bowl, the Dolphins against Washington. The film did me a lot of good; I slept through it. I fell asleep in the first quarter and I woke up in time to see someone carrying Don Shula off the field.

My wife, Elaine, flew in today, along with my friend Neil Walsh, an insurance man from New York. Our management has a smart setup this week for the wives. They're all staying in the Red Carpet Inn, about five miles from where we're staying. Harry Peter gave us tonight off—no meetings—and extended our curfew to midnight. Tomorrow night, it'll go back to 11.

The last time the Vikings played in a Super Bowl, four years ago, when I was still with the Giants, the management made the mistake of letting the wives stay at the same place as the players. One of the guys moved his whole family into his room, and the night before the game, he slept on the floor.

We won't have that excuse this time.

Saturday, January 12

We worked out in Rice Stadium this morning, concentrating on special teams, the kickoff and punting units. I played on the kickoff team—position L-2—when we practiced kickoff returns, and I was a guard on the punting team when we practiced punt returns. I'm a terrific guard. I never miss a block. Fortunately, I never make one, either.

After lunch, Grady Alderman and I went to see *Papillon,* the movie about a Frenchman who is imprisoned in a Lombardi training camp. After watching Steve McQueen eat cockroaches, I won't complain about our pre-game meal. It was a depressing movie, but the acting was good, and it wasn't as depressing as going to see the double feature that's playing a few miles from our motel: *Day of the Dolphin* and *Don't Look Now.* I didn't like the combination.

At our dinner meal tonight, about 20 of us wore special T-shirts that my friend Neil Walsh had made up. The shirts carried the Ultra-Brite slogan, "My Mother Never Told Me About. . . ." Under the slogan, Neil had put the words, "Bud Grant," and a picture of Harry Peter—smiling. Harry Peter wasn't upset. In fact, he asked me if I could get him a dozen of the shirts.

I'm glad the week is almost over.

Sunday, January 13

At our pre-game meal this morning, just before Harry Peter gave his talk, Carl Eller raised his hand. "Coach," he said, "I just want to say a few words."

The whole room quieted down. Last month, when we were losing to Washington at halftime, Eller broke a blackboard and screamed at us. When Carl Eller talks, you listen.

Carl stood up. "All I want to say," he said, "is let's not get caught with our pants down."

Carl was naked from the waist down. He had slipped off his pants during the meal. The whole room broke up laughing. He had wanted to break the tension, and he succeeded.

Harry Peter's talk was moderate, as usual. He reminded us that earlier in the year he had told us we had the ability to be the best team in football. He said he still believed that, and he said we had the ideal setting in which to prove it—facing the defending world champions. "They're a great team, a well-coached team," he said. "You've got to play your best game to win."

Harry Peter doesn't lie. If we're playing a team that's not good, he'll say so. When he says a team is great, it means something.

The feeling of excitement built up fast. We had a police escort to Rice Stadium, and I could see the crowd swelling, and I saw the Dolphins arriving, and the adrenaline began to flow. Then, when we got out on the field, just before the game began, I started watching two helicopters and the Goodyear blimp circling overhead. Some guys were leaning out of the helicopters, and I started wondering whether they'd fall out—or whether there'd be a collision.

I got so engrossed in watching the aerial duel that by the time I started looking at the field, we were losing, 7–0. Then I went out on the field for just three plays until we had to punt. I'd like to think we gave up the ball so fast because I wanted to get back to watching the helicopters and the blimp. The real reason, I'm afraid, was the Miami defense. It was the best-coached defense I'd ever seen. People talk about comparing the Dolphins and the old Packers, and I'd have to say that offensively they're about even. But the Dolphin defense has it all over the Packers. The Dolphin defense is different: They won't make the spectacular sack. They don't even try that hard to stop you in your own backfield. They control the line of scrimmage. They'll give you two yards every play, but that's it. They are incredible.

So is Larry Csonka. I don't think I've ever seen a fullback have a better day than Csonka had today. He just may be the best man ever at what he's paid to do: Get five or six yards at a clip.

By the end of the first quarter, I could see that the momentum wasn't going our way. I wasn't about to give up, but down deep, I wasn't feeling too cheerful. Statistically, I had a decent day, and my two running plays worked perfectly—one for about an eight-yard gain, one for a touchdown and no damage to my body. But statistics never compensate for victory. I'm sure that O. J. Simpson would have happily given up half of his 2000 yards this season if, in exchange, he could have been playing here in Houston today.

I'm disappointed, but I'm not remorseful. I still don't think the Dolphins individually are any better than us, but today they executed better. They beat us on technique, and they beat us good. My desire to win couldn't have been any greater, but I'm still going to wake up happy tomorrow morning. I got to the Super Bowl, and a lot of great players didn't, and I've still got most of my life ahead of me.

I'm going to sleep well tonight, even if I have to go to sleep counting Csonka, Csonka, Csonka. . . .

5/CONERLY

The Most Beat-Up Man in Football

By W. C. Heinz

Charley Conerly quarterbacked the New York Giants in the years Dwight D. Eisenhower quarterbacked the country. Like General Eisenhower, Conerly had some good years and some rough ones. He heard the cheers of his countrymen, and he heard their jeers. More than a decade has passed since Conerly last passed, but he still holds one record that may endure forever: So far, he is the only quarterback ever to marry a sportswriter.

Actually, Perian Conerly wasn't a sportswriter when Charley married her, but she became one while he was playing for the Giants. She was handicapped in her profession by being unable to enter the team's locker room, but she compensated by getting exclusive interviews with the team's leader, very exclusive. Incidentally, Conerly's roommate, when he wasn't at home, also went into the business of covering sports. On road trips, Charley roomed with Frank Gifford.

Conerly and his roommate—Gifford, not Perian—were central figures in what many people consider the best and most dramatic pro-football game ever played, the 1958 championship game between the Baltimore Colts and the New York Giants. The Colts won the game in sudden-death overtime, 23–17, and almost everyone remembers how John Unitas boldly and deftly guided his team to the winning touchdown.

Not so many people remember Conerly's heroics, without which there would not have been an overtime. The Giants were losing, 14–3, at the half, but in the third quarter Conerly hit Kyle Rote with a long pass, and when Rote fumbled on the Colt 25-yard line Alex Webster scooped up the ball and carried it to the Baltimore one. That set up the Giants' first touchdown. In the fourth quarter, Conerly completed a 46-yard pass to Bob Schnelker, and then teamed up with roommate Gifford on a 16-yard scoring pass that forced the game into overtime.

Unitas wound up with the victory, but Conerly wound up with the more efficient passing statistics: The Giant quarterback completed 10 of 14 passes for 71 percent, 187 yards, 13 yards per attempt, one touchdown and no interceptions; Unitas was 26 for 40 for 65 percent, 349 yards, nine yards per attempt, one touchdown and one interception.

The following season, Conerly was, statistically, the leading passer in the National Football League, not bad for an old man in his 12th pro year.

W. C. Heinz, who wrote the Conerly article, was for many years one of the finest sportswriters in the country. Then he became, simply, one of the finest writers. He has written three remarkable novels, The Professional, *about a boxer,* The Surgeon, *about a cancer surgeon, and most recently,* Emergency, *about a hospital emergency room. In the late 1960s, as a favor to a friend who had served as a doctor during the Korean War, Heinz helped the friend put his experiences down on paper. The result was* M.A.S.H. *He could have used that title on Conerly, too.*

At dinner one evening last week Mr. and Mrs. Charles Conerly, who own a 225-acre cotton farm four miles from Alligator, Miss., were discussing the problems common to couples contemplating their middle years who suddenly realize that the world is moving rapidly around them and, too often, right over them.

"The trouble with us," Mrs. Conerly said, "is that we don't assert ourselves enough. We always let everybody walk all over us."

"Oh, I don't know," Mr. Conerly said. "I wouldn't say that."

"Of course we do," his wife said. "They're always saying that the laundry isn't ready, or the cleaning won't be back until next week."

It was characteristic of Mr. Conerly that he would not agree with his wife's analysis of their plight, but the fact remains that people have been literally walking all over him for the past 11 autumns. He is the quarterback and passer of the New York football Giants. At 37 he is the oldest player in the National Football League and, although there is no precise way to measure such things, it is probable that no one in the game today has had to submit to such a cumulative beating.

"He's taken more beatings than anybody I've ever seen," says Dr. Francis J. Sweeny, who has been the Giants' physician since 1930, "but he resents it whenever you ask him where he hurts. I've seen Charley a mass of bruises, black and blue on his elbows, his arms, his shoulders, his back and his chest, his ribs. He's been bounced so much that I can't tell you how many spinal concussions he's had. Charley's been a battered man."

In addition to the physical punishment he has absorbed, Conerly has probably been the most abused player in the league's 36-year history. Five years ago, when the Giants were struggling through a season in which they won only three games in 12, the fans displayed banners reading: "Goodby Charley," "Get A New Quarterback" and "Back To The Farm, Conerly." This October, when Conerly completed only seven passes out of 22 in a game the Giants lost to the Chicago Cardinals, the New York crowd booed him vociferously, and the following week Conerly sat out the game.

"Some years it was so bad," Conerly admits, "that my wife and I just wouldn't go out evenings. I'd be recognized, and it doesn't matter to me so much what they say, but I didn't want my wife embarrassed."

Despite all the suffering, Conerly has repeatedly come up with outstanding performances. This season, two weeks after he was hooted off his home field, he led the Giants to remarkable upset victories over the two best teams at that time in pro football, the Cleveland Browns and the Baltimore Colts, both previously unbeaten and both favored. The following week, with five rookies in the Giant lineup, Conerly took another pounding in Pittsburgh as the Giants lost, 31–10.

In the Cleveland and Baltimore games, Conerly completed 24 of 41 passes, four for touchdowns. As has been true throughout his career—during which he has thrown more touchdown passes than anyone except the famous Sammy Baugh—he did not see three of these scores because he was flat on his back. Once, against Baltimore, he was submerged under half a ton of opposing linemen. As a result he has again set observers to wondering how, over the years, he continues to survive and perform.

"When he came home from Cleveland," his wife Perian says, "he looked like he'd been in a fight. Somebody had trampled all over one of his shins. Somebody else had gotten a fingernail in—'unintentionally,' of course—and ripped his nose right near his eye."

Conerly's closest companion on the Giants is halfback Frank Gifford. He and Conerly shared a bedroom on the train home from Cleveland.

"I was supposed to get the lower berth," Gifford says, "but after that beating he took I went to bed first and climbed into the upper. Charley likes to make you think he doesn't give a damn, but the next morning he could hardly get out of that lower."

All passing quarterbacks in the professional game are primary targets for the opposing players as they drop back and cock their arms to throw. Conerly, who is just over six feet tall and weighs 185 pounds, has suffered more than any other, however, because over the years he has lacked consistently good blocking and outstanding receivers. In addition, if the opposing linebackers are joining the rush against him, he will strip himself of a blocker to get an extra man down the field as a potential pass-catcher.

"When you see that thundering herd charging you," says Jim Lee Howell, the Giant coach, "and when you know you're going to be knocked down, it takes guts to stand there and not panic. Charley has that courage, and he has a lot of other things the public doesn't appreciate, too. He'll throw a pass that looks bad and they'll boo him. What they don't know is that Charley knows his receiver hasn't got a chance, so what he's doing is grounding the ball rather than take the seven- or eight-yard loss we'd get if he still had it when they hit him. He does that so well, though, that the officials can't call it grounding and impose a penalty.

"The guy has been our meal ticket for ten years," Howell adds. "On this club we don't send in more than one play in ten from the bench. That means that he not only takes that pounding but he gets up and calls those plays and runs that team."

"The mental beating," Conerly says, "is as much as the physical. If we get beat, it's my fault. At least that's what the people think. After a game I'm mentally exhausted."

Conerly's football injuries began with a broken nose in high school in Clarksdale, Miss. The nose was broken again while he played for the University of Mississippi, from which he graduated in 1948 after having been named to a number of All-America teams. In his first two games of professional football he was knocked out, losing an upper tooth in one and suffering a depressed fracture of the right cheekbone in the second.

But like most professional athletes who manage to survive in contact sports over a long period of time, Conerly is unable to recall many of his injuries. He does not know exactly how often his face has been cut, how many stitches it took to close the cuts or how many times he has had the wind knocked out of him.

In the manner in which he dismisses his injuries, Conerly has also dismissed his two and a half years in the Marines. As a corporal he landed on Guam with the third wave and saw his gunnery sergeant killed as they stepped out of the landing craft. Later, on patrol, his carbine was shot out of his hands by a sniper. Only with a few of his closest friends has he ever discussed these experiences. Such reticence, coupled with the poker-faced manner in which he takes the physical beatings and the criticism without complaint, has made him appear to be a nerveless, impassive, combat-hardened ex-Leatherneck. Actually he is a shy, sensitive, introspective perfectionist.

Once, although no one saw him do it, he cried in the locker room—in 1950 when, after having beaten the Browns twice during the regular season, the Giants lost to them in the playoffs. On the night before and the night following every game he requires sedatives to get to sleep.

"At home I can sleep nine hours every night," he says, "but this is something that just builds on you. I'm sure I've never been nervous about being hurt in a game. I don't like to get hit any more than the next guy, but I just don't think about it. You can't be worrying about that, because that's not your job. You're liable to hurry your throws."

The build-up starts with Conerly each Tuesday. That is when the Giant scouts who have been following the next opponent report in to the coaches and the team.

"They run over who's going to play against us," Conerly says. "They give us the weights—250, 260, 280 pounds—but it doesn't make too much difference. They're all big guys.

"You know that if the running game doesn't go too good you're going to have to pass a lot. And if you start to hit with the passes they're going to get at you. I can't do anything about that. When they do get me, I relax. There's no use for me to try to fight 'em.

"I guess you learn how to fall, too. You feel the shock, but there's no pain unless something's torn or broken. It's on Monday that you're sore, but that's gone by Wednesday."

There have been games in Conerly's career when, with the

Giant ground attack functioning satisfactorily, he has not been down all afternoon. On the average, however, he is flattened between 15 and 20 times a game.

"I guess what you see when they come at you," Conerly says, "is just bodies. Even though you know some of them, at that moment they're not personalities. Now you take some club we're playing—like Pittsburgh. Billy Ray Smith, I know him, because I used to see him fight in the Golden Gloves in Memphis, when he was at the University of Arkansas. That boy Stautner, I played against him for about nine years and I had a few beers with him once at an all-star game. Dodrill and Tarasovic, they've been around for a few years, too. Maybe the rest of them I don't know. I mean, if I saw them on the street I wouldn't recognize them.

"What I do is take a look at who's getting off me. If I don't recognize the face right away I look at the number. That way I know who should have got him—who's not doing his job."

With all the beatings he has taken over the years, Conerly has only once voiced his anger. When he is buried on third down he usually expresses disgust simply by throwing the ball back over his head before he walks off the field to let the punting team take over. In the first half against Cleveland this year, however, after a 237-pound linebacker bounded in on him untouched, he let go in the huddle with some tough talk. At the end of it he asked, "How would some of you guys like to stand back here and try to pass that ball?"

"I got real ugly," he admits, "but mostly you want to keep those boys up there blocking for you. You want friends in front of you. You say in a nice way, 'If you can just keep 'em off me a little longer this time I think we can get a T.D.' If you get them mad at you, hell, they might let them come through some time on purpose. They're good boys, though, and many times, when a man gets through, somebody'll apologize. They don't want to see me hurt, either."

"Sometimes," his wife says, "they'll even apologize to me."

After the disastrous 1953 season when, at least to Conerly's wife, it seemed that her husband had spent the whole autumn on his back, he informed the Giants that he was quitting. With a childhood friend from Clarksdale he was operating a liquid fertilizer business, and he also had an offer of better money from a Canadian team. In June of 1954, however, Howell, newly appointed as Giant coach, flew to St. Louis and drove to Bowling Green, Mo., where, at 9:30 in the morning, he found Conerly at a railroad siding loading equipment.

"He told me," Howell says, "that it wasn't a question of money. He just said, 'I'm not going to take that pounding. There's just no sense in it. I've got to have some more protection.' We told him we'd get him some, and we did. Of course, we've got new personnel this year, so he's getting knocked down more again."

"Every year," his wife says, "he's so tired of it that he thinks about quitting. Then you start to forget the bad things and remember the good. In December and January the newspapers tell what college players have been drafted and by what clubs. That starts it, because we look at that, and I'm always trying to see what guards the Giants get who'll make it easier for Charley. We've usually had such light guards."

"I'm looking to see," Conerly says, "what quarterbacks they've got who think they're going to take my job."

Conerly's black hair is streaked with gray. The age lines show now, deep across his forehead and spreading from the outer corners of his pale blue eyes. Of the 35 Giants now on the squad only one—Em Tunnell—saw Conerly come up. That first year against the Steelers in Pittsburgh he completed 36 passes, still a league record for one game. Three were for touchdowns, and one of those was thrown while he was flat on his back.

"The money is good, sure," he says—the Giants pay him at least $20,000 a year—"but that's not it. I couldn't do it just for money, and I don't see how anybody could. So you try to figure out what it is.

"I think about how we come up to New York every year, the places we go and the people we meet that we wouldn't meet otherwise. The big thing, though, is hard to explain. It's a kind of feeling. Take this year when we went out to Cleveland. There were 78,000 people there and they knew Cleveland was playing somebody but they didn't care who. They were just wondering how many yards Jimmy Brown was going to make. So we beat them.

"Every time I throw a touchdown pass or call the right play I get that feeling. If I could find that somewhere else I'd be doing something else. I just don't know where else to find it."

6/TITTLE

Y. A. Tittle's 176th Game

By Jimmy Breslin

The quarterbacks assembled in this book are, if nothing else, distinctive, and Y. A. Tittle is no exception. He has at least three distinctions: He holds the record for longest first name drawn by a quarterback (Yelburton Abraham Tittle). He is, so far as I know, the only quarterback ever featured in a speech delivered in a play written by an Irish actor about a German war criminal (Robert Shaw's The Man in the Glass Booth *offered a lyrical description of Tittle's passing). And he is a principal in one of my favorite trivia questions: Who is the only man ever to hit a home run off Sandy Koufax and catch a touchdown pass from Y. A. Tittle? The answer is Alvin Dark, who played with Tittle at Louisiana State University.*

Beyond that, Tittle was a magnificent quarterback, and of all the quarterbacks who completed their careers by 1965, Tittle ranked statistically behind only three—Otto Graham, Norm Van Brocklin and Sid Luckman.

Tittle had already put in ten seasons with the San Francisco 49ers when he joined the New York Giants in 1961. During his first three seasons as a Giant, the team won 33 games, lost only eight, averaged more than 400 points a season and won three straight Eastern Conference championships. It was the finest three-year period in the half-century history of the Giants.

Jimmy Breslin's story on Tittle's painful final game is the only newspaper story in this collection. It was written in 1964 for the New York Herald Tribune *where Jimmy and I shared an office, and it is an impressive display of how good a newspaper story— written on deadline, completed only a few hours after the event —can be. This story was not written at leisure; it was written in heat, in passion, the way Breslin, America's most gifted reporter, writes everything—his articles, his books and probably even his ad libs.*

They both woke up before the hotel operator rang for them. Y. A. Tittle didn't move. He looked up at the ceiling. This was the last time he would wake up to play a game of football because he had made up his mind to retire. "Costello dogs," he said to himself. He could see the No. 50. A brown 50 on a white jersey. Vince Costello, the Cleveland Browns' linebacker, red-dogs the passer a lot and it was the first thing Y. A. Tittle thought about when he woke up in an eighth-floor room of the Hotel Roosevelt Sunday morning.

It is like that after 27 years. You don't wake up and say "I'm playing today"; you wake up and say, "Costello dogs."

Aaron Thomas, the end, was in the bed closest to the door. He got up and walked past Tittle and went to the window.

"Rain," Thomas said.

"Heavy?" Tittle asked.

"Enough," Thomas said. Thomas opened the window. Tittle could hear the taxicabs down on Madison Avenue, their low pressure tires whining on the wet street. He reached over to the night table and picked up a thick blue-covered looseleaf note-book. The complete set of Giants' plays are on diagram sheets in the book and Tittle turned to a sheet that said "double dive 35" on the top. It is a straight ahead play and Tittle began to study it. You use straight ahead plays on a muddy field and Y.

A. Tittle began to go over every one that the Giants use. The amateur whines and curses the weather that's going to bother his passing. Y. A. Tittle looked up football plays that should be used in the mud.

He studied his plays through brown horn-rimmed glasses that were perched on a big nose that caves in halfway down the left side. Patches of shaved gray hair ran down the sides of his bald head. In the back of the neck, the grey ran into deep criss-cross lines. He says he is 38; the deep wrinkles in the back of the neck tell you that the 38 is just a number that he puts down when they ask him how old he is.

He had spent Saturday night the same as he has spent every night before a game since they put television sets into hotel rooms.

Right after dinner, Tittle came back to the hotel room, took off his clothes and sat down to watch television. He was dressed as he always is for television on the night before a game. In his shorts with the glasses on, a filter-tip cigarette in his hand and his socks on. The socks always are on.

"Lot of years," somebody said to him.

He shook his head. "Twenty-seven," he said. "That's just about my whole life."

"What do you do after tomorrow, give it up?"

"I don't know," he said. "I haven't said anything about it. But this game tomorrow is important to me for a lot of reasons. A lot of reasons. I want to have a good day tomorrow so much. . . ."

He wanted to have a good day because it was going to be his last. Y. A. had made up his mind that he was through. The last thing they like to do is stand and tell strangers who work for newspapers that they are finished with the business. But they tell each other, and Y. A. Tittle had told them in the dressing room that this was going to be his last game. That would do it, he told them, and on Saturday night Tittle sat in his hotel room and watched television and he kept thinking about the last shot he would ever get. No comebacks. No Cleveland next year. It was Cleveland now, and the career now, so go out right.

Now, it was 9:15 Sunday morning and Tittle put down the playbook and got up and got dressed for breakfast. He put on a white shirt and solid black tie and dark slacks. He reached into the closet and took out an olive green checked sports jacket.

"Still raining?" he said to Thomas.

Thomas looked out the window. "Raining pretty good," he said.

He took the elevator down to the lobby and walked into the Roosevelt Grill. It is a supper club, but the Giants use it for breakfast. Red-coated waiters served steak and scrambled eggs and the players ate quietly. When they were through, Allie Sherman, the coach, stepped up onto the bandstand. He smoked a cigar and he was in shirt sleeves. A green blackboard had been set up, with red stagelights playing on it.

"Now, once we get to pinch blocking, let each other know when they go back into a zone," Sherman began. He chalked in plays on the board.

In the background, Andy Robustelli's voice could be heard. He was in the back of the room, with the defensive team.

"Remember," his voice said, "we got to kick his rear end in. Remember, kick his rear end in for him."

When Sherman finished, the players filed out. Then Tittle moved over to Sherman's table, put the playbook on it and sat down. Gary Wood, the young one, sat on a chair behind him.

"Well, what do you think?" Tittle asked.

"The Green Bay special should be the best," Sherman said.

"Uh huh."

Sherman put the cigar in his mouth and waited for another question.

"How do we block on the slant 34?"

"Two-on-one," Sherman said.

Tittle picked up a knife and ran it across the tablecloth. "Now, the biggest frequency of dogging . . ."

"Costello," Sherman said.

"I know," Tittle said.

"This isn't a game you win with the big play," Sherman said. "We have to go straight ahead at them. The longer we have it the less he does." He was talking about Jimmy Brown; when they are as big as this one, they say "he" and never his name.

"Certain types of screens wouldn't be advisable today," Tittle said.

"What ones do you mean?" Sherman asked.

"Well, I don't think to the Frisco side is advisable."

"The Frisco side is all right here."

"I guess I keep thinking of Chicago," Tittle said. He meant 1963 in the championship game. He tried to throw a sideline screen pass to Phil King and Ed O'Bradovich, a Chicago lineman, intercepted it and ran for a touchdown.

Sherman smiled. "No, it's different here," he said.

Tittle nodded. "I guess I keep matching a play with a game," he said. "I got a game I can remember for every play that we got. That's the trouble when you've been around a little while. You remember too many games."

It was just like a business conference. There was no talk of "we've got to win" or no worry about getting hurt or how hard he belts when you let him get going for two or three steps. Just two guys sitting at a table and calmly going over technical things.

Football, when you do it for money, is like this. It is a trade, a job for money, and in all of New York few people ever have done their jobs better than Y. A. Tittle. They brought him into this town to pass a football and he did it well enough to bring the Giants to three championship games. But this year, with age taking a step away from him, and leaving him standing there a target for a lineman, he has done little.

John Baker of Pittsburgh got to him in the second game and tore two of his ribs loose, and after that the Giants were through and Y. A. Tittle had to gasp for breath every time he tried to pass. For the Browns, he was ready. The pain was gone, and there was a shot of cortisone in him to keep it out. The Browns were coming in for a game which meant the league title for them. Tittle was coming in after something, too. He wanted to go out of the town on top.

"You only know what it's like to play around here if you've played someplace else first," he was saying at the table. "This is the city for an athlete. I don't think I can remember a game I think is as important as this one to me."

The bus left for the ballpark at 11:15. Tittle sat in the back, on the right, a thumbnail between his teeth, looking out the window. He ran a hand over the glass so he could see out. He looked down at the sidewalk. Rain splashed into a puddle alongside the doorman.

Tittle began to move his lips.

The opener, he was saying to himself. Open with a double dive 39. Wheelwright right at them. Straight ahead. And watch Costello. Watch what he does.

In the stadium, in the light green-carpeted dressing room, he put on a gray sweatshirt and sat on a stool and looked down at his legs. Tittle's legs are smooth-shaven, so tape can be put all over them and then ripped off once a day. His toes stick together, with corns on the sides, the toenails black from 260-pound linemen stepping on them all year.

"I saw you in the first game you ever played here," somebody said to him. "It was on a Thursday night, against the Yankees." Tittle smiled. The guy was talking about the old football Yankees.

"What about the kids?" he was asked. "Do they think it's funny that this might be your last game?"

"I don't know," he said. "They're used to this business. Kids can adjust when they're used to things. My daughter now, she takes American history here. Then next week we get back to Palo Alto, she'll be having world history. Everything changes and she just keeps up with it."

Then he got up and started to get dressed, and the thumbnail came up to his teeth again and he began to think about another play.

At 12:45, a buzzer rang in the room. It meant the players had to get up and get ready to go on the field and everybody came around and tapped Y. A. on the shoulder and wished him luck and he sat there quietly and said thank you, and pulled on a cigarette he had cupped in his hand so photographers wouldn't catch him smoking. It was, it seemed, just another working day for him.

Then you shook hands with him and your hand closed on wetness. His whole palm was wet.

"What's this?" he was asked.

"This?" He smiled. "This is the business."

And a few minutes later, clapping his hands together, Tittle came trotting out of the dressing room, down the runway to the baseball dugout and then up the stairs and onto the field and there was a huge roar from the crowd when he came running through the goalposts and over to the bench. He waited while the Giants took the kick-off and when that was over, Y. A. came running on the field for the last big shot of his career. He wanted to go out of this city the way the good ones always do. The field was all right, and the rain was almost gone. He had a shot at it. A good shot at going out of this town on top. He bent his head into the huddle and called the first play of the game—a double dive 39.

Tittle took the snap, spun, handed the ball to Ernie Wheelwright and then kept going back, faking a pass. He kept looking over his shoulder at the Browns as he did. What he saw was no good. Their line jumped the Giants on this first play and Wheelwright ran into three or four white jerseys and right away you could see Y. A. Tittle was going to have trouble.

For the Browns kept getting that first step on the Giants' line and they stacked up runs and their halfbacks were all over the Giants' receivers. And on offense, they simply shoved everybody out and let him smash. He smashed and spun off them, Jimmy Brown did, and they were defenseless against him.

In the second quarter, with the Browns ahead, 3-0, Tittle went back and saw nobody open and then he said the hell with it. He took off on his own to the right and got to the Browns'

18. Ross Fichtner got to him near the sideline and tried to break him in half. Y. A. went down face first into the mud, but he pulled himself up right away. The referee was yelling about a personal foul and the ball was going to be put on the Cleveland 9. Now Tittle didn't hurt from the tackle.

On the second play, somebody was after him from the side, and Tittle ran straight up. Then he stopped and threw to Dick James, who was a yard behind the goal line. That put the Giants ahead, 7–3.

The Browns came back and scored. Ryan, their quarterback, was having a big day. Then Tittle was on the field again and he hit Joe Morrison on the Browns' 49 and now noise came down out of the three-decked green stands. Tittle clapped his hands and bent down in the huddle. He wanted Gifford this time, he told them. They broke out of the huddle and Tittle loped up to the line, looking over the Browns as he came.

Mickey Walker's gray pants were straining as he bent over the ball. The others were there, too. Bookie Bolin, Darrell Dess. At the snap, they would be coming back to make a pocket for Y. A. Tittle. Gifford was out on the right. Tittle put his hands down. The Cleveland halfbacks, Walter Beach, over on the left, and Bernie Parrish, on the right, were deep. They go even deeper when you show pass. Good. Tittle had called Gifford on a square-out to the sidelines.

Y. A. got the ball on the two-count and went straight back. Walker, Dess and Bolin came back with him and the white jerseys rushed at the three and grunted and slammed and tried to get through. Tittle turned around and held the ball up. Here was Gifford faking deep, throwing his head to the left, then cutting in one motion and running for the sideline, and Y. A. Tittle threw it at him and everything he wanted out of the afternoon was in that pass.

Gifford was at the Browns' 34 and he had his hands out and the ball was coming right to him when Parrish came running right by him and grabbed the ball and took off down the side-lines.

Tittle already was on his way over to the sidelines. You learn how to do this back in high school, in Marshall, Texas. You always get over there and cover the sidelines when you throw a pass out there. Y. A. Tittle put his head down and ran straight for the sidelines, at the Giants' 30, and Parrish was trying to get past that spot and into the open. Tittle came up and threw his body at Parrish's legs, and Parrish went up in the air and came down on his shoulder. The two of them skidded in the deep mud and then Parrish jumped up and clapped his hands.

Sometimes, it goes like that. Everything can be all right and you can know just what has to be done and how to do it, and you've done it a lot of times before and it has worked, and then when you do it this time the whole thing falls apart. It is like that in any business office in the city. Even the best in the place falls apart on something. Y. A. Tittle, who worked at his trade in New York as well as any ever worked, had just blown it all on a play called a square-out.

At the end, Tittle was on one knee in front of the Giants' bench, a blue hood thrown over his shoulders, his hands scraped and mud caked. The lights were reflecting off the puddles in the mud around him. Out on the field, Gary Wood was running the team and the Browns, scoring nearly every time they got the ball, ran up a 52–20 victory.

"How is it?" he was asked.

He shook his head.

"I'm sorry," somebody said to him.

"I'm sorry I couldn't give you something better," he said. "You people here have been awful nice to me."

He walked out of the stadium an hour later, in a black raincoat and black tyrolean hat with a red feather in it. He carried a brown-leather attache case and he looked like a businessman coming home from work, which was what he would be from then on. This was the last shot of a career that went 27 years and he blew it on a play called a square-out. Y. A. Tittle said he was sorry he couldn't have given the people a little more. Professionals think that way.

7/STARR

Pride of the Packers

By Leonard Shecter

As a man, Bart Starr is a model of good behavior. As a quarter-back, he was a model of efficiency. Through his 16 seasons with the Green Bay Packers, from 1956 through 1971, Starr completed 57.4 percent of more than 3,000 passes, a record for accuracy that still stands. In a stretch spanning the 1964 and 1965 seasons, he threw 294 consecutive passes without an interception, another record, and in 1966, he allowed only three of his 251 passes to be intercepted, a third record. Because his percentage of comple-tions was so high, and his percentage of interceptions so low, Starr acquired a reputation as a conservative quarterback. In a sense, he was—as conservative as any quarterback would be with such running backs as Jimmy Taylor and Paul Hornung to call upon. But Starr could be daring, too; his specialty was the long pass on third-and-one, and today, whenever a quarterback facing third-down-and-short-yardage falls back in the pocket to pass deep, any observer with a notion of football history is reminded of Starr. He could rise to heights under pressure. Starr was the Most Valuable Player in each of the first two Super Bowls, and the second award came after a very shaky start to the 1967 season, the season during which the late Leonard Shecter wrote the following story.

Shecter was, at heart, a debunker. He once wrote an article
about Vince Lombardi that stripped away Lombardi's saintliness
and angered all of Lombardi's players. Later, Shecter helped
Jim Bouton write Ball Four, *a book that stripped away baseball's*
protective coating and angered almost all of Bouton's ex-Yankee
teammates. But, writing about Bart Starr, even Shecter couldn't
debunk. All he did was strengthen the legend of Saint Bart.

It was a warm day in February in Green Bay, Wisconsin,
which is like a snowy day in July anyplace else. Instead of
hard-packed winter snow cuddling the landscape in the usual
polar bear white there was slush—deep, gooey, mud-flecked
slush. On his way home from school, little Bart Starr, nine years
old, had to slog through the muck which oozed over the tops
of his boots and made his feet wet and cold. When he came in
the side door, he was hurrying and did not think to take off his
boots. As he squished across the dining room rug, he left a thick
trail of wet, dirty footprints.

Before he reached the kitchen, he had been seized from behind by his father, the quarterback of the Green Bay Packers.
In short order he had found out a great deal about that good
right arm his father has. It was being applied with vigor to the
seat of his pants. Cherry Starr, Bart's wife, knew her eldest son
was home when she heard him crying.

After she had cleaned the glop off the rug, she called her
family in to lunch and the first thing little Brett Starr, three
years old, did was knock his glass of milk off the table—splash!

"Now that was just plain careless," said Bart Starr to his
young son. He lifted him off the chair and paddled his little rear
until he, too, was in tears. Then he sent him to his room.

"By the way," Bart Starr said to his wife. "You get off those
letters I asked you to do for me last night?"

"Not yet," Cherry Starr said.

"Well, for gosh sakes," Starr exploded. "If I knew it was

going to take you all that time, I would've done it myself. You *know* I wanted to get them out right away." He was practically spluttering.

"Now what in the world's gotten into you, Bart?" his wife said. "Hitting the children, shouting at me. What are you so edgy about?"

Bart Starr calmed down. "Well, I got a jillion things to do today," he said, "and I'm running behind. And I got to go over to Appleton tonight for a dinner."

"What kind of dinner?"

"Well, they're giving me a nice-guy award."

"Bart Starr," his wife said. "You got to be kidding."

Starr, blond, his intelligence glinting from his deeply set eyes, is the very model of a modern T-quarterback. And he tells this story as an answer to those who suggest that if he has a failing it's that he's too nice a guy. "I'm not all that nice," he says. "Just ask my wife."

The niceness of Bart Starr is legendary. And like most legends it is not exactly accurate. The story is often told that once, in huddle, in a burst of fury at Max McGee, the end, Bart Starr said, "Oh, hush up." It's a nice story, started by Gary Knafelc, who used to play for the Packers and room with Starr. It's also not true. What Starr *did* say to McGee was: "Dammit, knock it off."

"I know," says Knafelc, a man good-looking enough to be an actor, which he was for a time, "I just thought I'd give Bart a little color. I made him a Phi Beta Kappa, too."

His justification, says Knafelc, who is rather a pixie (if anybody six-feet, five-inches tall can be any kind of pixie) is that Starr *could* have been Phi Beta Kappa if he'd had as good grades his first two years at Alabama as he had his last two. "Maybe," Starr says with a laugh. "But the first two years I wasn't married."

What *is* true about Bart Starr is that he is what he has to be. There were times when he felt he was indeed too nice a guy and he reached down inside himself and filled the soft spots with steel. There was a time when he would rather face a firing squad than an audience, and he forced himself to become a calm, practiced, interesting, even amusing after-dinner speaker. There was a time when he was drafted 17th by the Green Bay Packers and knew so little about being a pro quarterback he was delighted just to sit on the bench—and in the years to come he made himself into the best quarterback in the National Football League, which is to say the world. The central fact about Bryan Bartlett Starr is that he has infinite ability to adjust, to become what his quiet but driving ambition demands him to be.

The importance of this ability in professional football cannot be overrated. The game is constantly changing, subtly shifting emphasis from running to passing, back to running again. Offenses are quicksilver, altering at the shout of a number at the line of scrimmage. Defenses adjust and readjust at the snap of the ball. The variations are almost as endless as those of chess, and the game of football must be approached with equal intellectual intensity.

It was in this spirit that Bart Starr had to set out this season to make his greatest and most significant change, from a man who used to lean on his team to one who must lead it. It is his most difficult change of all.

Starr was most comfortable when the team revolved around the powerhouse running of Paul Hornung and Jim Taylor. He was most comfortable when he was merely an extension of the overwhelming will of Vince Lombardi, the harsh-voiced coach with ego to match. He was most comfortable when he needed the team more than it needed him, and when Zeke Bratkowski, the number two quarterback, could slip into the game and hardly anyone would notice there had been a change.

Slowly, inevitably, the Packer style has been changing. "In recent years, the burden has fallen more and more on Bart," says Jerry Kramer, Green Bay's astute, articulate guard. "Always before it was Jimmy and Paul, Jimmy and Paul. And our offensive line was big and strong and it could overpower almost anybody. Now Jimmy and Paul are gone and the burden is on

Bart Starr. It's all on Bart Starr. He carries the whole thing and we're not as strong and as quick as we used to be on the offensive line either."

This is not to say that it is time to say a prayer for the dead over the Packer dynasty. "Coach Lombardi drives us so hard, gets so much out of us, drives himself so hard, that this club can never really go bad," says Kramer. "But we're all a little older and, well, our running game for instance." Kramer, a massive man with a golden coat of fur over his thick forearms, leaned back in the easy chair of his large and comfortable basement playroom; a color television set gabbled softly in a corner. It was Saturday afternoon before the Packers' first game of the season, the worst day of the week for a professional football player—the work done and the waiting begun. ("Saturday, all I can do is watch television," Kramer says. "Anything. Kiddie programs. Cartoons. I can't concentrate enough even to read a paper.")

"The running game," he said. "The other day Gale Gillingham (the other starting guard) and I were talking and he said, 'I bet Grabbo gains a thousand yards this season.' (Grabbo is Jim Grabowski, the pride of Illinois and one of the last of the wealthy bonus draftees.) And I said he hasn't got a chance. Gillingham was a little miffed. He thought I was knocking Grabbo. And I explained that he won't have the ball to run that much. Taylor would carry 17, 18, maybe 20 times a game. But now with Bart as precise and accurate as he is, I think Grabbo would be lucky to carry the ball 15 times a game."

By the second game of the season Kramer had been proven wrong. Grabbo carried the ball 32 times against the Chicago Bears and gained over 100 yards. Yet even while he was wrong, Kramer was right. Grabbo carried the ball so many times largely because Starr was hurting. He went into the game with his ribs wrapped in miles of tape and foam rubber. He also had an injured hand and a pulled thigh muscle and a feeling that fate was conspiring against him. "I never started training in better shape," Starr was saying one day during the training season. He was seated in the living room of his modest ranch home in a bulldozed development a quick kick away from Lambeau Field. "And I never had so many annoying little injuries."

Starr's performances in the season's first two games were called, by understatement, astonishingly poor. All last season he had thrown only three passes that were intercepted. In two games this season he threw nine, a 300 percent increase. Why? No one could say for certain. In the first game, in which Green Bay managed to pull out a 17–17 tie against Detroit, Alex Karras of the Lions set up light housekeeping in the Packer backfield.

In the game against the Bears the following week, which was pulled out, 13–10, with a long field goal, Starr had a good deal more time to find receivers. Still, he threw five interceptions and when he tried to settle for a ground attack, Grabowski fumbled the ball away three times. The Packers little deserved to win that game. They seemed to do it only out of habit.

All of which goes to prove that the Packers can expect to go only as far as Bart Starr goes, and no farther. Starr has said many times that he does not consider himself a giant of the gridiron in the Johnny Unitas mold. He never believed he had the sheer physical talent of a Unitas or that he could carry a whole football team with the stamina and accuracy of his throwing arm. The very idea that he might one day have to sent shivers up his back. Yet that day has arrived and no matter how much he wriggles and squirms, Bart Starr understands it.

Two things are involved here. One, of course, is leadership on the field. This means building in 39 other men the certainty that when extraordinary performance is called for, it will be delivered. The other thing is more subtle.

"Say you back up five years ago," Starr said, sitting on the edge of the couch in his simply furnished living room and leaning down to pet his elderly dachshund, Heidi. "At that time I wouldn't go up to a rookie to urge him to do the best job he could on the special teams, the kicking teams and so forth. Or

I wouldn't say something to some guy who may not even be in the game. Like: 'Look, if you get a call, be sure you're darn ready, be prepared.' I wouldn't find myself saying these things because at the time there were other people to be saying these things to him. You were *not* a senior ranking member of the squad. (Starr often refers to himself in the second person singular and the third person plural, "we," as though he were ashamed to use "I.") But as time goes on and you become a senior member of the team, you realize that it's your responsibility to do those things or they won't get told. You know, the coaches can say only so much to a player. After that it's the responsibility of the guys on the club."

All the time, though, Starr keeps in mind what Lombardi wants of him. It is the vanity of the coach, general manager and deity in residence at Green Bay that he has altered the course of professional football. Lombardi, conservative to a fault some say—among them Fran Tarkenton of the New York Giants— believes in his heart that a football is to be run with. He realizes the pass is here to stay, but nothing brings such a blissful smile to his face as a halfback gaining seven yards through tackle. "Basically football is a running game," Lombardi says in that gravelly voice of his that strikes terror into the hearts of rookies and obedience into the most suave veteran. "I happen to enjoy a well-executed running play more than a well-executed pass. We're usually about 50–50 with our plays. So are most of the other teams. When I first entered the league there was a great deal more passing than running. I take a great deal of pride in being the influence that changed that."

Yet it was obvious early in the season that if the Packers were going to make it as big this year as they did in the past, Starr was going to have to throw a lot. In the first game Starr handled the ball 26 times in the first half; 18 of those times he threw pass plays. It was not a successful half, but it showed the direction Starr must go. What it adds up to is pressure. It means he must make adjustments, almost as many as it took for him to become an after-dinner speaker.

When Starr first came to the Packers he spent more time looking at the tops of his shoes than into people's eyes. He was painfully shy and people said he could never become a leader of men. Yet almost from the very beginning he managed a transformation as soon as he bent down over the broad beam of his center.

"There is a softness in him," says Kramer. "A sort of gentle manliness. But there is also an iron-hard spirit. I recall when we were playing the Bears about five years ago. Bill George came through and hit Bart in the mouth. A real good shot. Blood all over. 'That'll take care of you, kid,' George said. You should have seen Bart. He snarled right back. Challenged him right there. 'You big SOB,' Bart says. And he's ready to fight. That's one thing about this game. You have to be ready to fight and Bart always is.

"A few years ago, if he felt he had to say something to one of his teammates, something like, 'C'mon, Jerry, let's go,' he'd come up after the game and say, 'Sorry, I didn't mean to holler at you.' Now he'll say, 'Dammit, you should have caught that ball,' or 'Hell, if I had a little more time I could've hit somebody with that pass.' He has the iron in him and he's more willing to express it."

It was this iron-hard spirit, no doubt, which Starr needed to call on when he was suddenly confronted not with a defensive line, but the scrubbed faces of a Rotary Club lunch. It is typical of him, though, that when he picked anecdotes to tell about the Packers they were uplifting ones, tales which were not only amusing but illustrated the *esprit* the Packers have built up over the years.

One of them is about a losing game. It was played against Detroit on Thanksgiving Day in 1962. The Packers went into the game puffed up with a ten-game winning streak. "But they almost beheaded us before we got out of there," Starr says.

In the third period, with the game gone, there was a time-out. The Packers had the ball, third-down-and-eight. Starr looked around at his backfield. Tom Moore was playing instead of Paul

Hornung that day. "Tom," Starr said, "what do you think about a sweep around right end to pick up this first down?"

Moore gulped. "You got to be kidding," he said. "We can't get eight yards on a run. They're just killing us. Darris McCord has been jumping all over me every time we try the sweep. Why don't you run Taylor?"

Starr looked over at Taylor. He was shaking his head. "You don't want to run me inside," Taylor said. "Roger Brown has pounced on me all day. I'm sore from my headgear to my shoes. Why don't you throw?"

Starr had been taking a terrible beating himself. He was frankly reluctant to pass and get knocked down again. But he steeled himself. He turned to Boyd Dowler, the end, and said, "All right, let's stop this foolishness. Run down at least ten or twelve yards, run a nice hook and let's pick up this first down."

"Bart," Dowler said, sincerely, "you're in a jam and I'd really like to help you. But Night Train Lane down there is covering like a blanket. Not only that, he's really hurting my ribs when I turn around. Throw the ball to McGee."

Max McGee, the other end, was by this time slinking away toward the sidelines. "He was," Starr recalls, "practically off the field and back on the bench."

Finally little Fuzzy Thurston, the guard, came up and took Starr aside. "Fuzzy had really had a miserable day with Roger Brown," Starr says, "and we tell this story on Fuzzy mostly because it's about a guy not losing his sense of humor in a crisis. He took me aside, just slightly, and said, loud enough for the whole squad to hear him: 'Bart, I've got a great idea. Why don't you just throw a long incomplete pass and that way nobody will get hurt.' "

The other story is on Max McGee. The Packers were playing the Rams in Los Angeles, needing to beat them to win the NFL's Western Conference title. Through the first half the game was very close and the Rams led by three points after three quarters. At that point Herb Adderley intercepted a pass and ran it back to the Los Angeles 25.

"As we were coming on the field," Starr says, "we were figuring this was just the lift we needed. And the thought was running through my mind that on first down if I make the fake to Taylor, have him make a real good fake into the line, pull it back and try to hit McGee over the middle we'd probably get him open. Sure enough we fake the ball to Taylor, he makes a beautiful fake and seven or eight of them gang him, figuring he has the ball. McGee was all alone down the middle. I threw the ball to him and it was on target. And he dropped it.

"We're back there thinking we want to shoot him. I mean shoot him on sight. Well, he strolls back to the middle and he gets about ten yards away and he just throws his hands up and says, 'My God, the smog is thick today.'

"We coulda killed him, but when he said that he just broke us up. The point is that we'd been playing poorly. We were so tight and so nervous we couldn't play well. But from then on we loosened up and played really well. We won going away."

One of the things Starr does better than tell funny stories, of course, is quarterback. Jack Christiansen, coach of the San Francisco 49ers, said last season: "Bart Starr has better timing on calling plays and taking advantage of defenses than anybody I've ever seen. He is probably the best quarterback in football today and when he retires, which I hope is soon, I expect that he will be recognized as the greatest of all time."

Christiansen's opinion is backed with impressive statistics. Bart Starr led the Packers to Western and World titles in 1961, 1962, 1965 and 1966. He was the league's passing leader in 1962, 1964 and 1966. Until this season, he held the NFL record for fewest interceptions (on a percentage basis). He holds the league record for most consecutive passes without interception —294. He holds the NFL record for highest percentage of career completions (going into this season—57.2 percent). He has a 69.9 percent completion record in AFL-NFL title games. (Of course there has been only one of these so far but this will do for a start.) He was the league's Most Valuable Player last season. And if the tell on a quarterback is how he does on third down in crucial games, try this on for size: against Dallas in the NFL title game last season, Starr completed seven of ten third-down passes. Against Kansas City in the Super-duper Bowl, it was seven of eight.

The strange thing is that there was no way to tell, when Starr was a lad, that he would ever become this kind of special light. The son of an Army sergeant, Starr grew up at an Air Force base in Montgomery, Alabama. This gave him a slightly marshmallowy drawl, the habit of calling everybody sir and none of the southern attitudes toward Negroes. "There was never any segregation on the base," he says.

He had a brother, Hilton, two years younger than he, who died a tragic death. Bart was 12 that summer and the two of them were playing hide and seek barefoot when Hilton stepped on a partly buried bone which punctured his foot. Although he received medical attention, the deep puncture led to tetanus. "For a long time I felt a real vacuum, a gap," Starr says, obviously still capable of feeling the old hurt. "An emptiness. We had a lot of fun growing up together. Of course, like any older brother I mistreated him a great deal. We used to fight and scuff and I was tough on him. But we played well together and I missed that a great deal. I hope this doesn't sound corny, but I've dedicated myself many times since then striving to do something *for* him. Because I think he would have been the better athlete of the two of us. He was much more fiery. My dad told me one time, 'If you had your brother's guts and your talent, you'd be all right.' "

Papa Ben Starr (the name, which could not be more perfect for a star quarterback, goes back to the Cherokee Indians of Oklahoma, there being Indian blood in the Starr line, blood which may account for Bart's high cheekbones) spent a lot of time with his young sons, teaching them the rudiments of football and baseball. "I can remember him coming home at night and going out and running with us and tossing a football around or hitting baseball flies to us. He played with us almost every day."

Nevertheless young Bryan Bartlett Starr (the middle name, which caught on, was the second name of the doctor who delivered him) did not develop into a high-school athletic star. He spent most of his time on the scrub team mumbling about the coach not recognizing talent when he saw it. Once he came home from school and announced he had quit football because he had not only failed to make the first team, he had not even made the traveling squad. "Fine," Ben Starr said. "That will give you time to cut down those old corn stalks in the garden and turn over the earth for spring planting." Bart promptly went back to being a scrub. "I hated gardening," he says, laughing his engaging laugh.

Starr did not play much as a junior and probably would not have played at all if the senior quarterback hadn't broken his leg. "That was, to make a pun," Starr says, "my biggest break. If it were not for that, I would not have played at all until I was a senior."

Looking back, Starr believes it was a matter of maturing slowly. He had more desire than ability and he was not very big. (Even now he is a rather slight 6–1.) At the University of Alabama, Starr got his letter as a freshman and helped beat Syracuse in the Orange Bowl. In the second year young Starr took his team to the Cotton Bowl. "After that we seemed to go downhill," Starr says, "the team and me as an individual."

In practice for his junior season he snapped a muscle in his back while punting and in short order he could barely walk. He wound up playing only a few games at the end of the season. It was not a good one for Alabama and there was a coaching change, Ears Whitworth replacing Red Drew. The new coach went for young blood and Starr sat on the bench. He admits to being resentful, especially since Alabama did not win a game all season.

Nor did it seem he would attract the attention of the professionals, although he wanted to. Indeed he never doubted he would be a professional. There is something almost mystical about Starr's determination. He has no reason to believe he is capable of certain things. He just *knows*.

It was Red Drew who told the Packers they would do well to pick up this fellow Bart Starr. The Packers did, but they were in no hurry, waiting until the draft's 17th round.

There was an offer to play in Canada for more money than the Packers would pay. Here again Starr's seemingly mindless pride stepped in. "I wanted to see if I could make it in the National Football League," Starr says. "If I didn't try, I would have always wondered. It's funny, though. When I agreed to play for Green Bay I wasn't even sure where it was."

Starr did not make it very quickly as a professional, either. In his first year with the Packers, 1956, he sat on the bench behind Tobin Rote. "I was glad to do it," he says. "I didn't expect to play that first year. But I've never had a pessimistic attitude. I wasn't doing anything or going anywhere, but I truthfully thought that things would change. I can't tell you why. I've been asked where I got the strength to overcome these things. I don't think that has anything to do with it. Things just worked out for me and I was able to step in, take advantage."

As Starr talked in his home, his older boy came into the room and showed his father a test paper with a perfect score, 100. "You owe me ten cents," he said laconically. Starr dug into his pants pocket and got it up. "You're going to break me," he said. The boy didn't seem to mind.

If one had to describe Starr's *Gestalt,* the whole of his personality, the words that would come to mind are modesty, will, intelligence, pride, drive, determination and courtly politeness. There are times when he seems rather a goodie-goodie, but this is deceptive. He is not, for one example, a member of the Fellowship of Christian Athletes, although he keeps a Bible beside his bed and is willing to match the depth of his faith with any man's. But religious proselytizing is not his dish of tea. His respect for every man's belief is boundless. At a quiet cocktail party in his home, after the Packers' first game (Starr himself drinks only beer but is a good host), a lot of the guests were watching a late football game on his color-TV in Starr's trophy-bedecked basement den. When the news came on at half-time, there was a shot of Father James Groppi, the leader of the

Negro fight for open housing in Milwaukee. Starr said that his minister had mentioned Groppi in his sermon that morning, compared him to Jeremiah and spoke of the strength of people who were willing to fight for their beliefs no matter how unpopular they were. Some of his guests reacted with what can only be called shocked silence. Later on Starr explained his position.

"The comment that our minister was making was that there are people in this country today who are forthright enough to take a stand on something that they believe in sincerely. They are willing to take this stand no matter how controversial. He said at least they can get their teeth into something, and he asked, 'How many of you would stand up, even, if necessary, to give your life?' He didn't say Father Groppi was right or wrong, but at least he felt strongly. Too many of us don't feel that strong about *anything*."

For all his sympathy for strong feelings, Starr seems to go through life trying to offend no one. He says that on the football field "I'll cut your heart out if I have to. I wasn't always like that, but I am now." Off the field, however, he remains the nice guy he always seems to be. So Jerry Kramer was asked if there was anybody he could think of in football or out of it who didn't like Bart Starr. He thought for a moment. "Nobody," he said. "Except maybe me. Sometimes he irritates me. Because he's too perfect."

One of Starr's perfections is his ability and willingness to compile enormous files on offensive plays and defensive patterns. From time to time, Lombardi will forget the way a certain play is run and he'll ask Starr. The quarterback invariably has it in his files and knows just where to lay his hands on it. His encyclopedic knowledge of the game leads many to believe that what Starr has in the back of his mind is a job as a coach. Ask him his ambition and he'll talk about this new business he is planning, the manufacturing of educational toys. (Starr also does public relations work for an automobile firm and he gives of his time freely to good causes, things like the Cancer Fund.

"Bart is very conscious of his image," says his friend Knafelc. "He's so conscious of it that he's very much like Lombardi. Both have to really force themselves to live up to their image. Bart even wants to go into a business that will be good and clean.") But underneath, Bart Starr does indeed think he would make a good coach. "My first love would be to stay in football," he says when pressed. He wants to have something solid for his family in the form of a business, but football can probably pull him away from anything.

An interesting possibility opens here. Vince Lombardi has been saying that the jobs of coach and general manager were too much for one man, yet he has found it difficult to relinquish either. In two years, though, when Starr will be ready to retire as a player, Lombardi will have a man available who has been a sort of an alter ego to him since 1959. It is an arrangement that Starr has encouraged. "I like to feel that the job I'm doing on a Sunday afternoon is that job that coach Lombardi would be doing if he were playing," Starr says. If there is any man that Lombardi could tolerate as coach under him, it would be this kind.

Starr and Lombardi enjoy an interesting relationship. They are not friends, to the extent that they do not socialize, do not go to each other's homes for dinner. It's a business relationship based on mutual respect.

The first time Lombardi saw Starr throw a football he growled at him: "One more like that and you're through here." It was in a club scrimmage and it was a bad pass, into a group of players, a pass-and-pray move. This is not Lombardi's style. "He scared me to death," Starr says.

It was under the rough, tough, top-sergeant coaching of Lombardi that Starr blossomed. "I don't want this to sound corny," says Starr, "but the greatest years I have had are the years I've spent under Lombardi." In those glorious years he seems to have sucked up Lombardi's attitudes through his pores. "I used to be for the underdog," Starr says. "But now I agree with coach Lombardi. I'm for the upperdog. I was for the underdog because I was one. Now I see the pressures that are on the upperdog. When you get to be an upperdog, you know the scratching and the clawing and the grabbing that everybody underneath does to knock you off your perch. The average fan cannot appreciate the pressure and the emotional peak you must reach each week to keep from getting knocked off your perch at the top."

There was a game in 1964, the year the Packers didn't win the championship, that Starr views as a turning point in his career. It was against the Baltimore Colts, and with less than a minute to go the Packers were trailing by a point. Lombardi sent in a play to Starr. He wanted McGee to go down on a pass pattern and turn in in order to take the ball into field-goal range. In the huddle, Starr let McGee talk him into a turn out instead. The pass was intercepted. There was no certainty that Lombardi's pattern would have worked better, but the coach insisted it would have. And Starr agreed with him.

"It was a crucial mistake," Starr says. "It got the Colts going and they just wrecked us. There was a time when it could have wrecked me. I used to harbor mistakes something fierce. You can't dwell on past failures. You have to shed them. But this was not something I was able to do. I felt so badly about this mistake that, and this may sound corny, I tried to dedicate myself to not letting that happen again. I still think about my mistakes, but I don't let them get me. If one play can be a turning point it was that one."

The dawning knowledge that he could not be a perfect player has made Starr more aggressive. "He has all kinds of guts on third down," says one NFL man. Because he can handle them better, Starr is willing to make mistakes and it makes him a more daring player. Not that Lombardi doesn't keep him in bounds. Starr has an ambition, for example, to play a ballgame without going into a single huddle. Teams do this at the end of games when they want to save time and often get off sustained drives by keeping the defense off balance. The plays are called at the line of scrimmage. "I've often thought about doing that,"

Starr says with a grin, "and perhaps one day I will. But if there is a weakness that I have—and I say this out of respect for coach Lombardi—it's that I hesitate to ad lib something during the course of a ballgame and say I'm justified because of this or that. I have done it a couple of times and coach Lombardi has backed me. He always would. But I have so much respect for his organizational ability, he leaves so little to chance, that there is very little reason to ad lib. There are times I know I should have done it and I haven't. I consider that a weakness."

There are not many weaknesses in Bart Starr. He is as close to a fanatic as a quarterback can become and still function as a human being off the field. When he talks about the function of a quarterback, the requirements of this difficult job, he becomes intense. He bunches up his shoulders and he speaks carefully and precisely. "You have to be totally dedicated to the game," he says. "I mean that sincerely. I can't stress it enough. You have to be willing to spend a lot of extra hours studying films, pass patterns, anything that will help you to be better prepared for the game. You have to have a good, retentive memory. You have to be able to think quick enough to make adjustments under pressure. You have to be unperturbed and unflustered mentally. You can't get mad or irritated and go all to pieces. You have to have a very high boiling point. Physically, you have to be able to throw the ball well, obviously. You have to be quick afoot, not necessarily fast, but quick-footed so you can move nimbly. You should be physically strong, so that you can absorb a certain amount of physical abuse. And most of all you have to have a sincere, burning desire to play the game. If you don't have a real love for it, you could never do the things you have to do in order to play this game."

What that is, of course, is a description of Bart Starr by Bart Starr. No one could have done it better.

8/ BRODIE

"I Experience a Kind of Clarity"

By John Brodie and Michael Murphy

It is probably only a geographic coincidence, but John Brodie, a Stanford man, is the first quarterback in this collection who did not go to school south of the Mason-Dixon line and east of the Mississippi. The Southeast dominates this book; of the 17 quarterbacks covered, nine went to college in the Southeast (Unitas, Jurgensen, Tarkenton, Conerly, Tittle, Starr, Blanda, Namath and Gilliam). The second largest contingent comes from California colleges—Morton, Kilmer, Kapp and, the top man in the quartet, Brodie. (How they must have loved it—all those gentlemen from warmer climes—when they took a snap from center in Green Bay, Wisconsin, with the temperature hovering around ten degrees.)

When John Brodie retired after the 1973 season, after 17 years with the San Francisco 49ers, he had thrown more passes and completed more passes than anyone in the world except John Unitas. Yet during his first 13 years in the National Football League, Brodie played for a San Francisco team that never won more than eight games in a season, and throughout his career, despite two chances in his last four seasons, Brodie never played for a team that won a conference championship. If Brodie was frustrated at times, and he must have been, he took out most of

*his frustrations on golf balls. He is the only man ever to play
quarterback in the NFL and play golf on the pro tour at the same
time. He is also the only man ever to play quarterback in the NFL
and write for* Intellectual Digest.

Brodie's 1973 contribution to Intellectual Digest *was a dia-
logue between the quarterback and Michael Murphy, the president and cofounder of the Esalen Institute in California, a center
that pioneered radical psychological and sociological therapies.
Judged by his words and by his thoughts, Brodie was certainly
one of the thinking quarterbacks.*

MURPHY: There are hundreds of thousands, maybe millions
of words written about football. There is a huge amount of
talent assembled to describe the game on TV and radio and in
sports magazines and newspapers. Supposedly, the best sportswriters are analyzing what the game means. Recently, there
has been an abrasive and "realistic" approach like Howard
Cosell's or in books like Jim Bouton's *Ball Four*. But it seems
to me, from my seat on the five-yard line, that there is a lot to
the game that has *not* been described by all these talented
sportswriters and analysts. All of these people are missing
something.

BRODIE: Many fans feel the way you do. A great many
football players do. I certainly do. There is a side to the game
that really hasn't been described yet—that "hidden" side of
sport you talk about in your book, things having to do with the
psychological side of the game, with what we might call "energy flows," and the extraordinary states of mind performing
athletes sometimes get into. I've been reluctant to talk to sportswriters about these things because I'm afraid they would reduce
them to categories they were more familiar with.

MURPHY: What are these writers and analysts looking
at when they describe football?

BRODIE: People tend to look at life—and at sport—

through their own experience and mental categories. When a person looks at a game of football, he tends to see a reflection of his own life. If it's mainly violence and getting ahead and winning at all costs, he'll tend to see that in the game. Or if life is mainly statistics and numbers and measurements, he'll tend to see that—many people have an incredible interest in football statistics. People look at the game and project their own reality onto it.

MURPHY: You could say that the two images that dominate our understanding of football now are the Beast and the Computer.

BRODIE: But many of the players—most of the ones I know—resent those images. They know there is more to the game than that. And I think there are many fans who see past those images and get glimpses of something more.

MURPHY: Can you give me some examples of the aspects that usually go unrecorded, some examples of the game's psychological side or what you call "energy flows"?

BRODIE: Often, in the heat and excitement of a game, a player's perception and coordination will improve dramatically. At times, and with increasing frequency now, I experience a kind of clarity that I've never seen adequately described in a football story. Sometimes, for example, time seems to slow way down, in an uncanny way, as if everyone were moving in slow motion. It seems as if I have all the time in the world to watch the receivers run their patterns, and yet I know the defensive line is coming at me just as fast as ever. I know perfectly well how hard and fast those guys are coming and yet the whole thing seems like a movie or a dance in slow motion. It's beautiful.

MURPHY: What happens to your performance in moments like that? Do you actually see what's happening more clearly?

BRODIE: Yes. Of course, some of the players on the other team may be in a similar state! Then the game moves up a level.

MURPHY: Are these things contagious? Sometimes it looks as if a whole team catches fire and starts doing things it couldn't do ordinarily. In the Washington Redskins game last year, something seemed to happen to the 49ers in the third quarter after you threw that touchdown pass to Gene Washington.

BRODIE: We had to *make* something happen then. That's why I went with that play. With third down and one yard to go on your own 22-yard line in a close game—and a playoff game, which leaves you with no second chances—you wouldn't usually go with the particular call I made. After I came to the line of scrimmage and started my snap count, I saw the defense shift into a position that might not happen in the game again. I gave the team a basic pass audible and gave Gene a little signal we had worked out, faded back and threw him that pass. When I threw it I *knew* it was going to connect.

MURPHY: When the play began it looked for a moment like the safety would make an interception. But then it seemed as if the ball went through or over his hands as he came in front of Washington.

BRODIE: Pat Fischer, the cornerback, told the reporters after the game that the ball seemed to jump right over his hands as he went for it. When we studied the game films that week, it *did* look as if the ball kind of jumped over his hands into Gene's. Some of the guys said it was the wind—and maybe it was.

MURPHY: What do you mean by *maybe?*

BRODIE: What I mean is that our sense of that pass was so clear and our *intention* so strong that the ball was bound to get there, come wind, cornerbacks, hell or high water.

MURPHY: In *Golf in the Kingdom* I discuss the "energy streamers" that a golf ball rides on its way toward the hole. I mean those lines of force that seem to emanate from the golfer when he can visualize and execute his shot in a moment of high clarity. Is that the kind of thing you are talking about? I know there are golfers who have had the experience.

BRODIE: I would have to say that such things seem to
exist—or emerge when your state of mind is right. It has happened to me dozens of times. An intention carries a force, a
thought is connected with an energy that can stretch itself out
in a pass play or a golf shot or a base hit or during a 30-foot
jump shot in basketball. I've seen it happen too many times to
deny it.

MURPHY: Is this something you can practice or develop? Can you learn to develop clarity during a game? Can you
strengthen your intentions?

BRODIE: Yes. Pressures that used to get me down don't
affect me to the same extent now. I've learned to shed certain
destructive attitudes when a game is under way. A player's
effectiveness is directly related to his ability to be right there,
doing that thing, in the moment. All the preparation he may
have put into the game—all the game plans, analysis of movies,
etc.—is no good if he can't put it into action when game time
comes. He can't be worrying about the past or the future or the
crowd or some other extraneous event. He must be able to
respond in the here and now. This is an ability we all have
potentially. I believe it is our natural state. But because most
of us lose it as we grow up, we have to regain it.

MURPHY: This sounds very much like Zen or other
spiritual disciplines. It seems to me that in many ways sport is
like a Western Yoga. I have heard mountain climbers, surfers,
sky divers and skiers who talk a language that is almost mystical, and now I hear you talking the same way.

BRODIE: Call it mystical if you like. For me it is simply
one of the elementary facts of experience. Here-and-now awareness, clarity, strong intention, a person's "tone level"—these
are things a lot of people who don't know anything about Yoga
or mysticism talk about. The trouble is, people don't make them
operative in their life as often as they could.

MURPHY: But some of the things you seem to suggest,
like a ball jumping over a defender's hands or time slowing
down, go beyond ordinary experience. In the East, and in our

Western religious traditions, there have been disciplines to develop these extraordinary powers and states of mind. But the modern Western world, for the most part, is lacking in such disciplines. They seem esoteric and alien to most of us. Maybe that is one of the reasons sportswriters and sports commentators find it difficult to comprehend the kinds of things you are talking about.

BRODIE: Not only reporters find it difficult, but oftentimes coaches do too. If a player begins to develop methods for tuning in to these deeper levels, many coaches are likely to criticize or disregard them. A player often has to be big enough to transcend his coaches' limitations. But then a coach has to deal with the team's owners and even with the fans and the media to some extent. The whole system works to build up certain attitudes about the way in which a team should be run. Take the computer for example: the way some teams worship it in the selection of their players and the creation of their game plans, you would think it was God. But computer-made game plans often lead a team away from the game itself. A team with a fixed game plan can be a brittle team, if it can't relate to the here and now of a game. The computer *can* be a helpful tool, as long as you don't expect too much from it. The same thing is true for certain programs of physical exercise: exceptions have to be made for the experienced athlete who has discovered training methods suited to his own makeup. A good coach will let him use those methods, even if they deviate from the fixed procedures the coaching staff has set up.

MURPHY: One of the problems coaches and players have —and it's a problem all of us have in talking about these things —is that our language about unusual powers and states of mind is so limited. We don't have commonly understood words to describe "energy flows" or what you call "being clear." These expressions don't make sense to a lot of people. I think the time has come to begin creating a language and an understanding about these dimensions of life.

BRODIE: Athletics could be a place where this kind of

insight is developed. Sport is one of the few activities in which many Americans spend a great deal of time developing their potentialities. It influences character, I think, as much as our schools and churches do. But, even so, it falls far below what it could be. It leaves out so much. I would love to see a sports team developed with a more fulfilling purpose.

One place in which you see the principle of self-knowledge work most clearly is with injuries. Two years ago I had a problem with my arm; I couldn't lift it above my shoulder—which is not good for a quarterback. Dealing with that sore arm led me into a process of self-discovery. Getting well meant *more* than getting the soreness out of my shoulder. I found out that my arm's condition was related to a very limited notion I had about myself and life. It wasn't enough anymore to simply play a better game of football. I had to change the way I perceived the world, the way I thought and felt, and the way I treated others. Life was a larger and more interesting affair than I had ever dreamed.

MURPHY: Why do you still play football? Sixteen years is a long time.

BRODIE: I play because I enjoy the game. After 16 years there is still an enormous satisfaction in it.

MURPHY: And yet so many people see football only in terms of winning at any cost, knocking the hell out of the other guy. Is that the only reason you enjoy the game?

BRODIE: No. It's important to win—there's nothing quite like it. It's important to go all out during a game. But there is a lot more to football than that. Involving yourself wholeheartedly, in the way we have been discussing, is a satisfaction in itself.

MURPHY: I get the idea that you and Gene Washington have a special kind of communication when a game is under way. Can you say anything about that?

BRODIE: Well, we room together, and we are good friends. We've worked out a series of signals that can change even after I've begun my snap count. But most of all, I guess, is that we read each other so well. He knows where I want him to be on a given pass play. Sometimes he will run a set pattern, but at other times he has to get to a place in the field any way he can.

MURPHY: Could that place be marked with a set of coordinates, say at a particular yard line? Or is it better to say that you meet somewhere in the field of existence, in the field of your relationship, amidst all the flux on the playing field?

BRODIE: I think the more poetic way says it better—it's a highly intuitive thing. Sometimes we call a pass for a particular spot on the field, maybe to get a first down. But at other times it's less defined than that and depends upon the communication we have. Sometimes I let the ball fly before Gene has made his final move, *without* a pass route being set exactly. That's where the intuition and the communication come in. But then we don't know what the other team, what those cornerbacks and safety men, might do next. That's part of the fun of the game, not knowing what they are going to do. The game *never stops.* You can never really take anything for granted—at least in most games in the NFL. And that's what's wrong with game plans so often—because you don't know where those guys are going to be a second before something happens. You have to be ready for the sudden glimmer.

MURPHY: Do you ever get the idea after one of these incredible pass completions that there was some destiny to the play, something more than skill involved? To me, as a slightly lunatic fan, there are times when it seems as if the script for a game has been written by God himself—or that it springs from someplace in the collective unconscious.

BRODIE: I know the feeling, but I don't know that we should call that kind of explanation an objective fact.

MURPHY: But isn't there a kind of communication, a kind of artistry, a kind of Being, if you will, that emerges during an inspired game? Something that isn't measured by grids or coordinates or statistics? Doesn't bringing forth this kind of quality depend upon something that one is not ordinarily aware of?

BRODIE: Yes, that's a good way to say it. I was reading

a statement by Alan Page [defensive tackle for the Minnesota Vikings, the NFL's Most Valuable Player for 1971] the other day in which he described the comedown when a game is over. He said it was a weird feeling adjusting back to reality, to sanity —having to be a person again. I understand that feeling. Life can feel like a box after a game. You can get into another order of reality when you're playing, a reality that doesn't fit into the grids and coordinates that most people lay across life—including the categories coaches, fans and sportswriters lay on the game.

MURPHY: When you are in a state like that you must be tuned in to an incredible number of energies and patterns, to all those players on both teams, to the crowd. In fact, when you begin your first offensive sequence, you seem to be deliberately tuning in to all of this. I sometimes get the sense that you are probing the situation before you work out your plan of attack. Are those opening minutes a time when you are learning what a game is going to be like?

BRODIE: Yes, we are tuning into the situation. And centering ourselves, dropping the nervousness, getting the feel of the game. We may have to drop useless emotional buildup and other distractions.

MURPHY: So you are saying you have to be both focused and sensitive. An effective quarterback has to have his radar working.

BRODIE: I equate creativity with awareness. It's a matter of simple knowledge. The more I know, the more I can do.

MURPHY: But knowing like this is more than the kind of knowing we are supposed to learn in school, more than verbal knowing or book knowing. It involves a tuning in to subtle energies and feelings and forces we can only come to through direct awareness. It involves the emotions and the spirit as well as the intellect—and the here and now, the complexities and subtleties of a given situation rather than preconceptions about it, or your rehearsals of it or what has been written in a book about it. It seems to me that this sort of knowing leads to a new kind of being.

BRODIE: You might say that. Football players and athletes generally get into this kind of being or beingness—call it what you will—more often than is generally recognized. But they often lose it after a game or after a season is over. They often don't have a workable philosophy or understanding to support the kind of thing they get into while they are playing. They don't have the words for it. So after a game you see some of them coming down, making fools of themselves sometimes, coming way down in their tone level. But during the game they come way up. A missing ingredient for many people, I guess, is that they don't have a supporting philosophy or discipline for a better life.

MURPHY: After hearing you talk, I gather that top athletes are people who are accustomed to altering time, who are accustomed to a higher state of focus and concentration, who are accustomed to altered perceptions of many types and to going with the inner flow of things. But I don't see any of this on the sport pages. Or in the sport books you hear about, or on the radio and TV programs. Our culture seems to screen it all out, even though such experience is at the very heart of a game so many of us love.

BRODIE: That's right. It's a case of experience being ahead of what we can say about it. Maybe if we could talk about it more clearly we could make it happen more. Sport is so important in creating values in America, it would be great if it could open up these inner dimensions for people. It's really what many coaches and players want to do, after all. They want sport to be more than winning at any cost, more than beating people up and making money and getting ahead over somebody else's dead body. But we have got to break out of this conspiracy to belittle sport and human nature.

MURPHY: Some critics of the game would say that its violence destroys the very things you hope for.

BRODIE: Violence is not the game's basic intention, even though some people think it is. The idea is not to hurt or damage somebody. But there is an intensity and a danger in football—as in life generally—which keep us alive and awake. It is a test of our awareness and ability. Like so much of life, it presents us with the choice of responding either with fear or with action and clarity.

MURPHY: I have heard some people say that all of this talk about "higher possibilities" and building character is fine, but that you don't need football to do it, that the game is a poor instrument in fact for accomplishing these things.

BRODIE: But that wouldn't stop us from playing or enjoying football. It is better to improve the game, I think, than to indulge in a lot of idle criticism of it. And when you look at its history you see that it has already gone through enormous changes. It is a much different game than it was in the 1920s or 1930s. It's a more complex and artistic game now, with all the offensive and defensive plays, with the game plans and the variety of skills involved. Why shouldn't the game go on changing? I see no reason why we should fix the game of football where it is, after the change it has gone through already. Why shouldn't it be a place to develop the mental and spiritual dimensions we have been talking about?

9/BLANDA

Alive and Kicking

By Wells Twombly

The year George Blanda started playing in the National Football League, 1949, less than 25,000 turned out to see the average professional game. In the years Blanda has remained in pro football, the average attendance has more than doubled. So has George Blanda's age. Of all the marks that have been set in pro football, none seems more secure than the first record in the record book, the one George Blanda holds: Most Seasons, Active Player—24, George Blanda, Chicago Bears, 1949 to 1958; Houston, 1960 to 1966; Oakland, 1967 to 1973. No other player has survived more than 18 seasons. Blanda's two other records seem almost as durable: Most passes thrown in a game (68) and most completed in a game (37). He also shares the records for touchdown passes in a game (seven) and in a season (36).

If you need further evidence of Blanda's longevity, consider this: He was playing professional football before many of his 1973 Oakland teammates were born; he entered the National Football League one year after Bobby Layne and Y. A. Tittle, neither of whom has thrown a pass competitively for a decade; he was twice discarded by the Chicago Bears, first a quarter of a century ago (he was a Baltimore Colt briefly in 1950), and again after the 1958 season, when he seemed to have outlived his usefulness.

Blanda sat out the 1959 season and if the American Football League hadn't come along in 1960, he might have ended his pro career at least 15 years prematurely.

The Blanda article is from the book Alive and Kicking *by Wells Twombly, a San Francisco columnist who treats the English language with the same respect Blanda accords his own wonderfully preserved body. As a San Franciscan, Twombly is treated daily to many of nature's most awesome sights. Blanda is not the least of them.*

In the entire universe, there is no more sorely misunderstood creature than canis lupus—the fluorescent-eyed, gray-muzzled wolf. He is the victim, not altogether innocent, of an exceedingly imaginative press. He does not, for instance, roam the snow-glutted hills in a snarling, disorganized pack. He does not attack for the sheer pleasure of splattering blood on the landscape. He is rarely guilty of reckless adventures, although his courage is well documented.

Rather, he is a part of a highly disciplined unit which follows a single leader, an animal which naturalists call the Alpha Male. There is no challenging the Alpha Male's authority. The pack follows him with a singular obedience, because he is the only sensible alternative to starvation. Always, the Alpha Male will find a way to survive, to secure food for his subordinates, to keep the pack together as a warlike group.

It is in winter that the leader's instincts grow keener and his skills become more apparent. There is a curious altruism in the Alpha Male's character, however. Despite his own strong urge for self-protection and his desire to dominate his peers, he is conscious of the common cause. Thus, he trains a younger wolf —called the Beta Male—to take his place someday. It is a pain to his pride, but it is necessary.

It is not in the Alpha Male's makeup to give way gracefully. He will hold on jealously. Only when it becomes absolutely obvious that he can no longer lead the hunt or supervise the denning period—when cubs are whelped—does he retire. Always he departs with sadness. Either the pack deserts him and follows the Beta Male, now moved up in rank, or he slinks away into the night and the cold.

In all of professional athletics there is no occupation quite so stimulating as playing quarterback. It swells the ego and ennobles the soul. Consider the atmosphere: The concrete decks of the stadium are clogged with humanity.

Television cameras peer over a man's shoulder while he stands in the middle of a huddle, telling ten other, larger men how they may grow in grace. He is absolute monarch on the field.

In an era when police are ridiculed and college presidents are evicted from their own offices, the professional football quarterback is the last living authoritarian. The nation is watching it, live and in color: The quarterback matches his massive intellect, his strong right arm, his semi-nimble feet against the monsters on the opposite side of the scrimmage line, men who would remove his helmet with his head still inside.

There he stands behind the center, counting cadence in a burly baritone. There he stands, the Alpha Male. The defenders are jumping around, performing some pitiful little ballet steps, designed to disturb, frustrate or confuse the quarterback. But he remains calm. He cannot panic. By experience he knows that the team—the pack—cannot survive, cannot win, cannot exist as an entity if he shows the slightest sliver of fear.

Now the ball is inserted firmly into his hands. Somewhere in that mass of noise and color and confusion a pass receiver is streaking along a prescribed route. Back goes the quarterback's arm. Now the ball is in the air. Now it settles softly in the flanker's eager little paws. First down!

Ah, the ecstasy of it! Ah, the agony! The crowd loses all its senses, save the power to make inane noise. Emotion spills over every seating tier, until it fairly floods the playing field. Now the quarterback leaps up off his pancreas and marches down to where the new scrimmage line is forming. Here is the Alpha Male strutting forward, to command again and again until age withers and custom stales his infinite variety. And on the sidelines, a field-to-press-box telephone set strapped across his scalp, stands the Beta Male—the back-up quarterback—waiting for all those autumns to pile up, waiting for the Alpha Male to slink out of the stadium and into retirement.

There can be only one first-line quarterback, only one Alpha Male. Is it any wonder that a quarterback in the National Football League is a seething mass of egotism? If he isn't he either goes home and sells insurance or he goes north to Canada, where standards are lower. A quarterback is asked to do the impossible every Sunday, in front of people who have paid seven dollars each for their seats and who think that professional football is some kind of scientific exercise. They ask him to perform miracles and if he falls somewhat short, the customers start braiding ropes and calling for an immediate lynching.

Only a person with a sizeable amount of confidence would volunteer for the job in the first place. Only an Alpha Male.

It is early in the morning of October 25, 1970, and destiny is waiting for George Frederick Blanda, the coal miner's kid, to open his gleaming lobo eyes. George doesn't stir. Why should he?

For slightly more than 20 seasons, Blanda has been waiting for destiny to find him. To hell with destiny! Where was it when he needed it, all those agonizing years with the Chicago Bears when George Halas, his fellow Slav, was attempting to bury him alive? Where was it when George Blanda was kicking all those field goals, gaining all those yards, throwing all those touchdown passes and never getting to call himself the Bears' number one quarterback for more than a few pitiful months?

Was destiny trying to catch up to him those first three years in Houston when he won two American Football League championships and just missed a third? Why, chances are destiny

didn't even know where George Frederick Blanda had gone to.
It probably didn't even recognize the new league.

Where, pray tell, was destiny when the crowds at Rice
Stadium wouldn't let the public address announcer get much
past "and playing quarterback for the Houston Oilers . . . No.
16 . . . George Bl . . ." before the boos would drown out the rest
of George's surname?

What was destiny doing on the morning when Houston's
psychedelic new general manager, Don Klosterman, called the
newspapers to report, with a note of boredom in his throat, that
five players had been given their outright releases? Let's see
. . . uh . . . center John Frongillo, tackle Rich Michael, fullback
John Henry Johnson, cornerback Bernie Parrish and . . . uh
. . . quarterback George Blanda. And when a *Houston Chronicle*
columnist who had always sort of admired George's swagger
suggested that the ball club ought to retire his number, was
destiny out to lunch when Klosterman called the paper to say
such an honor would be an "impossibility"?

And why hadn't destiny permitted the nation to know that
George Blanda was sneaking up on some incredible records—
Most points scored in a lifetime, Most field goals kicked, Most
extra points? And how many people were aware that of all the
quarterbacks who ever sweated and bled, only Baltimore's
sainted John Unitas had ever thrown more completed passes
into the enemy's end zone?

Club owners and sportswriters and coaches had spent the
better part of two decades trying to push George Frederick
Blanda into a corner and forget him. His accomplishments were
ignored. His sins magnified. They never talked about all those
points he placed on the scoreboard, only about the interceptions
he'd thrown.

So the bloody hell with destiny! Let it go find some slick,
lanky quarterback just graduating from college and anxious to
make $300,000 in quick bonus payments. At age 43, how much
does a man still hunger after fame? Better to take the money
and let somebody else's wife worry about scrapbooks.

Ah, but this was destiny's day, a moment right out of Bill Stern's book of fables. Remember how it was back in the 1940s? The whole family—or at least those Blanda brothers and sisters who happened to be living at home at the time—would tune in the Colgate Shave Cream Man every Saturday night at the white house on South Third Street in Youngwood, Pa. How did Bill Stern used to say it? Oh, yes . . . "Portrait of Destiny Catching Up with the Quarterback Nobody Loved."

So, on the murky gray morning of October 25, 1970, with wild geese honking in the air above his apartment located on a lagoon near the western shore of Alameda Island, George Frederick Blanda staggers to his feet and starts his rendezvous with destiny by going to the toilet.

Breakfast is bubbling in the other room. The routine never varies on the morning of an Oakland Raider home game. In fact, it never varies during the week before. It is always the same. George Blanda is not a superstitious man. He makes that perfectly clear. He just doesn't change his routine. He eats at the Grotto in Jack London Square every Thursday night. He attends the race meeting at Bay Meadows across San Francisco Bay in San Mateo every Friday afternoon. He eats the same dry cereal, drinks the same juice (orange!), consumes the same amount of toast, has the exact and proper number of cups of coffee on the morning before a game.

There is no change this morning, even though destiny is only a yard behind him and closing fast. Inside of eight hours he will, after only twenty years and four months in the game, be on his way to becoming an overnight sensation. Publicity will overwhelm him. George Frederick Blanda, whose national fame has heretofore been predicated upon two minor stories in the *Sporting News,* one in 1956 when he was with the Bears and another in 1964 when he was with the Oilers, will become the most sought-after interview in the entire commercial sweat industry. Magazine writers will call at incredible hours, begging two or three days of his time. Television commentators like Walter Cronkite and Heywood Hale Broun will come trailing after him, microphones flopping in the dust. His fee for speaking will double and then triple. Everyone will want him to say that he smokes their cigarette or drinks their beer or splashes his jutting jaw with their cologne.

He will endorse only two products, the breakfast food he eats every Sunday morning and is eating right this moment on October 25, 1970, and the after-shave lotion he has just got through using. He will tell everyone else that he cannot accept money to say he likes something he has never used.

Because of his age, he will become the towering hero of the Support Hose Set. One columnist, nationally syndicated, will describe how her husband kicked his tonic bottle 32 feet after a George Blanda field goal. Another will scold him for taking the alibi of age away from every man over 40. And yet another will say that he has become a bigger sex symbol to the middle-aged man than the 63-year-old company president who gets his teenage secretary pregnant.

Through it all, George Blanda will behave with his own brand of spectacular ambivalence. On the one hand, he will talk like the brass-plated old football hero that he knew of and read about as a small boy in western Pennsylvania. He will say that what he has done was exactly what he was paid to do, no more and no less. And on the other hand, he will shimmer in the golden glory that has avoided him for so long. He will enjoy every opportunity to speak to a reporter from a national publication. He will give away so much of his spare time that the Oakland Raiders' publicity director, Tommy Grimes, will be amazed.

But ever faithful to his image as the last of the old-style quarterbacks, who spit out teeth and drew plays in the dirt and who responded to serious injuries by suggesting that the best cure for a broken arm was to strap a ham sandwich on it, he will turn to Arnold Hano of *Sport* magazine and say, as if Arnold were destiny itself, "Where the hell were you when I needed you twenty years ago?"

And Hano will echo, "Yes, indeed, where was I twenty years ago?"

It is October 25, 1970, early in the morning and the Raiders are about to play the Pittsburgh Steelers at the Oakland-Alameda County Coliseum, just across the water. This will be the beginning of the most amazing season any football player ever had. George Frederick Blanda, whose father worked all week in the mines and drank too much on weekends, will make miracles for the entire nation to see. He will kick field goals from awesome distances with seconds left to play. He will throw touchdown passes. He will move the Oakland offense . . . move it magically, majestically.

"When George is on the field, the rest of us listen pretty good," guard Gene Upshaw will say. "It's like listening to your father. I mean, George speaks from experience, so much experience you hate to argue with him over the slightest little thing. Some of the guys on the team weren't born when he was a senior in college. He played against people like Steve Van Buren and he played with Sid Luckman. Those are names out of the distant past to most of us."

It has been raining for several days, first a sleazy drizzle, then a lashing, drenching purgatory of a storm. Now the water is all in the ground. The clouds are swirling off toward the Pacific Ocean, which lies crouched behind the San Francisco peninsula only eight miles away. Quarterbacks worry about the weather. It is part of their instinct. Sometimes wet turf means poor footing, so passes must be thrown short and flat, ball carriers must pound straight ahead on quick, secure handoffs. Deep mud would favor the Steelers, under ordinary thinking, because the Raiders worship the extravagant play—the long forward pass, the breakaway run. It is a reflection of the style of their number one quarterback, Daryle Lamonica, whom the literary set refers to, snidely, as the Mad Bomber.

With waterfowl still flapping in the dank atmosphere, Blanda backs his leased car out of the carport and leaves the parking lot at the Coral Reef Motel. He turns right on Doolittle Avenue and spins along in silence. Music on the car radio is for other, more frivolous times.

"I still like this game," he tells a newsman riding with him.

"I love the routine. People say that football meetings and game films are boring. Hell, I love both of them. I like getting up for the 'big one.' I like doing calisthenics. I like the action on the sidelines. I like being with other football players. I don't want to coach when I'm through with the game, but I don't know how I could get away from this. It would be hell leaving the routine. Coaching would be a way of staying in the game, wouldn't it?"

The car turns left on High Street and rumbles across a low, flat bridge. The neat 1930-style bungalows of Alameda give way to warehouses and oil tanks, boat yards and rubble-pitted heaps of Bay fill. It is still too early for the Nimitz Freeway—that merciful stretch of highway that takes a motorist right through Oakland without ever getting him dirty—to be clotted with traffic. It is almost serene, if a freeway can ever be described just that way. The Coliseum is less than two miles from the apartment Blanda rents during the season for himself, his wife of 22 years and their 15-year-old daughter, Leslie. Alameda is comfortable, white, middle class and conservative. It is culturally distinct from Oakland proper with its hard hats, its housing developments, its Hell's Angels and its burgeoning black population.

Life is not peaceful for the Oakland Raiders. They are 2–2–1 and this is not to be tolerated. Defeat is sinful because the Raiders are an Organization (always with a capital letter). They stress, according to their management, "pride and poise." The words are stenciled everywhere. There are only two commandments with the Oakland football club. Thou shalt have Pride and thou shalt have Poise. Thou shalt also make damn sure thou win, too.

Other teams approach professional football from other angles. The Raiders are a paramilitary organization, about as frivolous as the Gestapo, about as lighthearted as the CIA. They are commanded by Al Davis, who believes that other people are watching. He may be right. Security is strict with the Oakland club. Nobody gets near practice without proper clearance. Squad cuts are never announced to the press. Reporters simply have to hang around and see who's missing. Player deals are Byzantine in nature. Taxi squads—the ready reserve units of the National Football League—are limited to seven athletes, but the legend is that Al Davis has 20 men hid out in the hills. Bartenders at the Orinda Country Club all weigh 285. Either that or they can get to your table in 4.7 seconds, even if it is located 40 yards away.

As a means of expressing their determination, their unyielding focus on victory, they dress in black and silver. No blues, no reds, no golds or greens. Just black and silver, convict colors, elite guard colors, men-living-together-in-an-insulated-group colors.

"I like The Organization," says George Blanda, who looks like country singer Eddie Arnold, who speaks with a voice that sounds like John Wayne, only in a slightly higher register. "Some players knock it. But they're part of the new breed. They don't want to work for a thing. They want it all passed out to them. I could have quit a dozen times. I damn near did. Betty, my wife, has been wanting me to get out since 1959, the year the Bears decided they didn't want me playing pro football anymore.

"But the Raiders are a strong organization. They don't panic. They don't yank you out of the starting line-up. They give you a job and even if you have a bad day and have to come out, you know you'll be back in the next week. They don't panic. So the ball club doesn't panic. Maybe that sounds corny, but it's true." For this reason, George Frederick Blanda cannot hope to start in this, his 261st professional football game. Lamonica is the Oakland quarterback, the number one man. Blanda will kick extra points and field goals. But he will not start. He is a natural freak, a man who has lived as a Beta Male, become an Alpha Male, only to lose and regain the status. Now he exists in a special category, neither one nor the other. He is a wolf alone, a solitary figure—an Alpha Male in winter. He should be dead, but he isn't. He is alive in a game designed for young legs, young backs, young muscles.

"My wife says that my career is 'Death and Resurrection' over and over again," says Blanda, chuckling at his wife's intellectualism. He much admires his wife. She paints seriously. She majored in the dance and has taught classes in the subject. She reads heavy books. She thinks swiftly and cleverly.

Indeed, there is truth in Betty Blanda's observation. She starts a new scrapbook every generation, she says, and the pages are littered with clippings from the *Chicago Tribune,* the *Chicago American,* the *Houston Press,* the *Houston Chronicle,* the *Oakland Tribune,* the *San Francisco Examiner.* The headlines rise and fall with the movement of the planets in and out of George Blanda's astrological chart.

"Blanda Benched! Bratkowski New Bears Quarterback!" shouts one. Two crinkled yellow pages later there is another story that says, "Halas Says Blanda Is Best Quarterback in Professional Football." The Houston years are similar. "As They Say in the West, Blanda's Back in the Saddle Again," says the *Post.* A month later, the *Chronicle* reports: "George Through as No. 1 Quarterback. Trull in Charge from Here on Out."

So it goes. Blanda has outlasted every single one of them. They are all either retired or hiding in Canada—John Lujack, Steve Romanik, Ed Brown, Ron Knox, Tommy O'Connell, Bob Williams, Jacky Lee, Charlie Milstead, Don Trull, Bobby Layne, Glyn Griffing, Randy Kerbow and, Good God, is that all? They brought them in by the planeload, in Chicago and in Houston. Old George survived. (Do you know they were calling him "old" in 1960 with the Oilers when he was a mere lad of 31?)

The parking lot is circular. It lies in a bomb-crater depression between the 54,000-seat Coliseum and the 16,500-seat Sports Arena. Neither is fancy, just grim concrete. The place where the athletes leave their cars is heavily guarded, lest some espionage agent from the New York Jets sneak in and bug somebody's dashboard.

The younger Raiders are not sure how to take George Fred-

erick Blanda. He is a figure out of the romantic past. He is fully
nine years older than their head coach, John Madden, who at
least has the decency to be the youngest coach in the NFL.

The children walk around George cautiously. He is too old
to be a player and, almost, too old to be a coach. Besides, he
has an ego-shattering presence about him. His face is hard, but
handsome. He walks with a strut. His eyes are demoralizing.
They are singularly lupine. They wither, accuse and challenge,
all at the same time. On occasion—not often—those gray-green
eyes have transfixed defensive players, rooting them to a spot,
while a pass whistles over their helmets. The gaze is so disturb-
ing that Blanda's sweaty, uncomfortable enemies have described him as "evil" and "sinister" and "manipulative."

"That's a lot of bullshit," Blanda says in that John Wayne-in-
Rio-Bravo voice. "I'm a pretty simple, straightforward person.
I'm independent. I like to compete. I say exactly what I think
and I guess that threatens some people."

On the way to the dressing room, several rookies, dressed in
jump suits and floppy hats, bow respectfully to the senior citizen. They look like curates caught suddenly in the presence of
the archbishop. Blanda smirks. The man has an eloquent smirk,
straight out of the Bowery Boys movies of the 1940s. He enjoys
the reverence they show. No one will ever tell those rookies
what a bold-faced young varlet George Frederick Blanda was
when he was new to the Chicago Bears, way back in 1949 when
Harry Truman was president and Milton Berle's television
show cleaned out saloons every Tuesday night.

Blanda wears mildly modish clothes now. His slacks are
flared. His shirts are reasonably fashionable. His sideburns ex-
tend far below his ear lobes. But they are neat and trimmed. His
face looks like nature meant it to wear a duck's ass hairdo. His
pants should be pegged and shoes should be white bucks. Still,
he assimilates well. He has been around so long that the snap-
shot of him taken outside Wrigley Field in 1950 wearing a
wide-lapel suit and a fat tie looks stylish. His clothes were out

so long that they are suddenly in again. George Blanda has transcended something so artificial as fashion.

Some of the athletes are nervous. They have pregame jitters. They are hiding them by wearing what cliché experts call "game faces." In other words, they are nervous as hell, so nervous they cannot work up a decent look of terror. Blanda is gray, both at the muzzle and at the ears. Standing in the corner, near where the other quarterbacks, Daryle Lamonica and Ken (Snake) Stabler hang their clothes, he is placid, imperturbable. It is nearly noon on October 25, 1970, and Blanda is about to become a national hero.

The sky is starting to clear outside. Pittsburgh coach Chuck Noll is concerned. If the sun shines, the Raiders can throw deep and run wide, and that ain't good.

"The bomb," he says, "is always on their mind. Oakland wants to go for that big one. Basically, they're a long-striking team. You have to worry about Lamonica all the time."

But not today. The game starts splendidly for Oakland and Daryle does get off a picturesque scoring pass to tight end Raymond Chester, a young man of real talent. The play covers 37 yards and soon afterwards Lamonica, who suffers physical torments that would impress Job, pinches a nerve in his back and retires. Now destiny, after all these years, has thrown a sweaty arm around Blanda's shoulders.

Where have you been, old boy?

Madden has two choices: (a) He can go with Ken Stabler, young, left-handed and impressionable or (b) he can use old George, elderly, right-handed and a born adventurer who could have saved a lot of interceptions over the years if he weren't so damned determined to throw the ball into the end zone.

In a situation so tense there is only one intelligent move for a coach to make: forget all the technical nonsense. A man has to go with experience. And who has more experience than George Blanda? Once again the Alpha Male, George stomps out onto the grubby field. The customers are dubious. Here is an ancient gent who has been primarily a place kicker. He had some interesting moments as a relief passer, but he has thrown the ball only 138 times for Oakland over a period of four years.

On his first play from scrimmage, he throws 29 yards to Chester. Touchdown! The crowd of 54,423 gets hyperactive. Whoops! Somebody has been holding. Pittsburgh gets the ball and scores to tie the game. Now the Steelers get a brilliant idea. What is the best way to detach a quarterback from his intellect? Simple. Just blitz him until he cannot think anymore. The blitz is a murderous device. The defensive unit forgets finesse and just sends kamikaze pilots roaring through the line. The idea is to kill the quarterback before he can get the ball in the air.

There is a tactical risk. In order to free men for the blitz, it is necessary to give up all pretensions of double coverage of pass receivers. It is strictly: one man—one ball catcher. Period!

"They don't know how much we love to have the other team blitz," Blanda says afterwards. "I got two touchdowns against that damned blitz and they decided to quit it."

Quarterbacks take a physical smashing, no matter how they enjoy throwing against the blitz. As soon as the ball leaves their palm—wham! bam! thank you, m'am!—somebody splatters them all over the turf.

"Do I give a damn about that?" Blanda asks. "I've been hurt only once in an athletic event. That was in 1954 when I got a shoulder separation that just about finished me as the Bears' number one quarterback. Don Colo came up on one side of me and Len Ford on the other. I don't even remember who won our last four games of the year that season. Other than that, I've never been hurt."

So Blanda stands in there against the fearsome charge. As the second period ends, he finds Warren Wells—a troubled lad, but a brilliant pass receiver—streaking for the horizon. The touchdown play covers 44 yards and George is all hyped-up. Seems like old times, he says later, humming the words to a long-dead popular tune.

Back he comes with a 27-yard field goal and a 19-yard scoring pass to Chester again, just before the half. Now the stands are overreacting. Now it is October 25, 1970, and destiny is getting just a little bit ahead of George Frederick Blanda. When it is all over, the statistics are impressive. Blanda has thrown a dozen times, completed seven passes for 148 yards. Three of his passes have gone for touchdowns.

The next afternoon's *Examiner* will refer to this game as if it had been something transitory. "Blanda's Day of Glory—Indian Summer in Oakland." Indeed, George has turned the winter of his discontent into glorious Indian summer. But his career is just starting to get good. What an incredible thought! Babe Parilli was a freshman at the University of Kentucky when George was a senior. Poor Parilli lasted only until he was 39. Now he is an assistant coach and Blanda is on the verge of becoming famous.

Afterwards, Blanda sits naked in front of his dressing stall, flashing those lobo eyes at wandering reporters. This is when he is at his snappish best. He has competed in a football game. He has done what they pay him to do. He stands above and a bit to the right of the rest of the world, waiting to reenter. He has competed. He has dominated. Now he cannot stop competing. This is something about the man that reporters have never come to understand. The game has just ended. Blanda's glands are still pumping. His jaws are still wet with saliva. How in the hell can he calm down and say nice, polite things to people who insist on asking the dumbest questions?

It is still mano-a-mano as far as George is concerned. Those writers, they bring up those insipid questions and they expect him to cool down and be calm, tactful, reserved—even chatty.

"Do you have any trouble reading modern defenses?" asks a writer from a suburban newspaper. The kid is young, not more than four years older than Blanda's son, Rick, age 19. It is an insulting, condescending question. Maybe it isn't meant to be. But it is. So George competes. He has been challenged. Now he responds. The answer is something of a put-on. After all, on the sidelines, before Lamonica's injury, he had noticed that

Pittsburgh cornerback Mel Blount could be had. On the long pass play involving Wells, he faked a running play and then watched with animal delight as Blount took a couple of fatal steps back toward the scrimmage line. By that time Warren Wells was off and running. By the time the pass reached Wells, it was apparent to Blount that he had been conned.

"Of course I don't read defenses," Blanda tells the insolent young writer. "If I watched them, I wouldn't be able to see my receivers."

Nearby, looking tall and serious as a Baptist deacon, is Hamilton P. B. (Tex) Maule, author, critic and retired trapeze artist. He takes it down, word for word, as if George is serious. It appears just that way in *Sports Illustrated,* the weekly magazine that makes sweat smell so sweet.

Now it is time to shower and leave. Nobody spends so much time in the bathhouse as George Blanda. Since writers rarely roll up their slacks, take off their shoes and walk through the rain drops, George takes long showers.

When it comes to newspapermen, Blanda is selective. He likes to talk to journalists whom he thinks make sense. He will spend hours talking to the *San Francisco Examiner's* Bucky Walter, who looks, sounds and writes like W. C. Fields. He considers Bill Feist, a kindly acting man from the *San Jose Mercury-News,* to be a personal friend. He tolerates the *San Francisco Chronicle's* bearded poet, Glenn Dickey, not because he likes him, but because Dickey says what he thinks and George admires that quality. He will speak to no one on the *Oakland Tribune* staff but Ed Schoenfeld, the paper's myopic, hard-working golf writer.

Blanda has his list and he sticks to it religiously. One flagrant violation is enough for dismissal. People rarely get second chances with George Frederick Blanda. Experience—starting very early when he was a small boy playing snooker in Buckley's pool hall in Youngwood—has taught him that as soon as a man shows his unreliability, it is best to leave him alone.

What is right is right, George thinks, and what isn't right is best avoided. So Blanda divides the world in half, a regular Papal Line of Demarcation—good guys over here, bad guys over there. John Wayne would be proud. In future weeks he will work miracles far more spectacular than those he has performed on this day—October 25, 1970—against the Pittsburgh Steelers. He will amaze millions of people and justify the expectations of those good, solid, beer-swigging lads back there at the VFW Hall in Youngwood.

No matter where George Blanda goes, no matter what he does, he is not far away, spiritually, from Youngwood. He remains a tough, competitive Slavic boy struggling—always struggling—to avoid the choking horror of the mines.

Now he is about to be recognized as a genuine, walking, talking, bright-eyed football immortal. In future years, jock historians won't bother to recall how close George Frederick Blanda came to quitting before the miracle season of 1970 ever got started. But it is true. You could look it up.

10 / LAYNE

"I Sleep Fast"

By Myron Cope

*Almost a decade after Bobby Layne ended his professional foot-
ball career, I worked with him on a television show that was
filmed at a country club not far from New York City. During the
show, Layne demonstrated his skill with a golf club, a billiard
cue and a football. We hung a lifesaver from the diving board
at one end of the country club's swimming pool. Layne stood at
the other end, a good 30 yards away, picked up a football and,
on his first try, threw the ball right through the center of the
lifesaver. Before the day was over—as a matter of fact, before the
morning was over—Bobby proved he hadn't lost his touch with
martinis, either. Layne was a wild, tough, talented and brave
quarterback, a man perfectly matched to the two cities in which
he spent most of his professional career. Layne was the last
quarterback not to wear a face mask, and the auto workers of
Detroit and the mill workers of Pittsburgh loved him for it.*

*In the early and middle 1950s, the Detroit Lions and the
Cleveland Browns were the dominant teams of professional football, led by the dominant quarterbacks, Layne and Otto Graham. Four times in six years, the Lions and Browns met for the
championship, and three times the Lions won. In 1952, Layne
ran for the game's first touchdown, Detroit never fell behind and*

the Lions won, 17–7. In 1953, Layne passed for the game's last touchdown, and Detroit came from behind to win, 17–16.

Layne ended his career in Pittsburgh, the city where Myron Cope, author of the following story, has built a splendid career as a writer and sportscaster. Cope is a little guy, but he has a lot of guts. Once he knocked on Bobby Layne's door shortly after dawn, and that takes guts.

With the possible exception of his coach, Buddy Parker, it was Bobby Layne, more than any other man, who made the city of Detroit one of America's hotbeds of pro-football enthusiasm. Television riches as yet had not begun to engulf the game when, in 1950, Layne arrived in Detroit, his third stop in the National Football League. Briefly in the mid-1930s, the great tailback Dutch Clark had attracted huge crowds in Detroit, even leading the Lions to a championship in 1935, but the club lost its momentum and did not really establish itself as a major spectacle until Bobby Layne had taken a foothold in the city. Blond and blue-eyed, a fast-living young Texan with an infectious grin and a rasping drawl, Layne not only quarterbacked the Lions to four first-place finishes and three league championships but also brought to the drab, industrial metropolis a flamboyant presence. He was flamboyant not in the sense that he *strove* to attract attention but in the sense that he was constitutionally propelled toward it. He never required more than five hours' sleep to be at his best. "I sleep fast" was the way he once put it. A jazz buff oversupplied with nervous energy, he loved to lead forth his teammates to a night on the town, and so he became a night figure, fair game for gossip columnists and hecklers. His temper complicated matters. He could not abide intruders. He experienced run-ins with fans, and although some of his best friends were cops, he occasionally clashed with the law. The combination of his good looks, his love of a good time, and his combustibility made him the most glamorous football

figure of his day. Yet sadly, it was that aspect of his career that
he hated. He speaks of it with great reluctance.

I came to know him on the downhill side of his career, having
become a sort of marginal member of his circle. Buddy Parker
had quit Detroit and become coach of the Pittsburgh Steelers
and in 1958 had brought Layne to Pittsburgh, my lifelong residence. Layne soon began frequenting Dante's, a restaurant
where I, too, spent many hours. Striving to make the best of a
sorry team, he would gather his offensive linemen around him
and work his psychology upon them endlessly. He would buy
another round of drinks and restate his position that offensive
linemen, in contrast to defensive linemen, were artists. "Hear!
Hear!" the giants around him would shout. Blocking he would
get.

He attempted to invest the Steelers with an *esprit de corps,*
and to a modest degree succeeded. He railed at them on the
field. Off the field, he led them in fun. Some players, to be sure,
resented his autocratic ways, but it is noteworthy that defensive
lineman Ernie Stautner, the club's greatest and most competitive player, at once became his fast friend and remains one to
this day.

Fifteen tempestuous years after he had traveled north in 1948
from the University of Texas to join the Chicago Bears, Bobby
Layne retired on the advice of his coach and friend, Buddy
Parker. "I hadn't realized it," he says, "but I was a hell of a lot
slower. It's what they call that one step. Yeh, that one step in
getting back to pass." He went home to Lubbock, Texas, and
except for brief stints as an assistant coach in St. Louis and
Houston, he left the bright lights of the football circuit behind
him. [*Here, Layne recalls his early days.*]

At the end of my first season of pro ball, George Halas, who
you'll recall was both owner and coach of the Chicago Bears,
called me in and told me that he thought for sure that Sid
Luckman was going to retire. He said, "My plans are for you
and Johnny Lujack to be my quarterbacks from here in." Mr.

Halas was being honest with me, I'm sure, but after I got back to Texas he called me and said, "I've got to trade you. Sid has served me well over the years, and he's decided he wants to play some more."

Mr. Halas said, "Here's another thing—Sid's Jewish and Johnny Lujack is Catholic, which means they're a hell of a drawing card in Chicago. And besides, I cannot afford to pay you three the type of salaries you're making."

I imagine the three of us together were making somewhere in the neighborhood of seventy-five thousand, and in 1948 that was a lot of money for a pro club to pay one position. A lot of pro clubs at that time were suffering. Mr. Halas was sold out every game and probably made money, but he didn't make a lot of money. So what he did was sell me to the New York Bulldogs, which was the beginning of quite an experience.

Ted Collins, who managed Kate Smith, the singer, owned the Bulldogs. He was bringing the club down from Boston, where it had been the Boston Yanks, and he hired a new coach, Charley Ewart. Ewart was a Yale guy, so they made the team colors blue and white and called us the Bulldogs, just like Yale. But the names on that team were not exactly Yale names. Those names amazed me. Sabasteanski! Domnanovich! Barzilauskas! Jarmoluk! Batinski! Slosburg! Phil Slosburg didn't weigh but 150 pounds and was our diving halfback. His daddy manufactured pants.

We played six exhibitions and twelve league games, and outside of tying the Redskins and beating the Giants, which I guess was the upset of the century, we lost them all. We didn't have a cut dog's chance. Charley Ewart was a nice young guy who had been coaching over in Philadelphia, and he believed in that Steve Van Buren type of football. But the trouble was, we didn't have any Steve Van Burens. "Run it!" Ewart would tell me. He liked a running game. But Collins would tell me, "Throw it!"

I'd throw it, what do you think? I listened to the man who owned the club.

Well, it was just a horrible year. Collins was always changing

coaches. He'd tell Ewart that he was still the head coach but
that he couldn't come to practice or do any coaching. Collins
would have Ray Nolting coach the team one week or Joe Bach
another week. We had fines for fumbles. In order that we
wouldn't get fined, we got to where we'd just pass the ball every
down. But our pass protection wasn't what it should have been.
Hell, I think I carried the ball more than anybody on the club
—but not from being *supposed* to, but from *having* to.

A lot of clubs, the Philadelphia Eagles in particular, had
great teams at that time, and some of those teams would be
beating us 40–0 and they'd still be clawing to get at us. Greasy
Neale had all kinds of bonus deals for the Philadelphia players.
He'd pay a defensive lineman ten dollars for every time he got
to the quarterback. An interception was worth twenty-five. The
Eagles had all those kinds of bonus offers, so, hell, they'd be
whipping us by forty points and still fighting to get at us. It was
some year, I'll tell you.

We made up pass routes in the huddle and used hideout plays
and anything we could think of. In a game at Detroit, a receiver
named Ralph Heywood hid out in front of one of the benches.
I think it might have been the Detroit bench, right near Bo
McMillin, the Detroit coach. Anyway, nobody saw him. Then
he ran down the sideline and I hit him for a touchdown. The
Detroit fans threw snowballs at Bo McMillin.

At our home games in the Polo Grounds, lor-*dee*, you'd look
up in the stands and there'd be about thirty people huddled
together up there. And that'd be our wives. If anybody hollered
you could hear an echo. Collins put on circus acts to get people
out to the games—he hired tightrope walkers and all that. But
he couldn't get anybody out. To cut losses, the club fired so
many players that by the end of the season we had only nineteen
players suited out. Guys were playing positions they'd never
seen before. I think that's the year the league put in a rule where
you have to have a certain number of people suited out. Lord,
I'd weighed two hundred pounds or maybe a little more at the
beginning of the season, but at the end I weighed 169. I drove

into Dallas to see my old high-school buddy, Doak Walker, who was in his last year at SMU, and Doak didn't know me.

I promise you, I would not have gone back to that club. I would have given up football first, 'cause it was just too tough there. But I had learned one thing playing with the New York Bulldogs—I found out that I wasn't gun-shy. I could stay in the pocket and get hit, and it would not bother me. I think you've seen quarterbacks that you'd say were a little gun-shy—quarterbacks that are expecting to get hit. I learned I could take it. But I wasn't going to go back there to the Bulldogs.

Now in the meantime, Buddy Parker had quit the Chicago Cardinals and gone over to Detroit as an assistant to Bo McMillin. Buddy had tried to get me for the Cardinals when I was still with the Bears, but there was no way Mr. Halas would let me go to the Cardinals. At the time, they were the Bears' crosstown rivals and were in the same division. Mr. Halas didn't want me coming back with the Cardinals and beating him, and anyway, he got Ted Collins to pay him a bunch of money for me. But when Buddy Parker got over to Detroit he still wanted me, and so one night while I was at a basketball game in Austin I got word that Buddy was trying to reach me. I'd been traded to the Lions. And that was the greatest thing that ever happened to me, because that same year everything just seemed to fall into place.

Detroit drafted Doak Walker. They drafted "Fum" McGraw, who turned out to be a fine tackle. Leon Hart, the Notre Dame end, was the club's first pick in the draft. Somehow McMillin got Bob Hoernschemeyer, a fantastic back, from the Chicago Rockets in the other league, the All-America Conference, which had just folded. Oh, gosh, we had some great players come up that year. So actually 1950 was the start of something big in Detroit, but it was a pretty confusing year because we were six and six, and we had a better team than that.

I liked Bo McMillin, but he was getting up in his years and was very outdated in his methods. For instance, he never would kick a field goal. Doak Walker was a darned good kicker, and

I remember many games that we could have won that year by kicking field goals from inside the thirty or inside the twenty. But McMillin wouldn't kick a field goal.

In those days, baseball and hockey were the big sports in Detroit. Football players were recognized around town by very few people. We didn't average but twenty or maybe twenty-two thousand a game. Early in the season we'd have to play our home games at Detroit University because the Tigers were still playing baseball at Briggs Stadium, and we had to work out at a place called Jayne Playfield, which was a public playground out in Hamtramck, a tough part of town. We'd go out there to practice and Bo would try to clear the neighborhood kids off the field and they'd tell him, "Go screw yourself!" Oh, lor-*dee!* Bo couldn't do a thing about it. Those kids stayed right out there while we practiced. 'Course, the players could have run them off, but we didn't care.

That was the coldest year you'd care to go through. Bo used to come out to practice in one of those flying suits—a real warm suit—and he'd be wearing flight boots and a flight cap and gloves. There wasn't anything to break the wind on that public playground, but he'd keep us out there three hours, maybe three and a half hours, and we wouldn't accomplish anything. We'd just freeze to death while he stayed warm in that flight suit. Lord, I used to hate those practices with him. You'd try to save yourself all through practice, 'cause you knew that at the end of practice he'd make you run. And *that* was just drudgery.

Furthermore, your opponents could drive right up to the playground and park there and watch you put in your formations. I remember one time we were getting ready to play the Bears. We'd already beaten them, *bad.* The second time around was going to be a big game for them because they needed it to win the division. Well, Bo came up with a Y formation and an X formation at the public playground, so now we're playing the Bears and he sends in word to put in the Y formation. We did, and all the Bear players yelled, "Y formation!" Oh, God a'- mighty, it was funny. They knew everything we were doing.

Well, there were eighteen guys who owned the Lions, and

what finally happened was that even before the season ended they called a group of us down to the Book-Cadillac Hotel for lunch. Doak Walker, Cloyce Box, and Les Bingaman were there. So was Johnny Greene, who was our captain, and I believe Hoernschemeyer was there, though I'm not positive. We sat down and the owners said, "How can we get a winner? What does it take?"

To a man, we said that we thought Buddy Parker could win with the team we had. So the owners fired Bo McMillin and gave the job to Buddy.

[*In the years that followed, a firm and constant relationship was to flourish between Layne and Parker, both Texans, both willful men. Enjoying Parker's full confidence, Layne came to run the Lions on the field with absolute authority, and with a disdain for enemy blows. Except for a helmet and a set of almost wafer-thin shoulder pads under a loose-fitting, short-sleeved jersey, he wore no protective paraphernalia—neither a face guard nor pads on his ribs, thighs, hips, or knees. "I like the freedom," he says. Both he and Parker were equipped with a genius for strategy; the mating of their minds produced significant change in coaching theory.*

Principally, Layne's burgeoning reputation for derring-do sprang from his ability to march his team long yardage to a game-winning touchdown or field goal while with utterly nerveless aplomb he ate up practically all the remaining time, thereby depriving his opponent of a chance to strike back. It was a talent that Parker exploited to the fullest. All along, it was Parker's conviction that many games were won or lost in the final two minutes of the first half or in the final two minutes of the game. So Parker became, in all probability, the first coach to devote large segments of practice time to what came to be known throughout football as "the two-minute drill."]

When Buddy took over in 1951 we became the happiest group of ballplayers I have ever seen in my life. Buddy was young at the time, and although he believed in performance, he also

believed in having fun. For example, you could go to Buddy in
training camp and say, "We're getting sick of all this," and he'd
say, "Well, all right. We'll skip tonight's meeting. Take the
night off and go to the track."

The players were crazy about Buddy. We worked our asses
off to win all the exhibition games that first summer under
Buddy. We were trying to get those fans fired up to buy season
tickets and get the club going, so we even worked hard getting
ready for exhibitions. But the result was that we hit our peak
too soon. And in the next-to-last game of the season, although
we beat Los Angeles, we had four or five key injuries. The next
week we just didn't have enough people available to beat San
Francisco, and so the Los Angeles Rams backed into the divisional title and we finished second. But we had gotten the city
of Detroit excited that year. And in the next three years—1952,
'53, and '54—we finished first in the division all three times and
in the first two of those years we won the National League
championship. I don't think anyone will ever have the type of
group that we had those two years.

I'm not saying that was the greatest team that ever played
football. I'm talking about the kind of *people* we had—the
individuals. It was the most amazing thing that's ever happened
to me in sports. Not long ago I got out the pictures of those '52
and '53 squads and looked them over, and I'm telling you, we
didn't have a single bad fellow on those squads. Well, maybe
one. But he was young.

Lord, we had got us some ballplayers. Doak was a winner.
Hoernschemeyer could run and block and think—he was just
one hellacious ballplayer. We had Les Bingaman, who weighed
about 340 pounds and was so big that when Buddy finally
retired him he told him, "I want you to quit, because I don't
want you dying on the football field." Bing couldn't lose weight.
He had little bitty feet—I'd say he'd wear a nine and a half or
a ten shoe—and he had to tape up his arches because of that
tremendous weight that he carried. But the guy was quick as
a cat and a brilliant middle guard. He was captain of our team,

yet he came to camp every year with a fear of getting cut. In scrimmages he was all eyes. He looked at everything. He'd spot something—he'd see someone in our offense tipping off the play, and just before the snap of the ball, he'd say, "Six hole!" And the defense would pile into the six hole and stop the play. I'd say, "Bing, goddamn it, tell me who's tipping the play. Tell me so I can get him straightened out." But he wouldn't tell me till after training camp was over—till he'd made the team. He was all-league practically every year, but he never did stop worrying about being cut.

We had a team of leaders. The fellowship between our players was practically legendary. We all thought the same way— you could have all the fun you wanted to, but when you went out to play you had to win. We looked forward to practice. We looked forward to games. We even looked forward to training camp. Goddamn, it was like going on a vacation when you went to training camp. Guys got there *early*, just to get up there and get their hands on a football.

After 1953 I saw this spirit start dwindling away, and today it's gone. I think the reason is money. When I was playing at Detroit in those early years, no ballplayer ever heard of the goddamn stock market, and they didn't have any money to put into it anyway. But now you see guys sit down on the edge of a secretary's desk and pick up her phone and say, "What's General Motors doing today?" I'm not saying this is good or bad, but I'm saying that we had just one interest in Detroit and it was football. Every son of a bitch on that team was all football.

We brought up our rookies much different than they do now. During training camp, if we went to a tavern for a beer and a rookie came in—well, he just didn't *dare* come in. Rookies found their own joints. There were good reasons for rules like that. Say, for instance, that a rookie came up from Texas and got cut. Well, if he could, he might come and try to cry on my shoulder. But I didn't want to hear that crap. After the season began we let the rookies come to team parties and we had them

perform for us—we had them sing for us—and it added a lot
to the closeness of the team, but still, we had a rule that you
were a rookie until the exhibition schedule ended in your second year. Joe Schmidt, who of course later went on to become
head coach of the Lions, had played about six games in his first
year when he was at a party one night and heard everybody
calling a tackle named John Prchlik "Jolly John." So Joe called
him Jolly John. But Prchlik turned on him and told him in no
uncertain terms that he was *Mr.* Prchlik. He really let Joe have
it. He scared him to bits.

It was just terrific the way everyone became a part of the
team. In 1953 chlorophyll had come out and you had it in
chewing gum and in everything. It was chlorophyll this and
chlorophyll that. So we had a slogan that year—"Chlorophyll
will put more sock in your jock!" We went on to beat Cleveland
in the championship game, and all our wives sat up there in the
stands wearing hats that they'd made from jockstraps dyed
green. Some tied a bow in 'em, some of them wore them as a
band. They wore those jockstraps just every possible way you
could wear one, and it was pretty cute. The wives were real
close in Detroit, you see, and that was a big part of our team,
too. That was one of the things that Buddy Parker always
insisted on, closeness among the wives, 'cause you get a bunch
of wives scrapping and you got hell.

Well, I guess I can't explain what it was that we had those
two years. It's an intangible thing. It's just the most difficult
kind of thing to explain. But not long ago I went up to New
York to be inducted into the College Hall of Fame, and I looked
around and Bob Smith had come there from Tulsa and Cloyce
Box had showed up from Dallas and Harley Sewell from Arlington, Texas, and Doak Walker and Dorne Dibble from Detroit, and I mean just a whole bunch of guys I'd played with.
Guys I didn't expect to see. They'd gone there to be with me.
It was fantastic. Men who played on those Detroit teams still
get together around the country, they still look each other up.

I don't know if you're going to see that happen with the teams you've got now. I don't know. I don't think so.

[*In the company of his teammates he was always the big spender. At that time, he may have been the biggest in sports. He had not come from affluent beginnings, having been reared from the age of six by an aunt and uncle because his widowed mother could not support him. But at the conclusion of his college-football career, he found himself in the enviable position of being bid for—by the Chicago Bears in one corner, and by the Baltimore Colts of the short-lived All-America Conference. George Halas handed a blank contract to Layne's college coach and adviser, Blair Cherry, and told him to write in a figure. So from the beginning, Layne was paid well by the standards of the times —a $10,000 bonus and $22,500 salary—yet actually he had signed for a figure somewhat lower than the offer Baltimore had made him. It was Cherry's feeling that the Bears, as a going concern that had won championships, offered values that could not be measured in dollars and cents. "That was great advice Blair Cherry gave me," Layne says appreciatively to this day, even though he lasted but a year in Chicago.*

In college he had married well. Carol Krueger, a pretty and delightful brunette, was the daughter of a brilliant, wealthy Lubbock surgeon, Dr. J. T. Krueger. So between Layne's own substantial income and his wife's background, he felt no pressure to hoard his dollars. When I revisited him in Lubbock—in a sumptuous three-room suite of offices from which he now manages his investments and the estate of his late father-in-law—I recalled to him the trail of smiling waiters that he left in his wake.]

You're talking about something now that was always exaggerated. You ask me, did I slip fifty dollars to headwaiters? Did I toss a hundred-dollar bill to the band? Yes, I've done these things, but not to the extreme that people say. I've tipped good but I've gotten good service. Where I didn't get good service, I didn't tip. I never owned a Cadillac. I never owned a boat. I have a hunting lodge, but I never had a diamond ring in my life and never wore any rings or stickpins or crap like that. I don't think I dressed fancy. But I did carry around a little spending money, because I felt I had to spend a little extra money around the ball club. I felt like I was supposed to.

For one thing, I was making more money than anybody else on the club. So I always allocated a certain part of my salary to spend on the players. I called it play money. I mean, I didn't try to pick up *every* tab, but I tried to pick up more than my share. Some of the guys just couldn't afford to go to nightclubs and hear good music or go to nice places to eat. They just didn't have the money. So I tried to see that they did a little of this. I wasn't trying to be a big shot, and I don't think any of them ever thought I was trying to be one. Lot of times I tried to pick up tabs in a way that they wouldn't know about it.

See, I was making good money—a heck of a lot more than probably most of the guys on the team. Whenever I went in to sign a contract with Nick Kerbawy, our general manager in Detroit, we never had an argument. We didn't spend thirty minutes signing a contract, *ever*. In 1955 our team did poorly —Lord, we lost the first six games coming off a great team in '54. We had some injuries and I knew in my own mind I'd had a bad year. So I went to see Nick and told him, "I feel like I ought to take about a $2,500 cut." Taxwise, with other income and me being in a certain bracket, it made only about a four-hundred-dollar difference to me. Well, I think the club appreciated it. The next year I had a real good season and led the league in scoring, and I got a nice raise.

I was very fortunate, because in pro football if you start high it's hard for them to get you down, but if you start low it's hell to get up. In the 1950s it was a difficult thing for even a Joe Schmidt or a Yale Lary to go from seven thousand, say, to ten thousand, and then from ten to twelve thousand. The general manager's job is to get the guys signed for as little as possible. But Nick Kerbawy was a tremendous person, and he was responsible in a lot of ways for those great teams at Detroit. He put us up in first-class hotels. When we'd go to the West Coast on a two-game trip, the club would slip us a hundred or two hundred dollars for spending money. Nick got boys out of financial jams and never said anything about it. And when the team was going through a letdown, I might go to Nick, or our captain might, and say, "Nick, we need to have a beer party or something." He'd be all for it, and at the club's expense. He was *for* the football players. A lot of them didn't think so for a long time, but they finally realized that he was for 'em.

(At Dante's, the restaurant in Pittsburgh, Layne continued to spend well, although he usually avoided the front cocktail lounge, confining himself to a table in the darkened rear dining room. Surrounded by teammates and cronies, he enjoyed telling a story or hearing one, but there was one surefire way to plunge him into an ugly mood. One needed only to mention the press.

The blood would rush to his face, and he would launch into a tirade that rambled on and on, while those around him waited silently for the storm to spend itself. Although he had a scattering of close friends among the sportswriting fraternity, he saw the press as one great mass of gossip-mongers waiting to feed on his traffic tickets and nightclub celebrations. His argument was that the press had no consideration for the feelings of his wife and two sons. On one occasion, while the two of us sat in a parked car outside his apartment at 3 A.M., he stated his argument plaintively, keeping a grip on his temper. But at the table in Dante's, he sometimes would turn on me, remembering that I was a member of the press, and denounce me in the strongest possible terms. I would leave the table and go to the bar. The next night he would beckon me to his table, and when I refused, he would insist. Finally I would approach the table. He would utter the beginnings of an apology, but then his pride would stop him and again he would explode with a denunciation of me. I would return to the bar.

Even at those times, I always liked him. One does not expect even temperament from genius, whether it be in the field of painting, letters, or quarterbacking. Another time, shortly after he had treated me to another blistering, he overheard a tipsy belligerent giving me a hard time at the bar, whereupon he appeared as if from a puff of smoke and with a finger wagging under the man's nose warned him that he had better settle down "or mister, I'll tie your tongue to your shoelaces."

Usually he appeared to be in hale spirits. But his bursts of anger came more frequently toward the end of his five years in Pittsburgh—partly because the fans had gotten on him for his failure to deliver a championship, and partly, I suspect, because he saw that time would run out on him before he could taste another one. There would never be another Detroit. He knew he would never recapture the good years with the Lions.)

Well, I was in Detroit long enough. In football you can't stay at one place a long time. It's kind of like a car dealer being in a town for a long time—sooner or later he's a son of a bitch. Have you ever noticed that? Well, it's the same in football. I don't care where you are, sports fans get tired of you. It's the damn truth, they get tired of you. I can't put my finger on the reason, but the only time a guy in sports really truly becomes worth a damn is after he quits. I got booed in Detroit when we were winning championships. But I went back not long ago and was introduced at halftime of a Lions game, and I got an ovation.

Looking back, I don't think I'd want to change many things, but it *is* something I've thought about an awful lot. Some of the past I don't like. The glamour image? Yeah—that type of thing. If I had it to do over, I would probably try to do something about that part of it. It's not good when you have kids growing up. I don't think it's hurt my two boys, but they've probably been conscious of some of the publicity I got. I used to be real happy when the Detroit papers would go on strike. I had a lot of experiences—sad experiences—with writers.

How would *you* feel if your name was in headlines and you weren't within miles of the incident? "Bobby Layne's Car

Caught Doing Sixty in a Thirty-mile Zone!" That was the head-line. But it was Hunchy Hoernschemeyer and Harry Gilmer that had my car. I was in bed. But when people see "Bobby Layne's Car," they know damn well that if it's his car he was there. How would *you* feel?

Listen, I've known some wonderful guys who were sports-writers, but the press can crucify you and get away with it. If I had those years to do over, I probably wouldn't exopse myself to that kind of treatment. Mantle learned how to handle it. In his later years he did a fantastic job of avoiding exposure. You've got to have some fun in football—it can't be all business —but I would make an effort to avoid the exposure.

Well, as I said, you can't stay in one town a long time. I spent better than eight years in Detroit and it was long enough. But I'll tell you what I really miss. What I miss is the guys. That's what I miss more than anything. I miss going to training camp. I miss the road trips and the card games. I miss the fellowship. The locker room, the places where it was a pleasure to be. The practice sessions. I miss the bar where we'd go for a beer after practice. I miss having that beer with the guys. I miss the ballgames. I mean, when you've got a whole team looking forward to everything, when you've got guys showing up for practice early and staying late—well, you've got something there. We had that perfect thing for a while. What I miss now is my teammates.

11 / RYAN

How the Unwanted
Quarterback Made Good

By Gary Cartwright

When Gary Cartwright wrote the following article about his fellow Texas intellectual, Frank Ryan was at the mid-point and high-point of his professional football career. Ryan spent thirteen years in the National Football League, from 1958 through 1970, but it was in the middle 60s, with the Cleveland Browns, that Ryan reached his peak. For three straight years, from 1965 through 1967, Ryan was selected for the Pro Bowl. About the time Cartwright's article appeared, in 1965, Ryan completed his doctoral dissertation. Dr. Ryan is the only former football player to serve as director of the House Information Systems Committee on House Administration, U.S. House of Representatives. No current quarterbacks aspire to the job.

His hair is thick as a welcome mat and brushed with premature grey. Frank Ryan obviously will not be a second Y. A. Tittle. His wife worries he might be a second Red Skelton. "Frank's sense of humor gets him in trouble. His humor is sometimes lost on people," says Joan Ryan, a tall, quick-witted mother of three with cornsilk blonde hair and a soft touch with sophistication. Or maybe he'll take up law, or biology; he will have exhausted the challenge of pure math if his paper, "Concerning the Set Asymptotic Values of a Holomorphic Function," is stamped QED by Rice University this spring.

It's axiomatic that Frank is easy game for a challenge . . . chess, guitar playing, television denouncing, jokes perpetrating, even editing. He is, in fact, editing his image right now, starting with the Official 1965 Cleveland Browns Press Book. All of the Browns have been offered an opportunity to revise the official biographies of them which appeared in last year's press book. Ryan has accepted the opportunity. Indeed.

1964 PRESS BOOK—*(Ryan is) refreshingly candid in interviews . . . (and he) predicted "I'll be a Tittle in two or three years" after the 1963 season.*

"A Tittle? A Tittle! That wasn't what I said." His imp's smile, the smile of a man enjoying a private joke, goes tight. Frank Ryan is a wry introvert, a dangerous combination in his business. When interviewers ask stupid questions (Do you anticipate you will be another Tittle?), Ryan has a fiendish urge to answer the same way. What he said, in effect, was "I'll be another Tittle in two or three years if I lose all my hair." Since he won't, the subtlety should have survived.

The only sportswriter Ryan completely trusts is a football-season columnist for the Cleveland *Plain Dealer* who began only last fall. The writer's name is Joan Ryan; she and Frank are related by marriage. Joan worries about Frank's emerging image—writers who before hardly bothered to represent him at all, now, in their panic to uncover and capture fragments of his fascinating personality, misrepresent. She also worries that he doesn't worry enough: "I think Frank should learn to say, no comment. He should preserve his humor for quiet evenings with friends or family. In his attempts to be extroverted, he becomes a regular Red Skelton, but he also loses some people." Ryan acknowledges this. But he finds contrary temptations irresistible.

1964 PRESS BOOK—*(Ryan) has rare sense of humor and is great kidder and prankster.*

"I don't have a rare sense of humor. I take a mad delight in a joke sometimes, but this is infrequently. That's the charm of it. For instance . . . Lou Groza and the dead sea gull. Groza is such a sympathetic figure. But before one road trip I put a dead sea gull in his kicking shoe, at the bottom of his duffle bag. On the plane to St. Louis I went to a lot of trouble telling this story about people dying of parrot fever . . . how no one is really safe with all those birds flying around. I thought it was pretty funny at the time, but Groza was very upset. He had to have his shoe disinfected before the game. I wasn't there when he found it, but they told me later that was lucky: He would have slaughtered me. That happened a couple of years ago. Last year I did nothing out of the normal. So I don't deserve that reputation based on one or two incidents."

1964 PRESS BOOK—*(Ryan) requested and wears No. 13 jersey.*

"They have really made something of that No. 13 business. It's this simple: When I came to the Browns I wanted No. 11, but Ninowski had it. The only other number they had was 18 and I didn't want that because it had become identified with Lenny Dawson, a perennial second-team quarterback. We had a rookie on the squad, John Furman, and when he got cut I grabbed his number. It was 13."

1964 PRESS BOOK—*(Ryan) is extremely bright with IQ near genius level.*

"He resents being called a genius," Joan says. "I have read that his IQ is anywhere between 132 and 167. I don't think he knows himself, and anyway an IQ is relative."

In stronger terms, Ryan says, "If it were true I wouldn't mind. There's no indication my IQ is above average. It bothers me that people think I have accomplished more than I have.

What people don't take time to consider is how much you can do with determination. That's the only virtue I have in excess —determination. It is embarrassing to be called Dr. Ryan or Professor Ryan, or a nuclear physicist. I'm not a doctor yet. I'm not a professor and I don't know if I will be (although that's the plan). I'm a mathematician. I told that to a writer last year and he wrote that I was an atomic mathematician, whatever that is."

In the three years that he has guided the Browns from third to second to first in the Eastern Conference—and ultimately to an NFL championship, which, according to Bobby Layne, is the only test of a great quarterback—Frank Ryan has emerged as a categorical freak, an egghead in a world that prefers its eggs scrambled. Again, sportswriters are the inno- cent villains. This is because it's easy to follow Ryan but hard to understand him. In his taste for perfection, Ryan is so calm, so perfunctory, that his flawless logic can be mistaken for banality. Reflected as he is against a world of physical violence, Ryan comes off too simple, too lean of wasted thought, for straight public consumption. It is more comfortable to dismiss him as flip, or zany . . . a suspect at large from science fiction.

There is a curious paradox which Frank Ryan does not try to explain. One side is deliberate, calculating, a self-directed pawn on the chess board of human dilemma, a man who can trace the origin of his own desperation back to his hunger for perfection, and who, however capricious he might appear, is in control of the situation. Riding against this is his private eval- uation of Ryan-the-quarterback.

Ryan calls himself "serendipitious." It's an obscure word coined by Walpole in allusion to a tale, *The Three Princes of Serendipity*, and it relates to a talent for finding valuable things which you have not sought. Instinct would be a cheaper term, although Ryan's word seems to remove all opportunity for error.

Ryan says, "The ideal quarterback must have serendipity.

Why does he make good plays constantly? By accident? By
coincidence? Or is it a sixth sense? The times I have felt best
on the field, then my mind was following no logical conscious
thinking pattern. There was no effort to analyze, to evaluate,
to review, to study patterns or tendencies. Something just came
to me, and it worked . . . not once or twice, but time after
time."

This quality nudged into Ryan's cerebrum in midseason last
autumn, about the time visions of championship danced in his
head. Oddly, it took form one Sunday after Ryan and the
Browns had "out-thought ourselves." It was in Dallas, where
the Browns won a game they should have lost, and this game,
everyone agreed later, was the cross-road to a championship.

Cleveland won the game when Bernie Parrish intercepted a
Cowboy pass and ran it back for a touchdown late in the fourth
quarter. But the Browns continued to win, says Ryan, because
of something they learned that day.

"We learned we could win with basic plays. We could win
by doing what we did best. We feared Dallas' defense and we
put in a lot of new formations to fool them, but what happened
was we fooled ourselves. After that we went back to basic plays
—with one exception, against St. Louis in the next to the last
game; we out-thought ourselves again. But we went into the
championship game against Baltimore believing we could beat
them with basic plays, and we did."

After near disaster in Dallas, the word in Cleveland was
"execution"—do less but do it perfectly. The trick, of course,
was having the physical tools to push opponents aside, and the
mental determination to do so. With fewer plays to clog his
instincts, Ryan began to concentrate on specific keys: "Suppose
Jim Brown is going to sweep right. Our left guard pulls and
leads the play, and if I'm smart I'll watch how their defensive
right tackle reacts. If the tackle takes off chasing our guard, we
have a counter play to fix him next time. If the tackle plays it
right, I'll take my second key from the safety: is he forcing
(coming in) too quickly. A play-action might stop that. This

is the thing: I still need to concentrate more on the whole posture and less on the path of the play (in progress). That's inexperience. If I were a Layne or Van Brocklin I wouldn't be watching Jimmy Brown run around end, I'd be breaking down the play right on the spot. This is sophistication. The more sophisticated I become in my on-the-spot analysis of the game, the better I'll be. To stay at an emotional peak without losing sophistication—this is the heart and soul of my football thinking now."

The result of this sophistication, of course, was that Ryan called fewer bad plays. Cleveland's elaborate check-off system became almost obsolete. Ryan says, "We didn't check-off more than eight or nine times all season. (Teams will frequently use that many in one game.) Our offense was that well conceived by (coach) Blanton Collier. He taught us to believe this: if you have done your homework, don't worry about strategy."

The first time Frank Ryan met Blanton Collier he fell madly in love. Ryan was with the Rams from 1958 to 1961 and, with them, his confidence sagged and so did his sense of direction. The Rams traded Ryan in 1962, accepting the conclusion that he wasn't their kind of quarterback, to which Ryan adds, "They weren't my kind of coaches."

He says, "Blanton was the first coach to give me something concrete. The others just accepted the fact I could throw a football, but Blanton reduced throwing to a procedure, a series of basic steps, so when things went bad I could check back and find out why—I was holding the ball too long, or not watching the right spot, or not looking quickly enough to my secondary target. I remember going to Bob Waterfield my last year with the Rams and telling him about a problem—a thing of getting tense while I was waiting back in the pass pocket. The more time I had to throw, the more nervous I got. Blanton would have had an answer. He would have told me to concentrate on my key. The point is, he gave me specific answers and

I'm a man who needs specific answers, even if they are wrong.
I need something to think about. Otherwise I flounder."

Under Ryan, the Browns' offense matured last year in direct
relation to this sophistication and serendipity. Collier had told
Ryan earlier: "You are lucky if you have two running plays,
certainly three, that will work consistently on a given Sunday,"
and after that scare in Dallas, Ryan tried something. Early in
the week he would divide all possible running plays into three
categories—inside plays, off-tackle plays and end runs. In each
category he would reduce to four or five the ones which should
work best against the defense he would confront the following
Sunday. On Saturday night, in a hotel room, he would ask his
offensive linemen which of the remaining plays would be the
easiest to execute.

"The upshot," he says, "was that we weeded 100 plays down
to nine—three in each category. Of course we might have to
eliminate or add as the game progressed, but our nine basic
plays worked . . . I'd say at least 75 percent of the time. Half of
making a play work is having confidence in it. We went against
New York in the last game of the season, a game which meant
the championship, and our attitude was that if we couldn't win
with fundamental plays, we didn't deserve to win the championship. Of the first 13 plays I called that day, almost all were
basic runs. It turned out these were not the best possible calls,
but they worked because we believed in them."

They worked for a championship. The championship was
the end of a frantic and sometimes depressing string of means
for Frank and Joan Ryan. The Rams made some big promises
when they drafted Ryan fourth and signed him in 1958, but
they also offered some colossal heartaches. "I was scared out of
my mind that first summer," says Joan. "I felt Frank would
never have his dream. It's hard to think of someone you know
intimately being in a league with Waterfield and Van Brocklin.
It's good now to know that he has had this small achievement,
that if he retired tomorrow he would have reached the one
goal that made the difference."

More objectively, Ryan says, "I think I proved something to myself: I can quarterback a champion. I have the feeling now that I can go anywhere, even back to the Rams, and somehow, by hook or crook, end up with a good team. I really believe this. I believe it because I would always be striving in the right direction. The championship is the proof of the pudding . . . QED . . . that which was to be demonstrated: our theory works."

Ryan came to the Rams with curious credentials. At Rice he had been a second-team quarterback, respected but always in the shadow of King Hill. Over some objection, the Rams drafted Ryan after the Cardinals had used their bonus choice to take Hill.

Tex Schramm, then the Ram general manager, remembers, "The feeling was that Ryan might be the better passer of the two, and, of course, we knew he was intelligent. On the minus side, he was considered a risk—you know, an atomic physicist and that stuff. Hill was bigger and stronger and a better athlete."

Ryan played little that first year. He played maybe a third of the time in 1959, and a bit more in 1960 and 1961 while the Rams were rummaging through quarterbacks like a fishwife at a firesale. Billy Wade . . . Zeke Bratkowski . . . Buddy Humphrey . . . Ryan. After the final 1961 game, Ryan confronted general manager Elroy Hirsch and, in front of the squad, delivered a "Trade me or I'll quit" ultimatum.

"The Rams kept telling Frank he had the No. 1 job, but he didn't," says Joan. "Those were terribly depressing years. The Rams were trading off their entire offensive line for Ollie Matson, who couldn't learn the plays . . . Waterfield was making Frank No. 1, then starting Bratkowski because Frank was supposed to be too nervous to start . . . and every time Frank did something wrong, one thing, they jerked him. Those last two years in Los Angeles, we went around with this horrible, whirling, dizzy feeling: what was wrong? Was it Frank? Was it the team? Was it the coach? Was the stadium facing the

wrong direction? If Frank has ever doubted he was a quarterback, it was then. One mistake and . . . zip! They jerked him.

"I'll never forget 1960, Waterfield's first year," says Frank.
"He came up to me and said, 'Frank, you're my quarterback.'
I played sloppy all during camp. I'm a slow starter anyway, too
absorbed with school work at first, I guess . . . all thumbs. I
was on the bench by the second regular game and I didn't play
again until the fifth game. At that time we had a losing streak
of about 13 games, stretching back to the 1959 season. We tied
the Bears that Sunday. We broke the streak because I played
well. As a reward Waterfield started me the next week against
the Lions and I threw three touchdown passes in the first half
alone. In the third quarter I threw an interception and he jerked
me and put in Wade. The next week he let me start again in
Dallas. The first pass I threw was a touchdown to Red Phillips,
the prettiest pass I have ever thrown, and we built up a 20-
point lead. Then I over threw Jon Arnett on a pass I should
have hit. . . . Waterfield jerked me. That really burned me.
After 14 games we were winning because I was playing quarterback, and he wasn't letting me quarterback."

Ryan asked to be traded to Pittsburgh where his pal Buddy
Dial was catching everything they threw, and where Bobby
Layne was nearing retirement. Instead, he went to Cleveland
where Paul Brown handled quarterbacks as robots and where
Ninowski was firmly dug-in as No. 1.

"The night we heard of the trade Frank just sat there with
his head in his hands," says Joan. "I reminded him they had
Jimmy Brown, Ray Renfro, men like that, and he reminded
me they also had Ninowski. I almost expected him to give up,
but he didn't. I have never admired Frank more than I did that
fall. He sat on the bench but he was very noble about it. I might
add that Jim (Ninowski) has been just as noble since Frank
took over."

"What bothered me that first year," says Ryan, "was the fact
that Ninowski got 75 percent of the work in camp and I got

about 25 percent. Brown had traded away Milt Plum (for Ni-nowski) and I guess he had to make it look good. Probably if Jim and I had a Mexican war right there he would have beat me, fair and square. But I was still bitter from my days with the Rams."

When Ninowski was injured in mid-1962, Ryan became the No. 1 quarterback. He remained No. 1 under new coach Blanton Collier in 1963. The Browns made a run at the title in 1963, Ryan's first full year at the wheel, but went aground near port. Ryan accepted the blame. Opposing coaches called him erratic, a view most of them wouldn't surrender until the final two games of 1964. The ghost of that tragic collapse in 1963 threatened resurrection in 1964, particularly when Cleveland lost to challenger St. Louis in the 13th game. Joan Ryan says she had never seen a team less composed than the Browns in St. Louis. Ryan says, "I wasn't feeling serendipitious."

"That's when I fully came to appreciate Dick Modzelewski (the veteran defense tackle acquired in a preseason trade)," Joan says. "He was a mother hen. He had played with a championship team and he knew that pot of gold wasn't as far as you think. They would look at Dick and say, 'Can we do it?' and he would say, 'yes.' "

From that 19–28 loss in St. Louis the Browns became a great football team, Ryan thinks. The following week Ryan threw five touchdown passes to beat the Giants, 52–20. The first conference title in a decade was assured. The championship game was just dessert.

"I have never been less nervous than I was before the championship game," says Joan. "It was one of those horrible, tacky, ugly feelings that make men gag . . . but I absolutely knew we would win it. Usually I can't even eat before a game. That morning I ate like a lumberjack."

The Championship was to be a classic collision of theories: Baltimore's short-fuse-bomb offense vs. Cleveland's conservative, containing defense, a defense which had allowed more yards than any other. Ironically, it was almost the reverse. Ryan

says, "Our defense went in with the idea of playing the receivers
real tight. Don't give them any room and hope the rush can get
to Unitas. There's nothing that bothers a quarterback more than
seeing a defensive back play just a few yards off his receiver. It
worked. By the time Unitas took a second look our defense
was on him."

While the Cleveland defense was stacking Unitas, Ryan
played his two pet cards: keep it simple, and go for the bomb
when the inspiration hits. Ryan led the league in touchdown
passes, 25, the same number he threw in 1963 when he tied
Otto Graham's club record.

"A quarterback kills a team (i.e.: an opponent) by putting
the ball downfield," Ryan says. "He rips a team apart that way,
throwing to a target 15 or 20 yards downfield instead of dunk-
ing it out there to the side. This is probably a fault with me: I
should dunk it out in the flat to Jimmy Brown or Ernie Green
more often, but I keep telling myself the immediate aim is to
get it downfield."

In tennis vernacular, Ryan goes for "winners." He went for
them against the Colts and hit three for touchdowns. The game
was not long in doubt.

Despite what this may imply, Frank Ryan is not by nature
an impatient man. He taught himself chess and normally keeps
20 games running by mail. He hates television but he taught
himself to use it. Says he: "It shuts off my mind. When I'm
worn out from studying, I watch a little television and go right
to sleep. It's really a weakness." He is teaching himself to play
the guitar, and he is even progressing in the dubious craft of
small talk, which he hates worse than television.

He says, "I am trying to not look bored when things are put
on a casual basis. I am actually antisocial. I can't chat about
the world situation because I don't have anything to offer.
Teaching (math) is the only social function I have prepared or
want to offer society. I abhor public relations. The idea of
drinking, mixing and being pleasant to a lot of people I don't

know or like . . . this is not something I enjoy is the best way
to put it."

What he does enjoy is sleeping late, smoking a pipe, solving
a puzzle, playing with his sons, Frank Jr. (Pancho), 6, Michael,
5, Stuart, 3, and their black and white spotted dog, Diddle-
Diddle; surprising his wife by coming home with no blue ink on
his handkerchief. He also enjoys tinkering around the Ryans'
two-story, four-bedroom home on a quiet, tree-hushed college
street three blocks from Rice.

And, of course, he enjoys the special satisfaction which
comes to "unwanted" men who prove their critics wrong.

Super Bowl VII:
The Drama and the Distractions

By Peter Gent

Billy Kilmer is not the most talented quarterback in this collection. In fact, he is one of the least talented. He is not a star so much as a survivor. He survived being a starter in his rookie season and being a substitute in later seasons. He survived playing behind John Brodie in San Francisco, and he survived playing behind a porous line in New Orleans. Then he got to Washington and passed the toughest survival test of them all. He survived competing with Sonny Jurgensen, the man with the golden arm, for the starting position on George Allen's aged and able Redskins. Kilmer is one tough man.

The story that follows is only partly about Billy Kilmer. It was, as the author Peter Gent indicates, supposed to have been entirely about Kilmer, but once Gent settled into the Super Bowl scene in Los Angeles in January 1973, extraneous events—distractions, George Allen called them—kept intruding upon the story. It's probably appropriate. Extraneous events have always intruded on Kilmer's career; he has always been accident-prone, and only a few of the accidents have been physical. Yet Kilmer has kept recovering, from psychic scars as well as an automobile crash, and he did manage to make it to a Super Bowl, which is more than a lot of quarterbacks with greater gifts can say.

Gent is the perfect man to write about Kilmer. In five seasons as a tight end and wide receiver for the Dallas Cowboys, Gent suffered his own share of psychic and physical damage. He purged himself of his suffering in a novel called North Dallas Forty, *a marvelous novel in which one of the two main characters is a quarterback named Seth Maxwell. Seth Maxwell deserves his own place in this book, but come to think of it, he is here, scattered around, disguised as reality, and a little bit of him comes through in Billy Kilmer.*

"Got on board a westbound 747,
Didn't think before deciding what to do.
All that talk of opportunities, TV breaks and movies
Rang true, yes it sure rang true. . . ."

—It Never Rains
in Southern California*

It's early afternoon in Port Aransas, Texas. I'm looking out across Mustang Island at the white Gulf of Mexico surf. I expect to die here and have asked for a simple ceremony. My body is to be shrouded in an NFC flag and dropped into the ship channel. Someone will release ten or 15 balloons and a couple of white-washed sea gulls. There will be a short statement absolving the people of California and Commissioner Rozelle of any complicity in my demise. Maybe the astronauts could say a few words over my watery bier (not too many words—they had an awful time with the Pledge of Allegiance). The coughing fits are coming closer and closer together. The end can't be too far off. But, let's begin at the beginning.

I had just finished watching Billy Kilmer and the Washington Redskins beat the tar out of Tom Landry and the Dallas

Cowboys and having little faith in things cosmic, I told my wife I would love to go to the Super Bowl and write a story about Billy Kilmer's rise from the ashes.

The last time I had seen Billy was on a hot Monday in the fall of 1969. I had been out of football for a couple of months then, and was trying to make a little money by selling printing. I had ducked into my favorite bar to escape the heat and fortify myself for a long afternoon of huckstering. The dark, airconditioned coolness felt good against my sweat-soaked body (a sweat that came of fear rather than exertion), and I was winding my way to a corner from which to drink and watch the ad execs hustle the local models. A familiar voice rasped my name from the darkness. I made my way to the shadowy sound hoping for a sale. Instead, I found Billy Kilmer. He had come to Dallas aboard a Braniff charter after it had dropped his Saints teammates in New Orleans. He was drunk and disgusted; the day before, he had been benched in favor of Ed Hargett.

I had always liked Billy and was sorry to hear that he had been benched, but, after all, I was out of the game completely, and I knew the end must come to us all. So we spent the day drinking Coors and riding around in my VW van. I tried to point out the advantages of civilian life but Billy would have none of it and kept vowing to show everybody's ass. I wished him luck, but figured he'd be in the car-wash business before the year was out. I mean, after all, he had been benched for Ed Hargett and most people figured Billy was playing on borrowed time ever since he smashed up that car and himself in 1963.

Since Billy Kilmer got to Washington, I have looked back on that Monday and his angry, ruddy, whiskey face and raspy voice and tried again to believe in fairy stories. The phone call asking me to go to the Super Bowl, all expenses paid, and write a story on the Redskin quarterback seemed to be setting the stage.

Well, my week is long since up, the game is long past and the only fairy stories that take place in Los Angeles are chronicled in the underground papers. Billy didn't win the Super Bowl. He

didn't even play well. I contracted Black Lung Disease from
what they laughingly call the California air. But I witnessed a
week that I shall never forget should I ever recover. That week
is my legacy, what I leave to the few generations that follow
before the end comes . . . and the end is coming. I know, I
glimpsed the face of the devil in the Polo Lounge on Saturday
night.

"Only in sports do you see real emotion."

—George Allen

The fishing boats are making their way slowly up the channel
from the Gulf, the sea gulls whirling and diving into the wakes
like sportswriters around a buffet table.

I arrived on Monday, Super Day minus six, and immediately
contacted my old friend John Wilbur (Redskin right guard).
John invited me down to Dana Point where he is part owner
of the Wind and Sea Restaurant. It was a beautiful place, and
I sat around a big square table with Wilbur and three other
Redskins: Walter Rock, the right offensive tackle, Len Haus,
the All-Pro center, and Billy Kilmer. I ordered a triple shot of
tequila to show I was still one of the boys and picked up the
conversation right where Billy and I had dropped it three years
before in Dallas.

"Your problem, Billy," I said, "is that you don't know when
to quit."

"*We* don't know when to quit," Billy laughed and indicated
his teammates. "You know that all the towels and bedspreads
in our hotel were blue? Rozelle was expecting the Cowboys."

"You tell 'em, Whiskey," Haus said with a grin.

"That's right, Zeke," added Rock. They all got great pleasure
out of savoring the Cowboy victory and you could tell these
giant linemen took pride in protecting their quarterback.

The rest of the evening consisted of Billy holding court as
various fans or the merely curious streamed by. He was always
polite and his ruddy face beamed. I hoped against hope that

Washington would win the Super Bowl. The triple tequilas
blurred the evening pretty quick and Billy slipped quietly out
before I got a chance to ask any relevant questions. John Wilbur
drove me as far as the Saddleback Inn in Santa Anna, the
Redskin headquarters. I made it back to my room at the Newporter in Newport Beach on sheer will and a lifelong fear of
vomiting in strange places. No problem. The week was young.

> "I'll kill for a dime."
>
> —Overheard in press-lounge poker game.

The Newporter Inn is a huge rambling resort hotel with its
own lighted golf course. It was press headquarters for the Super
Bowl. My room had two king-sized beds, a color television, and
a combination basket of wines and cheeses with a card that told
me the NFL wished only the best for me and mine. The rooms
at the Saddleback where the Redskins stayed, or the Edgewater
Hyatt House in Long Beach, where the Dolphins stayed, were
about the size of one of my king-sized beds. They lived two to
a room. The media lounge at the Newporter had free drinks and
food available about 18 hours a day with six hours set aside for
the help to drag the sportswriters out to dry in the sun. The big
treat for the Redskins was to buy their own Coors and ice it
down in their bathtubs.

People who still think of the Super Bowl as a game between
the two best teams in football to determine the best team in
football just haven't been paying attention these last seven
years. The Super Bowl VII was a National Football League
Public Relations Spectacular complete with 20,000 balloons,
4000 racing pigeons, three astronauts, The Little Angels from
Chicago, 80 football players, 1500 sportswriters and 85,000 fans.
(The 90,000 attendance figure was a sham; there were 5000
no-shows.) That count doesn't include the myriad of pom-pom
girls, the Pro Bowl Band, the drivers for the motorized football
helmets (cost per helmet: $5000) and the University of Michi-
gan band.

During the course of Super Bowl Week, the National Football League force fed the attending members of the press incredible amounts of food, drink and football. The press in turn dutifully passed on the football to the readers. The teams were forced to spend a week in Los Angeles "to be available to members of the press" who after the first ten minutes on Monday began to repeat the same questions over and over at an embarrassing rate. The players jammed in the Saddleback or the Hyatt Edgewater were required to leave family and friends behind and live in the stultifying atmosphere of a one-ring circus. And people ask why the game was so dull.

The National Football League spent $35,000 to entertain the press for one night on the Queen Mary. I would be afraid to guess what the halftime box lunches for the sportswriters cost, but they started passing them out right after Miami's second TD. The menu listed: California avocado stuffed with crabmeat, one-half California lobster, cold California artichoke, homemade peda bread, California apple and cheese and, for dessert, baklava (a 40-layer Armenian delight). All this was packed into cute little monogrammed Super Bowl overnight bags which became property of the writer as soon as he stuffed himself with the food.

"He is the fiercest competitor I've ever met. While he was laying in the hospital bed he was already making plans to be a sports car driver if he could never play football again. He was a great athlete. He swore he'd play again but I don't see how. One leg is that much shorter than the other."

—Ex-coach Red Hickey on Kilmer (1964)

Wednesday, I drove over to the Saddleback to see Diron Talbert. I hadn't spent time with him in a couple of years and he had invited me over to drink beer. I found Diron with Walter Rock, Len Haus and Billy. There was Coors iced down in the sink. I opened one and sat to talk to Diron. Billy was on the phone. Everytime he'd hang up the phone would ring again. Diron's eyes were bright and dark; the pupils were dilated. He was ready to play; they were all ready. It was only Wednesday.

Allen would try and keep them like this till Sunday, but a man can't maintain a state of alarm indefinitely.

Diron and I talked of his three brothers and two sisters, his mom and dad, and himself. He was in good health and spirits and couldn't wait till Sunday. I looked around at these giant men, trapped by curfews, this tiny room, love of the game, and the desire to be the best team in professional football. Back at the Newporter, the sportswriters would be digging into the second half-ton of onion dip while the non-stop poker players ordered more free whiskey and the editor from Omaha tried to call the waitress he had met from Thousand Oaks; he had to hurry, his wife would be in Friday.

"It's the old guys that hold this team together," Diron was saying as we sped through traffic on our way to meet Myron Pottios and Ron McDole at a bar. "The old guys are the heart." The words seemed strange coming from Diron; I could remember him as a junior from the University of Texas coming up to Dallas to visit his brother Don playing with the Cowboys. That is the nature of time. "All we talk about is football. We might start talking about something else, but we always end up on football and I love it."

"What about Billy?" That was the only question I asked during my entire stay.

"Man," Diron winked at me with a look that comes of years of knowing someone. "He's the real Don Meredith."

That's all I needed to know.

The Beverly Hills is a sprawling pink hotel located on Sunset Boulevard in Beverly Hills. Inside, just past the lobby, is the Polo Lounge; frequented by both mogul and star, it is the place to be if there is further purpose to your eating beyond nourishment. Some of the producers of Super Bowl VII, that special of specials aimed at the 75 million, hung out at the Polo Lounge. I had breakfast at the Polo Lounge. It was like old home week. At the table next to me was Wellington Mara, owner of the New York Giants, the last man to have the pleasure of firing me. Also at the table was his nephew, Tim.

Across the room, in a booth, sat young John Rosenbloom, son of the ex-owner of the Colts; two discreet booths away sat Don McCafferty, the ex-coach of the Colts. In McCafferty's booth sat Howard Cosell. While I was eating a light breakfast (out of deference to hemorrhoids developed from hours on the freeways) Weeb Ewbank came in, looked around, called me Bob and wandered out. Outside by the pool Jack Whitaker was soaking up some sun.

As I was leaving I ran into the whole NFL films crew. They looked like high-class bus boys in their monogrammed polo shirts. I tipped everyone within range, climbed into my car and sped off. I would return.

The tide is coming in from the Gulf of Mexico. The flotsam that the sea wouldn't swallow washes up on the rocks around the breakwater. It reminds me of the buses unloading writers at the Newporter after the *Queen Mary* Party.

"At first they thought it was John Brodie in the car. Billy was wearing a pair of tennis shoes with Brodie's name on them. If Billy hadn't had that accident, Red would still be in San Francisco."

> —Mrs. Red Hickey to a news-
> man at the *Queen Mary* Party

"Well, the NFL finally did what the whole German Navy couldn't do. They sank the *Queen Mary.*"

> —A disgruntled sportswriter who had to eat his free
> dinner sitting on the floor

I'm driving up the Newport Freeway for the zillionth time. That's the thing about southern California, you just follow these concrete strips until you get where you're going. There is no real sense of direction. It's Friday afternoon and I'm making my last social call on the Redskins at the Saddleback. There have been rumors that the Redskins are going to make a political statement after the game condemning Nixon's bombing of North Vietnam. The smog has been heavy all week and the late afternoon sun has become a dim orange ball behind its curtain. My lungs have been burning since Wednesday. This morning I started a hacking cough. I don't smoke. I began to count the hours until kickoff. The carnival is wearing thin. It is noticeable in everybody's eyes. The NFL is risking public relations over-kill.

"Are you guys gonna make a statement?"

"Not the team, just individuals. I mean, it wouldn't be fair to speak for the team. At first there was gonna be a group of us, but now it's just up to the individual."

"It would be dynamite. The No. 1 fan's team rejecting him."

"Yeh, but it wouldn't be right, you know what I mean. To take that moment, if we win, and use it for politics. After all, that's *our* moment, man. It's our profession, our bread and butter, you know. And this *is* the Super Bowl. I mean, I think it would be wrong to take that moment of victory and make a public statement, you know? That moment belongs to the *team;* it's ours, man. We worked all year for it. It's the Super Bowl, you know?"

"Yeah, I know."

It's later Friday night. I'm at a party in Beverly Hills standing next to Max Baer Jr., who is explaining that "they" are after him. The house is jammed and there's a guy running around naked. Nobody is paying any attention to him. My eyes burn and I want to lie down.

"One good thing came out of the car accident; they quit trying to make a running back out of me."

—Billy Kilmer

"Never lose interest in life."

—President Richard M. Nixon on the occasion of his 60th birthday

It's Saturday night and the pregame tension is terrific; it's difficult even to find a seat at the Polo Lounge. The room is jammed with the great and near-great; all are getting ready for The Game. I order a triple tequila; by now, my body needs it. Timmy Mara walks by looking strangely horrified. Frank Gifford comes in looking younger and more beautiful than ever. Weeb Ewbank wanders through like someone's abandoned child. Someone says Pat Summerall is there or has been there. Mr. Iselin, the owner of the Jets, makes his way to the back of the room. A girl in suede asks me if I was at the Puma-Shoe Party earlier in the week. (The Puma-Adidas Athletic Shoe War has spread here from the Olympics.) I nod that I was and check her feet. I recall what Kilmer said: "If we don't win the Super Bowl, then it was all for nothing." My chest aches and my fingers have gone to sleep. I never get to bed and Super Sunday is on me before I know it.

"That was a fine game . . . one of the best Super Bowl games ever."

—President Richard M. Nixon

My seat is 71 rows up on the 45-yard line. It's the auxiliary press section. The game gets started late as there are all sorts of timing problems with the U. of M. band, the astronauts and The Little Angels from Chicago. The astronauts louse up the Pledge of Allegiance. A plane flies over carrying a banner warning the "Ramskins" that "Vince is watching." Sonny Jurgenson is propped up by his crutches on the 20-yard line. He looks lonely. I'm coughing a lot now and have broken into a cold, shivery sweat.

Finally, the game begins. Billy doesn't look sharp while Griese hits everything he tries. The Dolphins are cool and methodical. They've been here before and know how to avoid the false starts and fake highs of Super Bowl Week. The Dolphins saved it all for today. By the time I get my free overnight bag with my half a California lobster for lunch, Miami is out in front, 14–0. They are never headed and Kilmer is smothered trying to pass on the last play of the game. Billy has been intercepted three times and his only chance for a touchdown pass hit the goal post. The game ends, 14–7.

I wait for the crowd to clear and then move from my seat toward the aisle. I wade through artichokes, avocados, baklava and lobster halves. My boots slip on crabmeat and mayonnaise. A black kid digs around under the seats for discarded "California apples and cheese." The red sauce for the lobster is smeared on everything; it gives the impression that there has just been a human sacrifice.

I go to the locker rooms out of a sense of duty, but ask no questions and stop only to visit shortly with John Wilbur. Blood runs from a gash on the bridge of his nose. The vacant look in his eyes drives me off after a few moments. On his way to the showers, Kilmer is trapped by a covey of writers. He patiently answers the same questions over and over. His red face strained, but composed, he shoulders the blame for the loss. I don't feel at all well. I walk through the tunnel to the sick gray air outside. I pass a couple necking inside one of the motorized helmets; the Falcons', I think. It would be the Falcons'.

Making my way to the car, I pass drunks being led away by friends and family. Oblivious to the game's end or outcome, they hoot and howl and stagger off. A couple of middle-aged men in orange cowboy hats keep up a steady chatter about Miami's victory, but most of the crowd seem on their way somewhere else, to some other distraction.

"I really love to see people get emotional."

—George Allen

It's Monday morning and I'm aboard Delta flight 10 to Dallas. The Pro Bowl contingent is to be aboard this 747 and I plan to try and interview Billy. Paul Warfield and Larry Little bounce aboard. In another section, I can see Chris Hanburger, but I can't find Kilmer. The stewardess closes the outside door and we pull away from the gate. I'm just as glad, I can barely breathe and wouldn't know what to ask Billy, anyway. Besides, I'd prefer to think that he was somewhere in Los Angeles, drunk and riding around in a friend's VW van, vowing to show everybody's ass.

13 / MORTON

Mr. Wonderful's Almost Wonderful Season

By Gary Cartwright

Craig Morton's story is Billy Kilmer's—without the satisfaction of beating out a Sonny Jurgensen. Craig Morton is a survivor, too, and perhaps when, and if, he starts a new career in the World Football League he will, finally, for more than a few fleeting moments, be a star. For Morton, the frustrations of pro football have far outweighed the fulfillment. It is ironic that here, in this book, if nowhere else, Morton has beaten out his Dallas rival, Roger Staubach. The collection of literature about Staubach is not nearly so dramatic nor so exciting as one of his scrambling runs. So Staubach was benched for this book and Morton was thrust into the starting lineup, his plays called for him this time by writer Gary Cartwright.

Remarkably, Morton merits the spot statistically. In the complicated official NFL rating system, Morton ranks seventh among all the quarterbacks active during the 1973 season, and of the six ahead of him, four—Jurgensen, Tarkenton, Gabriel and Unitas—are included in this collection. Four who rank behind Morton—Brodie, Kilmer, Namath and Blanda—are also included. Morton's most impressive statistic—an average of 7.86 yards gained for each of more than 1,300 pass attempts—places him second among all active quarterbacks. But as Tom Landry

*has been telling Morton for years, directly or indirectly, statistics
aren't everything. Morton is in here for his personality and his
suffering, more than for his accomplishments.*

Gary Cartwright is also the author of a football novel, The
Hundred Yard War. *He is a member of the dominant school of
journalism represented in this collection, the Texas school, personified by Cartwright, Larry L. King, Dan Jenkins, Bud Shrake
and Peter Gent (who qualifies by style, if not by birth). Morton
is a Texan, too, by residence, like the men who died at the Alamo.*

Craig Morton arrived in Texas in 1965, a little too late to help
out at the Alamo, but just in time to save the Dallas Cowboys.
Which was what he was supposed to do.

Morton was a real California Golden Boy, the son of a glass
blower, up from the prune orchards of Campbell, California, by
way of the ski slopes of Lake Tahoe. The Cowboys shelled out
$148,000, to be spread over three years, to get him, and he was
going to make the whole Southwest forget Don Meredith.

"Is it true," said a friend of mine named White, "that they
found him in a manger wrapped in swaddling clothes?"

His rookie year, Morton and some other bachelor Cowboys
rented apartments in a swanky building in a part of town where
airline stewardesses were thick as sitting ducks. Another friend
of mine, a young financier named Skidmore, found himself
poolside one day at the Cowboys' place. As Skidmore told the
story, he was just sitting there, enjoying the gin and scenery,
when this uncommonly handsome man with bulging muscles,
blue eyes and curly blond hair leaned over his chair and, in a
voice so warm and sincere it might have been Temptation itself,
asked, "Can I get you anything?"

"I knew right then," Skidmore said later, "that here was Mr.
Wonderful. Morton is really, truly, genuinely, authentically
wonderful. He is too wonderful to admit it, but I am here to tell

you. He wears wonderful clothes on that wonderful body, and
he smells like a candle shop. He dates wonderful women, and
he treats them like queens. He has a wonderful stereo and a
wonderful collection of records. He has read Ken Kesey. Is that
not wonderful?"

"What I want to know," said White, "is can he hit the side
of a barn with a tractor?"

"Who cares?" cried Skidmore, and now there was no way
you could miss the sarcasm. "Don't you see? He's *wonderful!*"

Before Craig Morton arrived in Texas, the Cowboys never
had a winning season. Since Craig Morton arrived in Texas, the
Cowboys have never had a losing season. If you think you
detect a cause-and-effect relationship, forget it. Ralph Neely,
Dan Reeves, Bob Hayes and Jethro Pugh arrived in Dallas the
same year; they flourished. Morton suffered. There came a time,
sure enough, when he couldn't hit the side of a barn.

His first four years in Dallas, Morton labored behind Don
Meredith. Then, in 1969, he became the Cowboys' regular quar-
terback. The same year, he wrecked his shoulder in combat.
The next year, he wrecked his elbow.

Some people say the elbow injury was a direct result of the
shoulder injury, that Craig pushed himself too hard, too fast.
(One story, never verified, was that a team doctor rewired the
damaged shoulder with a section of muscle transplanted from
Morton's big toe; the story is probably untrue.) Strange things
began to happen. Craig would drop back, set up and fire a
well-placed bullet—into his center's butt. Or a linebacker
would shoot in from the blind side and, in a perverted variation
on the old Statue of Liberty play, take the ball from Morton and
gallop for a touchdown.

Other things happened, personal things. Morton made the
mistake of picking a fight with the wrong guy in a New York
bar; when Craig stepped outside, Mafia thugs beat him up. His
best friend and business partner tapped the till, and Craig was

forced to declare bankruptcy on two campus bookstores in California. The Internal Revenue Service found great gaps in his tax returns and began camping on his doorstep.

What followed was shellshock. A less complicated man—a Roger Staubach, for example—might have overcome pain and humiliation and even betrayal by the simple expediency of forgetting everything that had happened. Not Craig.

He did it differently. He submitted himself to hypnosis in the hope that post-hypnotic suggestion would give him confidence and free his skills. It was a legitimate experiment, and one that was supposed to be confidential. "The object," explained Edward J. Pullman, director of the Southwest Hypnosis Research Center, "was to relieve Craig of game pressures, boost his confidence, free him from further injury by conditioning him to relax on the instant of body contact, to keep his elbow from being a conscious hindrance, and just generally to open up the full potential of his abilities."

But after the Cowboys' wretched performance against Baltimore in the Super Bowl in January, 1971, the story got out. Future generations of athletes and fans may come to regard post-hypnotic suggestion with the same indifference they now accord the whirlpool bath and cortisone injections, but coming when it did, in the stench of the worst-played Super Bowl ever, the revelation was like Darwin walking into a Ku Klux Klan rally and announcing, "Guess what, gang? Our relatives swung by their tails."

The bitter irony was that Morton lost both his public trust and his self-esteem by playing in the 1971 Super Bowl. Normally, leading a team to a Super Bowl, even one that is eventually lost, is not the worst thing that can happen to a quarterback (witness the ups and downs of Earl Morrall), but it was a common belief that Morton followed rather than led his team to Miami.

"I don't know about everyone else," Lee Roy Jordan said after the game, "but I can't get over the feeling we won. I know one thing: We'll be back next year, and things will be different."

Jordan was right. The Cowboys did return to the Super Bowl, and things were different. Dallas crushed Miami. Roger Staubach was the quarterback.

Still, after the Super Bowl, Craig was not without his defenders. A magnanimous Staubach said, "It's really something when a guy can come back from *two* operations involving his throwing arm. If I'd had Craig's problems, I'd be a cook on a ship somewhere." Staubach's praise didn't come out quite so kind as he had intended. Staubach is actually older than Morton, but at the moment he seemed to be saying: Boy, I hope I look that good when I'm Craig's age.

Then came the 1972 season.

"And Now a Word for Morton," read the headline in the Dallas *Times Herald*.

"One Year Later: Craig's in Control," proclaimed the Fort Worth *Star-Telegram*.

This was November, 1972, and for the moment at least, Craig Morton was among the hottest quarterbacks in the NFL. Back in August, the thing that everyone had said would happen happened: Staubach ran into trouble (the Rams' Marlin McKeever) and dislocated his shoulder. They dusted off Craig Morton, inserted him in the Tom Landry relay station behind center as you might change transistors in a space age toy, and the Cowboys went right on winning.

The headlines were apologetic, as though to say: Mr. Wonderful, we knew it all the time. By November, Staubach had recovered, but Landry said: "Craig's our No. 1 quarterback and he's in there to win it or lose it." This statement seemed directed to that embittered section of fans who persisted in booing each time Morton's name was called over the public address.

"Sure, I heard them boo when I was introduced," Craig said after his three touchdown passes nailed Detroit. "It's a free country. I'm not telling them who to vote for. [Though Staubach had played only a few downs, he nevertheless held a wide lead in the Most Popular Cowboy contest sponsored by a local dairy.] I'm not telling them who to applaud.

"When I'm throwing touchdown passes and the Dallas Cowboys are winning, I can live without the cheers."

When the situation had been reversed—when Staubach was throwing the passes and Morton was just another lonely figure in a blue raincoat—Craig had been wonderfully gracious. Now, in victory, he was even more gracious. He talked to any and every reporter who approached him, and they never seemed to tire of his litany.

He praised (1) the Dallas organization, (2) Landry, (3) Landry's staff, (4) the offensive line.

"There are a lot of guys on this club who have faced many trying moments," Craig said, and you could almost hear the pale voice of Tom Landry quoting his favorite philosopher, the Apostle Paul, who claimed that suffering brings on endurance, endurance brings character and character develops hope. Hope for what? More suffering?

Craig continued: "It's a great credit to our organization and head coach because the thing everybody is concerned with first is our team being No. 1. I just think things are going to work out your way if you work hard enough."

Again, there was the echo of Tom Landry: "Take away winning and you take away everything that is strong about America. If you don't believe in winning, you don't believe in free enterprise, capitalism, or our way of life."

If there was a dark spot on the season, it was an early loss to arch-rival Washington, a defeat that was blamed not on Morton, who played well, but on that one-time paragon of dependability, the Doomsday Defense. No, Craig had done his job. Except for his 21 season interceptions (he tied Archie Manning for the most interceptions), he would have ranked among the top three passers in the NFC. As it was, he finished seventh.

The Craig Morton of the November headlines, the one in control, was not a helpless giant tossing firecrackers; he was the legendary California bomber who had created so much anticipation seven years earlier. For the 1972 season, he had 15 touchdown passes, and at least four other TD passes—three of them in critical situations—had been dropped. (His detractors said that only went to prove Morton is a Jonah on the ship of destiny.)

Off the field, too, Morton finally seemed healthy. During the season, he and two new business partners opened a bar called Wellington's. It had a patio level and a discotheque level and a conversation level and a penthouse level, spiral staircases and piano bars, bartenders in velvet waistcoats and barmaids in hardly anything. The place was packed each night with beautiful people. Morton did, indeed, seem to be in control.

Morton's Cowboys went into their final two games of the season—against Washington, which had clinched the Eastern Division title, and against New York—needing only one tie and one victory to wrap up the wild-card spot in the playoffs.

When I visited the Cowboy field house a few days before the Washington game, nearly everyone had something good to say about Craig. "People don't realize what kind of job Craig has done for us since Roger got hurt," said Ray Renfro, the assistant coach who oversees the passing game. Linebacker D. D. Lewis added, "It was in the back of everyone's mind Craig would fold. But he took the challenge. Instead of folding, he got tougher."

"Craig has had a lot of shots thrown at him, and he's weathered them all," said tackle Ralph Neely. "Most of us can remember a couple of years ago when you'd walk into the training room and there would be Craig, day after day, soaking his arm in ice just so he could work out.

"We're a mature club. It doesn't matter who's quarterbacking. How can you define leadership? When Landry first started sending in the plays, it bothered us. At least it bothered me. But Landry took us to two Super Bowls. You can't argue with that."

I found Landry in his office, sitting alone in the dark. At first I thought he was watching films, then I realized he was just sitting there with his arms folded across his chest. Maybe he was talking with God; I couldn't guess about what.

"Without Craig," Landry said, switching on the lights and drawing back the drapes by activating a panel of buttons behind his desk, "we'd be nowhere."

When Landry observed that Morton had matured considerably in recent months, I couldn't help but think of Don Meredith. That word—*mature*. Landry never considered Meredith mature, because Meredith didn't believe in the same things Landry did.

Meredith quit pro football at the age of 30 after Landry pulled him in the 1968 playoff game against Cleveland, replacing him with young Craig Morton, the nonplaying hero. The story is that Meredith went to Landry's office in the offseason, hoping for some reassurance. When Meredith told Landry that he was seriously thinking of retiring, he fully expected Landry to talk him out of it. Instead, Landry said, "Don, I think you're doing the right thing," then invited Meredith down on his knees for a prayer.

There had been speculation that Morton would retire or, more likely, demand to be traded before the start of the 1972 season. Instead, Craig *matured*. He had, as Landry noted, abandoned his "playboy image" and joined the Lovers Lane Methodist Church, a sister church to Landry's own.

"It was a decision he alone had to make," Landry told me, meaning Craig's return to the team, not the church. "He wanted a chance to win back his job. As it developed, he didn't have a chance to win it back. Roger was hurt and suddenly Craig was our only quarterback."

I asked Landry about his policy of sending in plays. Didn't that make his quarterback something less than a leader of men? I mean, this was a delicate situation. Not as gregarious as Meredith or as singleminded as Staubach, Morton had to lead by example. Morton had told me, "When you're faced with certain situations (a bum shoulder, for example) it's hard to offset it when you're not calling your own plays. A quarterback only succeeds when he does what he believes in. Take Kilmer.

His arm is not that strong, but he knows what he can do. He defeats them with his strength . . . with the thing he does best."

Landry had heard the question many times. "The execution of the play, not the selection, is what gains confidence," he answered. "It's how you handle yourself in a tough situation."

After the Cowboys demolished the Redskins and clinched a spot against the 49ers in the playoffs, Morton walked around naked, shaking hands with his offensive linemen. Craig had not had a spectacular game—seven completions for 61 yards (four others were dropped)—but Dallas controlled the ball with a running game that accounted for 246 yards, executing Landry's game plan to perfection. Long after the others had dressed and gone, Morton was still in front of his locker, answering questions from the press. Finally, there was only Morton, me and the cleanup crew.

"You've got your God-and-country line down pretty good," I told him.

And for a moment, his good-old-boy grin relaxed, and he said with a thin trace of bitterness, "The only questions they ever ask me are about Staubach."

Anyone with a TV set knows about the Miracle of Candlestick Park, how Roger Staubach came off the bench and threw two touchdown passes in the final four minutes and beat San Francisco in the first round of the playoffs. Until the resurrection of St. Roger, the 49ers had things their own way, having converted a Morton fumble and a Morton interception into 14 points.

You may have seen it on your TV screen, too, when Landry walked over in the fourth quarter and told Morton he was through. Morton said, "Okay." Then he went over and wished Staubach luck.

Landry made his decision to pull Morton after Bob Hayes dropped a sure TD pass, a fact that may or may not be significant to the story of Craig Morton, but one that was central to the hubbub of guessing and second-guessing which led into the

NFC championship game the following week in Washington.

All week before Washington, Landry played games with the press, with George Allen, with his own players, and maybe even with himself. Morton or Staubach? The man who got them into the playoffs, or the man whose miracle kept them there for at least another week? It seemed incredible that after all these weeks—all these years, really—Landry still couldn't make up his mind.

I never doubted that Landry would go with Staubach. My conversations with the Cowboys that week dictated that judgment. The tributes to Craig that had come so naturally one wee earlier stuck now in the Cowboys' throats.

"For Godsake, don't quote me," said one player, "but it's this way: Morton can go along with the trend of the team, but he can't change it. Staubach can. We saw it all last year, and we saw it last week."

I asked Bob Hayes what he thought would have happened if he had caught that touchdown pass from Morton; and Hayes, who didn't catch a touchdown pass all year, rolled his eyes and said: "We'd have lost."

The only principal who thought Craig Morton should start against the Redskins was Craig Morton. Reporters confronted him on Wednesday at the Cowboy Club where he had come to accept his award (a vacation for two in Acapulco) as the Most Popular Cowboy; ironically, a surge of more than 1000 votes in the final week had pushed him ahead of Staubach.

Craig analyzed the situation perfectly. He told the reporters, "I've always played well against the Redskins. You have to be very careful. You have to know and be alert which way their linebackers and special defenses are going. You have to keep yourself out of second-and-nine and second-and-eight situations."

Landry would announce his decision after Thursday afternoon practice. Radio and TV men, and sportswriters from Dallas and Washington, hung around the practice field, mingling with kids and housewives with new Christmas Instamatics. George Allen himself could have walked in and watched practice. The only secret was locked in the mind of Tom Landry.

Inside the field house after practice, before the announcement, Morton and Staubach sat at adjoining lockers and tried to joke with the writers.

"You mean he hasn't told either of you, either?" asked a writer. "That's a hell of a way to run a railroad."

"Depends on who's the conductor," Staubach smiled.

Morton wore his smile, but said nothing.

"How about a statement?" said a writer.

"If it's me," said Staubach, "quote me as saying it's tremendous . . . the most exciting day of my life. If it's Craig, then say I'll do everything in my power to help the team."

"Well said," said Morton.

"Now," Staubach said, slipping into his overcoat, "you won't have to phone me tonight. I can watch films, study my notes and play with my kids."

An hour later, in the Cowboy publicity office, Landry announced that Staubach was his man. "The reason primarily is that Roger brought us to this game," Landry said. "My feeling is he ought to have his chance to see what he can do. This decision is based only on this one game. It doesn't mean Craig is now No. 2."

"Wait a minute," I interrupted, "if Roger wins this game, there's no way you'll start Craig in the Super Bowl. If he loses, then there is no tomorrow."

"I didn't say that," Landry answered. "You said that."

After the press conference, I downed two quick whiskies and drove to Craig's house in an upper-middle-class neighborhood not far from the practice field. It was a large, modern home of thick carpets, a walnut stereo that ran the length of the living room, a wine rack, a swingout bar, leather-covered furniture, a mobile of autographed game balls hanging above the fireplace —not the sort of place you would expect a bachelor to have. There was a permanency about it.

Craig was rubbing his elbow as he admitted me. "I just hit my funny bone on the corner of the table," he said.

Craig poured me a drink and we talked about the future. How he wanted a wife and a family. He had been married briefly in college, but it didn't work. Wellington's was making money, and should make more in the future. He had almost recovered from bankruptcy. "I'm a truster of people," he said. "I tend to judge people as I judge myself. It hurts when you learn you can't trust people who are very important to you."

By now the news of Landry's decision was on radio and TV. People were already reacting.

"I used to think I knew what was going to happen," he said. "Now . . . it's like when Bob Hayes dropped the ball in San Francisco. . . ."

"I saw it on TV," I said. "You fell flat on your back, as though you had been shot. What was going through your mind?"

"I was thinking: What *else* can happen. Then today . . . something else did happen. What can I say? I'm very disappointed. Having Roger come in and win was great, but this decision should be based on more than just those few plays."

"Landry says you've matured."

Craig smiled, this time a private smile. "I have. When I first came here, I was restless. I wanted something to happen and I wanted it right then. I had no goals, no purpose. What I did have was a super ego. But I've had my thrills and I've had my disappointments. I used to worry what people thought of me, but that's all in the past."

"What now?"

"I'll have to wait and see. Maybe Roger won't do so well against Washington. Maybe I'll come in like he did and save the game."

"And if that doesn't happen? Say, just for the sake of argument, that Dallas loses and you have to watch the whole thing from the bench."

Craig shook his head as though he saw the absurdity of his

hopes, as though, after all this time, he knew that faith was just another word for nothing else to lose.

"I'd have to wait and see," he said.

It was time for Craig to go pick up his date, a beautiful woman named Brent. "Stay here and finish your drink," he said. "I'll be right back."

I made a fresh drink and sat in front of the Christmas tree, reflecting on disappointment, recalling something Craig had said: "You can't blame others for your shortcomings."

Then who can you blame? In a country where being big, handsome and talented is a national virtue, where honor is equated with victory, and victory is presumed to be the reward for hard work, is there in fact *blame?* Damn right, I decided.

The door bell rang. I opened the front door and looked down on a chubby girl in glasses and a Sewer Queen sweatshirt. She told me her name was Gina, and she had come to see Craig Morton.

"I just heard it on the radio," she said. "I was so shocked I jumped right in my car and drove here."

"Are you a friend of Craig's?"

"I interviewed him once with my college journalism class," Gina said. "He told us to come see him any time. He was so wonderful."

Anyone with a TV set knows what happened against Washington. Staubach bombed out, and the defending Super Bowl champions were humiliated in a style reminiscent of the 1968 Cleveland game that finished Don Meredith's career. There was one big difference this time: Landry didn't pull Staubach.

For whatever consolation it was worth, this was one they couldn't blame on Craig Morton.

He never got off the bench.

14 / MEREDITH

A Cowboy Named Dandy Don

By Edwin Shrake

Poor Don Meredith. While almost every other outstanding quarterback in National Football League history lasted for at least a dozen seasons, he could survive only nine. If he were as durable as Dawson, Jurgensen, Unitas, Morrall or Brodie—all of whom started in pro football before he did and all of whom were still playing in 1973, five years after his final game—Meredith would still be a Cowboy and might be earning $150,000 a year. Instead, Meredith is struggling along as a television personality, earning a reported $250,000 a year, covering football games on Sundays in the fall and filling in as host of the Tonight Show *on weeks when Johnny Carson feels a need for R & R. Don Meredith never won a Super Bowl, never even an NFL championship, but, somehow, it's still difficult to feel too sorry for him. Thanks to the job he did on ABC's* Monday Night Football, *singing and needling and, in a memorable moment, referring to a football-loving president as "Tricky Dick," an all-around performance that earned him his next job at NBC, Dandy Don's name will certainly outlive Slingin' Sammy's, even in Texas.*

Edwin "Bud" Shrake, who knows Meredith as well as he knows the English language, wrote the following story for Sports Illustrated *at the start of the 1968 season, when neither the*

author nor the subject suspected that the season would be Mere-
dith's last. According to Texas lore, it was at the end of the 1968
season that Meredith went to Coach Tom Landry and said he
had decided to quit, fully expecting Landry to talk him out of
his decision. Instead, Landry said only, "Let us pray." I don't
know what Meredith said in his prayer, but whatever it was, it
sure worked.

The scene is at the mansion of John D. Murchison in Addison, Texas, a few miles north of Dallas, adjoining the grounds of the exclusive Preston Trail Golf Club. A party is in progress to celebrate the start of the first Byron Nelson Classic tournament. Although many guests are dancing to music by strolling musicians, others have already gone through the buffet line and are seated at their tables. A lady in a green dress approaches one table where a young man is eating with his pretty blonde wife and several friends.

LADY *(pointing finger at young man):* You have simply got to do something about this. I was out there all day today, and I didn't go once. Not once! Let me tell you, it wasn't because I didn't need to. But I will not use those things. They don't even have mirrors!

YOUNG MAN *(looking up):* Listen, ma'am, I'm sorry, but I don't have the slightest.

LADY: Those Port-O-Sans.

YOUNG MAN: Those what?

LADY: Those toilets on the course. I can't bring myself to use one. I want you to go over there tomorrow and tell the guards to admit me to the clubhouse.

YOUNG MAN: But ladies are barred from the clubhouse. It's the rule.

LADY *(with fierce stare, pointing again):* You *are* Don Meredith, *aren't* you?

YOUNG MAN: Yes ma'am.

LADY: Don't tell *me* that *Don Meredith* doesn't know what to do about a *silly rule* when he sees one. *(She whirls to join her group, then looks back.)* I knew you would understand. You're not like the rest.

There is a notion, held by many, that Don Meredith can do almost anything better than almost anybody else—from throwing a football to amending the rules of country clubs. Meredith tries to believe that himself, because his job requires a stupendous amount of confidence. One night last spring Pete Gent, a Dallas Cowboys pass receiver and close friend of Meredith, drove over to Mount Vernon in East Texas to have dinner with the quarterback, with Meredith's wife Cheryl and with Meredith's parents, Jeff and Hazel, who run a dry-goods store. Sitting in the living room after finishing the blackeyed peas, fried chicken, cream gravy, biscuits and pie, Gent began talking about basketball (he was a three-year varsity man at Michigan State). Don Meredith did not play basketball in college, although he once set a single-game scoring record of 52 points in the Dr. Pepper High School tournament in Dallas.

"Jeff," said Gent, "there's one thing you have to admit."

"What's that?" Jeff said, reading the evening paper.

"Jeff," said Gent, "You have to admit I was a better basketball player than your son."

Jeff did not answer.

"You have to admit that," Gent said. "I was a better basketball player than your son."

"Maybe you were. On some days," said Jeff, turning the page.

The first game of bumper pool I ever played with Meredith at his home in Dallas, I beat him. Thereafter, I made a number of other mistakes, forgetting to knock his balls away from the pocket, missing shots, using poor strategy. But Meredith played carefully and won the next eight or nine games before I won another that I suspect he allowed me. "I wanted to make sure the first one was an upset," he said. A few weeks later Dave Marr, former PGA golf champion, was staying at Meredith's house, and when I walked into the den they were playing bumper pool. We were late for dinner. "This guy won't let us go until he's convinced he's a better player than I am," said Marr, laughing. "There's no such thing as a friendly game of bumper pool for me," Meredith said some time afterward. "Any game I play, I have to win. When Chigger [his wife] beats me at bumper pool, it kills me. And the little rascal is really good at it."

Don Meredith—also known as Dandy, Dandy Don, Slim, Joe Don (his real name), Joe Jim Dandy, Jim and Jimmy, a variety of names that sometimes results in one teammate not knowing to whom another is referring—lives with Cheryl, their baby son, Michael Shayne, and a menagerie of animals, including a pet coyote called Lisa, in a house that befits the president of Don Meredith Incorporated, a new firm that handles his dozens of business ventures, endorsements and investments. It is the sort of house you might expect to see on a bus tour of the stars' homes in Beverly Hills, with the driver announcing: "On your right, behind that high iron fence with the big gates, you see the yellow, Spanish-style home built and first occupied by Vilma Banky in 1923, later used for exterior shots in the film *Sunset Boulevard.* . . ."

Sprawled on a lawn chair beside his fountain, which shoots four colors of water, gazing at the ducks swimming on his semiprivate lake, which is stocked with bass, perch and catfish, gazing across at the "country home" of his neighbor—the fabled millionaire, Colonel D. Harold Byrd, who gave the world's biggest drum to the University of Texas band—Meredith recently was pondering how he came to occupy a house that has an elevator opening into the master bedroom, stained-glass windows, two balconies and more bathrooms than the Cotton Bowl.

"Everybody's got to live someplace, and I've wanted this place since 1956, when I was 18 years old," he said. "At the time

I was dating a girl who lived down the road. I was getting $10 a month from SMU on an athletic scholarship, and I'd look at this place and tell myself, 'No, Dandy, what would an East Texas boy do with something like that?' Then, on my thirtieth birthday [last April 10] I got very depressed. When some people are depressed they go out and drink a lot or eat a lot. When I'm depressed I buy something. So I bought the house, because your thirtieth birthday can get you down. I might have overdone it. But if I ever get rich, I'll be good rich. I'm too gregarious not to share it. I certainly wouldn't want to sit alone and count it."

It is difficult to imagine Meredith ever being by himself, although being alone is quite another matter. In the past three years—with a Playoff Bowl, two NFL championship games, two Pro Bowls and, in 1966, the Bert Bell Memorial Award as pro player of the year—he has become a celebrity rather than merely a well-known football player. He is instantly recognized on the streets in New York or Los Angeles. In Dallas he is followed by autograph hunters; his doorbell and telephone (the number of which Cheryl changes several times a year) constantly ring. Playing golf in a pro-am the day before the Byron Nelson Classic, Meredith drew as big a gallery as Jack Nicklaus or Arnold Palmer. Steve Perkins, pro football writer for the Dallas *Times Herald,* suggested the PGA should put Meredith on the tour to increase its crowds. Ralph Neely, the Cowboys' All-NFL offensive tackle, says, "He has leadership qualities you may find once in 10 million men. People get a kick out of being around him."

Cheryl is less than delighted with the demands made on her husband's time. She has one baby, another expected in January, the vast house and gardens to look after, as well as three schnauzers and a coyote, and she has had an untamable raccoon and an ocelot named Pepe that ran wild in the neighborhood—Marr calls Cheryl "Mrs. Dolittle"—but she would like to see Meredith a bit more.

"We've been married six years," she says. "Really, it's only three, but every year seems like two years. The off season is a

different year than the season. Both years are fast and hectic.
I'm not really looking forward to Dandy quitting football. I
used to think I was. But it won't be much different when he
does. He'll get into something just as challenging. He'll still be
gone all the time. He's got ants in his pants. In the off season,
he's gone physically. During the season, he's gone mentally.
He'll be sitting right beside me, but he's somewhere else. Sometimes he tells me he hates football, but I know he loves it. He
says he doesn't like being a leader, accepting responsibilities,
but I know he likes that, too, or he wouldn't do it."

From Mount Vernon—where he performed in one-act plays
and served on the Future Farmers of America state championship shrub-judging team, as well as being an outstanding athlete
—Meredith found his way to Dallas and Southern Methodist
University, and eventually to the Cowboys and a splendid
manse, only after wavering between three other schools that
might have sent him in very different, but perhaps equally
successful, directions. Although his parents owned a farm, he
was anxious to get the boy out of the country. Still, he was
almost lured to Texas A&M, in barren College Station, by what
he calls the "magnetic charm" of Bear Bryant. "I told him I
wanted to throw the ball," says Meredith, "and he said, 'Son,
if you can throw well enough to win games for us, we'll throw
the ball all you please.' If he had been coaching anywhere but
Texas A&M, I'd have gone with him." At the time Meredith
thought he wanted to become either a preacher or a lawyer. The
University of Texas law school had a powerful appeal. He also
visited Texas Christian University, where his older brother,
B.J., had been a quarterback. At TCU, Meredith was assured
he could keep wearing his boots and Levi's and be as country
as he wished. "But that wasn't my dream of college," he says.
"I don't know exactly what I thought college would be. I had
some vague picture of boy-girl relationships, stuff like that, and
SMU seemed to be it. I didn't know what fraternities and
sororities were. But I went through rush because I wanted to
go to college so much that I would do anything to get there a
week early."

As a freshman, he was an outside linebacker in a 5–4 defense. SMU had seven quarterbacks, and Meredith was far down the line. But one quarterback signed a baseball contract, another was hurt, and Meredith kept moving up. He started against Texas as a sophomore, threw two passes for touchdowns and ran for another, as SMU won 19–12. From then on he was the SMU quarterback. He led the nation in passing that year, operating a rather free-lance offense that depended on Meredith's uncanny knack of avoiding tacklers—he is a very good runner for a quarterback—and his quick arm. "I sort of ran all over the place and then usually threw the ball. I hated regimentation," he says. It was during that period that Meredith began to divide the Dallas audience, some of them cheering madly for him, others claiming he was the worst thing that had happened to SMU athletics since the bleachers collapsed at old Ownby Stadium. "They all wanted another Doak Walker," he says. "To my mind, Doak Walker was at one place and the rest of us were at another. They were expecting me to be something I could never be."

Feeling as he did about regimentation, it was a pure cold shock when he went to his first Dallas Cowboys camp in 1960 and began to work for Tom Landry. Clint Murchison Jr. had signed Meredith to a personal-service contract, and the Chicago Bears had drafted him to be traded to the Cowboys, who were just setting up in business. Meredith had also been drafted by the Dallas Texans (now the Kansas City Chiefs) of the AFL but says he did not ever receive a firm offer from Lamar Hunt.

"I was happy with that personal-service contract, anyhow," he says. "I never thought I could be a Unitas or Starr or Jurgensen, I mean as good as they are now, and I still don't, even with people telling me the last couple of years that I'm in their class. But then I never considered it. I knew with that personal-service contract I'd have a good job in the Murchison organization. So I went to camp. Landry is a hard person to get to know. Now I love him to death, but that first month I wasn't sure if I could take him.

"But I did feel I ought to be the Cowboy quarterback right

away, and it kind of hurt when they traded for Eddie LeBaron.
Now I know that the guy who must have been upset the most
was Don Heinrich, since he was a veteran and was counting on
being the regular. But I thought I was supposed to step in
immediately. Don and Eddie helped me a lot. LeBaron is a man
I thoroughly respect. He got the most from his ability, and very
few ever do that in any field."

The early years with the Cowboys were torturous. The players had come from the NFL's first expansion draft and from a
few trades. The club did not participate in the college draft its
first season, a tremendous handicap considering the bonus-pick
treatment given the Minnesota Vikings the following year. Le-
Baron, Heinrich and Meredith were buried by pass rushers.
Crowds at the Cotton Bowl—where Meredith is now playing
for his 12th season counting the three at SMU, making him far
more familiar to Dallas fans than any other man who has ever
played there—became professional enough to start booing, and
their target frequently was Meredith. For a while Landry used
LeBaron and Meredith in a shuttle, alternating them every
other play. Neither quarterback liked it. Meredith was resisting
Landry's system of playing football and organizing people.

Finally Meredith became the starter in 1964 and endured a
season that could have broken him. He had a list of injuries that
would fill a page on a prescription pad. Playing with a weak
team, he received erratic protection. He was splitting up with
his first wife, Lynn, whom he had married at SMU, and was
anguishing over losing custody of his daughter, Mary Donna.
Although he is 6′ 3″, Meredith had always been frail, with very
skinny legs, and the beatings he took on Sundays were painful
even to watch. Grudgingly, some of the booers began to applaud. And gradually Meredith's teammates began to appreciate him.

A friend was telling him, then, about some experiences riding
in country rodeos as a teen-ager. "One night I was thrown off
a bareback bronc, and I lay in the dirt, not scared and not
especially hurting but knowing there was no reason in the world

why I should ever ride a wild horse again," the friend said.

"I know how you felt," Meredith said. "I know exactly. Sometimes when I'm lying on the ground at Yankee Stadium or someplace, and some guy like Sam Huff is pounding my poor thin body, I tell myself, 'Dandy, why did you ever take this up as a career? Why don't you get a decent job? You're too nice a person for this to be happening to, Dandy. Why don't you go back to East Texas where you belong? Let the other fellows play football. You don't need it.' "

Now, looking back at that 1964 season, Meredith says, "It did hurt. It hurt a lot. People kept saying, 'How can the kid do it?' They talked about me having great courage. I'll admit I liked getting that sympathy. But it wasn't really a matter of courage as much as of determination. Nobody is going to beat me. I knew if I didn't get up they would have beaten me. I couldn't stand the thought of that."

By 1965 Meredith was emerging as a team leader at last. But he slipped in a puddle of water in the hall of the training-camp dormitory that summer, fell and hurt his right shoulder and elbow. "I was missing my passes by six inches to a foot," he says. "That doesn't sound like much, but it's too much." The Cowboys won their first two games that season. "I didn't throw well, but I was playing well. At least, we won," says Meredith. St. Louis beat the Cowboys in the third game. "A guy dropped a pass that would have won it for us, but I missed five receivers who were open for touchdowns. You're not an NFL quarterback if you do that. So I was benched." Rookies Craig Morton and Jerry Rhome took over at quarterback. Dallas lost three more games. In the seventh game Meredith started again, and the Cowboys lost their fifth in a row. "That was against Pittsburgh," he says. "The worst game I ever played in my life. I wasn't throwing bad, but everything else was bad. I was trying so hard. After the game I saw Tom Landry cry. He wasn't crying so much about the game as he was crying about me. He had been fair, more than fair, to his mind, and he wanted so much for me to do well, and I was awful. I'm no good at pep

talks, but I got up in the locker room, that dismal locker room
at Pittsburgh. The players had their heads down, couldn't do
anything, couldn't remember how to take off their uniforms. I
told them I was going to work harder and we were going to
win."

Landry was not so sure of that. Sunday night, all day Monday and Monday night he tried to make a decision. "I had to
think about it a long time," Landry says. "Meredith's career
with us was in the balance. We had spent five years on him.
Now did we want to junk it all and go with rookie quarterbacks? It's tough to start all over. I never had any real doubts
about Meredith's ability. My only doubt was if he could stand
up physically through an entire season and win a championship."

On Tuesday, Landry called Meredith into his office. "I didn't
know what the word would be, but of course I was going to try
and take it like a man," says Meredith. "You know, be cool no
matter what. So Tom looked at me and said, 'Don, you're my
quarterback. I believe in you.' And we both started crying
again."

"That decision pleased a lot of players," says Frank Clarke,
a Cowboy receiver for eight years. "We had come to understand
the pressures on a quarterback, and we knew sticking with one
would remove some of the uncertainty. Meredith had to be our
leader. He used to be thinking, 'It'll come.' Then he found out
it was here already, and he had to do something with it."

Since that Landry decision in midyear of 1965, the Cowboys
have a 22–10–1 record in regular-season games. They won five
of their last seven in 1965, despite Meredith's being hit so hard
in the 13th game that he could not recognize old friends or
remember teammates' names in the locker room. He fell in his
New York hotel the following week and had to be hurried to
the hospital for X rays of his skull. But the Cowboys finished
second in the East. In 1966 Meredith stayed reasonably well,
threw 24 touchdown passes while directing the league's best
offense. The Cowboys won the East only to lose 34–27 to Green

Bay in the NFL championship, failing to score from the two-yard line in the final minute of a game that Meredith has replayed many times in his mind.

Last year pain found Meredith again. He hurt his arm and shoulder in the exhibition season, twisted a knee and had his nose broken by a fist that got past the face bar. After the first Redskin game, which Dallas won on a 36-yard Meredith pass to Dan Reeves with 10 seconds to play, Cheryl called an ambulance to their home, and he was put into the hospital with pneumonia. He lost more than 20 pounds and was extremely ill, isolated in a room with a sign on the door warning hospital personnel to stay out and let him rest without bothering him for autographs. He missed three games. "Very few people realize how serious Meredith's condition was," Landry says. "An average man, even an above-average man, wouldn't have made it back on his feet for months, much less back to playing football. Courage is what did it. It was February before he ever felt good." The Cowboys, however, put together a 9–5 record, won their second Eastern title and again lost to Green Bay (21–17) when the Packers scored on a quarterback sneak in the last few seconds on a frozen field with the temperature 13° below zero. "I can't describe how cold it was. All I can say is it hurt just to breathe," says Meredith. After the game, Meredith and Bart Starr went on the Johnny Carson show. Carson asked whether the Packers would have had time for another play if the quarterback sneak had not been successful, and Starr replied that he didn't know. "You wouldn't have," Meredith said, as though ice was still cracking on his face. "You sure wouldn't have."

"That field was so bad," Meredith says. "We thought we had an advantage in our speed, our quickness, our multiple formations. We had studied hard and knew what to do. Suddenly we couldn't do anything we had done all season. Our game plan was gone down the ice."

This season, having signed a new three-year contract, Meredith reported a week early to a motel near the Cowboys camp in Thousand Oaks, Calif., while an impending player strike was

being settled. Meredith was somewhat overweight from a practice of reordering entire Tex-Mex dinners at Casa Dominguez,
a Dallas restaurant owned by his friend, Pete Dominguez, and
from high living at such places as Majorca—where he went to
pose for Jantzen ads—Palm Springs, Reno and other comfortable wateringholes to which his enterprises took him between
January and July. At camp he went on a severe diet and stopped
smoking cigarettes at the same time, an undertaking which
caused him to look a bit crazed. Landry had decreed that
Meredith should play at 200 pounds or less, five pounds under
his weight of last season. The idea is that Meredith, who like
the other Cowboys is on a continual weight-lifting and isomet-
rics program from training camp until the last game, will be
more alert and nimble, and maybe more enduring.

"Landry thinks, and Meredith agrees, that we have been
lacking a little something extra in the fourth quarter," says
Ralph Neely, a Dallas tackle. "The way to get it is to work
harder. Meredith is setting the example. He nearly ran my legs
off the first week we were out here, before camp started. Some
days I'll be draggy and tired, and I see him working hard. That
makes me think if he can do it, I can do it. So I work hard, too.
If we are going to win the championship this year, he's the man
who will do it for us. He's the leader. If he comes into the
huddle and calls a triple reverse, there's not a man in our
starting offensive lineup who doesn't believe it's the greatest
play anybody ever thought of. He's got authority. In our preseason game with Chicago this year, a linebacker smashed him. He
came to the huddle and said, 'O.K., let's cut that out; I'm not
going to put up with it,' and we kept that linebacker away. The
kind of offense we have if we're going good will average about
four yards per rush, and if we're going bad we'll average less
than two. On those bad days, Meredith is the one who keeps
us together."

Cowboy President Tex Schramm has been in intimate contact with Meredith for the past eight years—not always to their
mutual satisfaction—and has watched his quarterback go

through the rather bruising process of growing up, by which Schramm would mean at least partially conforming, coming around to accepting the Landry way. "It's easy to say Meredith has matured. But what form does that take?" says Schramm. "When he first came to us he thought if we just gave him the ball he would find somebody and throw it to him. That's how he played, and that's how he approached life. The significant thing is that now he understands there must be a plan and a reason, and it's reflected in both his life and his football playing. He's planning for the future, making investments with a purpose. He hasn't totally accepted what we tell him or completely disciplined himself to what needs to be done, but he recognizes what we mean. Little by little, the self-discipline will come, he'll see that he does have certain weaknesses—one being his physical makeup—and to be a success, to attain what he wants, he has to work at it. This year he has stopped many of his performances and personal appearances beyond his radio and TV shows and a few other things in order to concentrate more on his job.

"Meredith has plenty of self-doubts," Schramm says. "That's probably the reason for the finger-snapping facade he puts up. That facade is not his real nature." Schramm laughs. He is fond of Meredith though often exasperated by him, a game they both understand. "What Meredith should be is a singer or something where he can do what he wants to excel in without having to do the practice."

Singers, of course, do have to practice. But the fact is, Meredith might have been a professional singer by now except that he is not all that good at it. He toured for a time in a show with Roger Miller and Molly Bee and found the routine disappointing. "I woke up one morning and said, 'Self, they didn't raise you to make a living in this business,'" he says. But he will sing anytime, anyplace. You can usually hear him coming—the strong and slightly nasal voice racketing out tunes like *God Made Me a Black Land Farmer, Hello, Wall, With a Little Help from My Friends* and *The Biggest Fool That Ever Hit the Big Time,* mixing in an occasional rock 'n' roll or soul song. Willie

Nelson, the country-and-western singer and composer, is among the friends who have stayed at Meredith's house. Meredith once made a record called *Them That Ain't Got It Cain't Lose*. However, Meredith will sing any sort of music. A few years ago we went into Asti's, a Manhattan restaurant where waiters and customers leap up and bellow opera. Meredith was going to test himself against that crowd, but I collided with a waiter carrying a trayload of dinners, and after the crash and the yelling we decided opera was not in Meredith's line, anyhow. There is no doubt that show business is, or could be. Meredith has been offered the leads in two new television series. Seeing him at The Daisy or La Scala or The Factory in Los Angeles, you would pick him out as a young actor.

"Meredith just doesn't enjoy practice," says Schramm. "I don't imagine he even spends any time on the practice tee at golf. When the season starts, he'll work hard. But not in April. If he would work for three months in the spring throwing sideline passes to a receiver, there's little limit to what a great quarterback he would be. But Don resents any attempt to change him.

"When you've got your future riding on one guy, a quarterback, you like to have him be a little serious," Schramm says. "You say be dedicated, pay the price, and he says I'm not Bart Starr, I'm Don Meredith. Well, we know we'll never make Don Meredith into Bart Starr. They're different personalities. Starr is the epitome of a hardworking, dedicated athlete. Meredith is like a Babe Ruth or a Bobby Layne. If Starr is Stan Musial, Meredith is Mickey Mantle. I understand that, but sometimes I get annoyed at his flippancy. Last spring I told him he had to join the adult world. He got mad and stormed out of my office. The next day he came back and said, 'I'm not gonna join your adult world. I'll live in my world and you live in yours.' " Schramm is laughing again as he thinks about it.

"Like most athletes, Meredith has an inner fear that when he quits playing, people won't like him so much," says Schramm. "All his investments are defensive, so he won't ever have to be

dependent on anyone or ever be poor. It would destroy him to
have to be dependent on somebody. He's his own worst enemy,
but he knows that. He knows when he's not doing things right.
He's tougher on himself than others are on him. But what he
doesn't understand is that if he worked harder and became as
complete a quarterback as Unitas or Starr, he'd make ten times
as much money as they do. Because of Meredith's personality,
he'd make Unitas and Starr look like peanuts."

Meredith enjoys being the sensitive poet-clown-athlete
touched by sadness and danger. He will do his imitations—a
flamingo, a lighthouse, a lighthouse with a snake in it, a cow,
a pig—and then will suddenly become very grave, almost
morose, but still be smiling, talking about the most desperate
matters as if he understood they were absurd and would eventually wind up as nothing. "He has these periods of intense
honesty," says Pete Gent, "when he gets you aside and tells you
at length what all is wrong with him." One thing Meredith has
wondered about—apart from the usual jokes after a bad day
when linebackers have dazed him, ends and tackles have fallen
heavily on him and cornerbacks have caught his passes and
brought them back in a direction he never intended—is why he
plays professional football. Money alone is never the answer.
"Money is part of it," Meredith says. "But I guess the main
reason has something to do with masculinity. Proving your
manhood. This is a very masculine game. It's hard to do that
frontier stuff anymore, fording rivers and so forth, but this
game sort of occupies that place for me. I've met a lot of
professional athletes, and they're all pretty much alike. Some
may be artists, some may be animals, some may be gentlemen,
some may cross you out, but they've all got something in common—coordinated bodies, love of competition, this feeling for
proving themselves. I really like this game. I need it. I must love
it, or Lord knows I wouldn't be playing it. I'm certainly not a
sports fan. In the last eight years I haven't seen ten athletic
events that I wasn't playing in. I don't read about sports in the
papers as a regular thing, except that I know a lot of golfers and

like to check and see how they're doing now and then."

When his footballing is finished—his contract expires after
the 1970 season, but he may decide to keep going another couple
of years—Meredith figures to be a moderately wealthy man,
perhaps more than that. With two partners he has bought a
2,300-acre South Texas ranch with a landing strip. He has
prospered in the stock market overall, has some oil properties,
is involved in several businesses, is about to become a partner
in a big Dallas restaurant called Dandy's, has a variety of
television offers to select from (he would be an excellent "color
man" on pro football telecasts, a field in which talent is sorely
needed, but he is not inclined in that direction at the moment)
and is hotly pursued by sponsors wanting him to endorse their
products. He fancies himself someday as a tycoon, a developer
of empires. Some of that may have rubbed off from working for
the Murchison brothers and knowing Jim Ling, director of the
Cowboys. "I've never played in that ball park, but I know I'd
be good at it," Meredith says.

But now he is entering a season for which he has, after his
own style, labored mightily. In California in July he turned
down several offers for endorsements because they would be
distracting. Although bothered by his customary sore arm in
training camp, Meredith threw the ball better in the early
preseason games than he ever had before in his career. Against
the Rams he hit three touchdown passes in the first half, two
of them perfectly thrown bombs to Hayes and Rentzel. The
coaches, the press and many of the players began to talk about
the "new" Meredith. "He has really worked this year," said
Bob Lilly, the Cowboys' All-NFL defensive tackle. "He's the
team leader, no question about that."

In many ways, though, he's the same old Dandy. Before the
opening exhibition game with the Bears, Meredith was sitting
in a quarterback meeting with Morton and Rhome while Landry drew diagrams on a board. Meredith was smoking a cigar
and also playing with it, twirling it in his fingers like a baton,
gesturing grandly with it, taking exaggerated puffs, pretending

to be a railroad president or a tin-mine baron from Bolivia. When Landry turned around to ask a question, Meredith stuck the wrong end of the cigar into his mouth. He coughed, sputtered, spat shreds of tobacco over his playbook. Morton and Rhome laughed, but Landry stared down at Meredith with as stony and humorless a face as he could manage, and Landry is quite good at that when he wishes to be. "You do understand what I'm telling you, Don," said Landry. Meredith nodded. The thing is, now he does.

15 / NAMATH

The Sweet Life of Swingin' Joe

By Dan Jenkins

Way back in the days before he hit 30 and before Mike Lucci of the Detroit Lions hit him, Joe Namath lived a very busy life. He had so much energy back in 1967, when he was only 24, that in one game that year he threw 60 passes; during one stretch that year he completed 15 straight passes; and for the entire season, he completed 258 of 491 passes for 4,007 yards. Only two men in football history have thrown more than 60 passes in a game, and one of the two is Namath himself; no one has completed more than 15 passes in a row; only two men have attempted more than 491 passes in a year; only two, the same two, have completed more than 258; and no other man has gained 4,000 yards passing in a season. Besides all that, Namath didn't need much sleep in 1967. Joe was at his peak then; from 1966 through 1968, he stayed healthy enough to become the first man in pro history to gain more than 3,000 yards passing for three straight years. Since then, of course, his career has suffered—from injury and from the absence of a championship. (The yardage he gained from 1966 through 1968 equals the yardage he has gained in his other six professional seasons.) Still, among football people, Namath ranks right up with Sonny Jurgensen as a pure passer—and right down with Sonny as a pure liver.

When Dan Jenkins, the author of Semi-Tough *and hundreds of equally comic articles, wrote this Namath profile for* Sports Illustrated *in 1966, Joe was just embarking on his glory years. Namath himself would be the first to admit that he can no longer keep up the pace Jenkins has so vividly painted. But he can try.*

Stoop-shouldered and sinisterly handsome, he slouches against the wall of the saloon, a filter cigarette in his teeth, collar open, perfectly happy and self-assured, gazing through the uneven darkness to sort out the winners from the losers. As the girls come by wearing their miniskirts, net stockings, big false eyelashes, long pressed hair and soulless expressions, he grins approvingly and says, "Hey, hold it, man—foxes." It is Joe Willie Namath at play. Relaxing. Nighttiming. The boss mover studying the defensive tendencies of New York's off-duty secretaries, stewardesses, dancers, nurses, bunnies, actresses, shopgirls—all of the people who make life stimulating for a bachelor who can throw one of the best passes in pro football. He poses a question for us all: Would you rather be young, single, rich, famous, talented, energetic and happy—or President?

Joe Willie Namath is not to be fully understood by most of us, of course. We are ancient, being over 23, and perhaps a bit arthritic, seeing as how we can't do the Duck. We aren't comfortably tuned in to the Mamas and the Uncles—or whatever their names are. We have cuffs on our trousers and, freakiest of all, we have pockets we can get our hands into. But Joe is not pleading to be understood. He is youth, success, the clothes, the car, the penthouse, the big town, the girls, the autographs and the games on Sundays. He simply *is*, man. The best we can do is catch a slight glimpse of him as he speeds by us in this life, and hope that he will in some way help prepare us for the day when we elect public officials who wear beanies and have term themes to write.

Right now, this moment, whatever Joe means to himself behind his wisecracks, his dark, rugged good looks, and his flashy tailoring, he is mostly one thing—a big celebrity in a celebrity-conscious town. This adds up to a lot of things, some desirable, some not. It means a stack of autographs everywhere he goes ("Hey, Joe, for a friend of mine who's a priest, a little somethin' on the napkin, huh?"), a lot of TV and radio stuff, a lot of photography stills for ads and news and continual interviews with the press. Such things he handles with beautiful nonchalance, friendliness—and lip.

Then comes the good part. It means he gets to sit at one of those key tables in Toots Shor's—1 and 1A, the joke goes—the ones just beyond the partition from the big circular bar where everyone from Des Moines can watch him eat his prime rib. It means that when he hits P. J. Clarke's the maître d' in the crowded back room, Frankie Ribando, will always find a place for him, while, out front, Waiter Tommy Joyce, one of New York's best celebrity-spotters, will tell everyone, "Joe's inside." It means he can crawl into the Pussy Cat during the late hours when the Copa girls and the bunnies are there having their after-work snacks, even though the line at the door may stretch from Second Avenue to the Triborough Bridge. It means he can get in just as easily at two of his other predawn haunts, Mister Laffs and Dudes 'n Dolls, places long ago ruled impenetrable by earth people, or nonmembers of the Youth Cult.

Easing into the clubs and restaurants that he frequents, Joe Willie handles his role well, "Don't overdo it, man," he says. "I can hang around till three or four and still grab my seven or eight." He sits, he eats, he sips, he smokes, he talks, he looks, and maybe he scares up a female companion and maybe he doesn't. "I don't like to date so much as I just like to kind of, you know, run into somethin', man," he says.

Namath is unlike all of the super sports celebrities who came before him in New York—Babe Ruth, Joe DiMaggio and Sugar Ray Robinson, to name three of the more obvious. They were *grown men* when they achieved the status he now enjoys. Might even be wearing hats. They were less hip to their times and more or less aloof from the crowd. Joe thrusts himself into the middle of it. Their fame came more slowly—with the years of earning it. Joe Willie Namath was a happening.

He happened first when he was a sophomore passing whiz who made Alabama Coach Bear Bryant change his offense. He happened again as a junior when he proved to be such an away-from-the-field mover that Bryant had to kick him off the team for drinking and carousing before the last two games of the season. He happened again when he returned to take Alabama to the 1964 national championship on a gimpy leg. Then Sonny Werblin, the owner of the New York Jets, made him *really* happen when he gave him that $400,000 contract on the second day of 1965. No football player in history had ever been worth half that much. But this wasn't all. He quickly had to undergo an operation on his knee to have a torn cartilage removed and a loose ligament tied. And, thanks to those splendid satirists, Robert Benton and David Newman, the hip line in New York became, "Sorry I can't make your party, Sybil, but I'm going to the tapping of Joe Namath's knee."

He was already a celebrity then, but his image grew throughout 1965 when a certain amount of suspense built as to whether he would be drafted, or whether his knee would allow him to play any football at all for Werblin's $400,000. During it all, the wisecracks flowed like cocktails.

"I'd rather go to Vietnam than get married," he said as the draftboard in his hometown of Beaver Falls, Pennsylvania, requested that he appear for his physical.

Then after he flunked it and a lot of superpatriots bristled, as they did at Cassius Clay's attitude, Joe said with brutal honesty, "How can I win, man? If I say I'm glad, I'm a traitor, and if I say I'm sorry, I'm a fool."

Once when he was asked to point out the difference between Bear Bryant and Jet Coach Weeb Ewbank, Joe grinned and unwisely said, "Coach Bryant was always thinking about winning. Weeb is mainly concerned over what kind of publicity you get."

When a writer tried to tease him about his classes at Alabama, asking if he majored in basket-weaving, Joe Willie said, "Naw, man, journalism—it was easier."

When he was asked to explain the origin of the white shoes that he wore—and still wears—during a game (and now endorses commercially), he shot back, "Weeb ordered 'em. He thought it would save tape."

But all of this was a year ago. Now in this season as he goes about the business of proving that he is worth every cent of his contract (he has thrown nine touchdown passes and put the Jets in first place in the American Football League's Eastern Division through five games), he is becoming the quarterback that Werblin gambled he would be—a throwing artist who may eventually rank with the best—and he is still a swinger. Namath may be Johnny Unitas and Paul Hornung rolled into one; he may, in fact, be pro football's very own Beatle.

He lives in a penthouse on New York's upper East Side, one that features a huge white llama-skin rug, an Italian marble bar, an elaborate stereo hookup, an oval bed that seems to increase in size with each glance, a terrace, and a couple of roommates —Joe Hirsch, a writer for *The Morning Telegraph,* and Jet Defensive Back Ray Abruzzese, whom he knew at Alabama.

Of Hirsch, Joe Willie says, "I got my own handicapper." Of Abruzzese, he says, "I got my own bartender," referring to Abruzzese's onetime summer job tending bar at Dudes 'n Dolls. And of his apartment, he says proudly, "I had the same decorator that Sinatra had for his pad."

He whirls around the city in his gray Lincoln Continental convertible, the radio blaring, parking by fireplugs whenever possible, wearing tailor-made suits with tight pants and loud print linings, grabbing checks, laughing, enjoying life, spending maybe $25,000 a year ("On nuthin', man") and wondering why anyone should be offended.

"I believe in letting a guy live the way he wants to if he doesn't hurt anyone. I feel that everything I do is O.K. for me, and doesn't affect anybody else, including the girls I go out with," he says. "Look man, I live and let live. I like everybody.

I don't care what a man is as long as he treats me right. He can be a gambler, a hustler, someone everybody else thinks is obnoxious, I don't care so long as he's straight with me and our dealings are fair. I like Cassius Clay, Bill Hartack, Doug Sanders and Hornung, all the controversial guys. They're too much. They're colorful, man. If I couldn't play football, I'd like to be a pro golfer. But I like everybody." Joe's eyes sparkle, as if he is getting ready to make a joke, and he says, "Why, I even like Howard Cosell."

Joe Willie's philosophy is more easily grasped when one realizes what he lifted himself up from in Beaver Falls. It is a picturesque but poor town in the hills about 30 miles outside of Pittsburgh. He was the youngest of five children, and his parents were divorced when he was in the sixth grade. His father was a mill worker. He lived with his mother, and there was little money, so Joe hustled. He shot pool, he shined shoes, he ran messages for bookies, he hustled; he got by. "Where I come from," he says today, "ain't nobody gonna hustle *me*, man."

As he prepared for his senior year of high school the idea of going to college was remote. An older brother, John, was a career man in the Army, a warrant officer in Vietnam. Joe was set on joining the Air Force and making it a career. What stopped him was a lot of touchdown passes and offers from precisely 52 universities, including Notre Dame—but not Alabama.

"I wanted to go to Maryland because I was stupid enough to think it was down South," he says. "I didn't know from outside Pittsburgh, man. All I knew was that I wanted to go South. I think a lot of kids from the East and Midwest do because of the climate."

Namath took the college board exams and failed them at Maryland. "You needed 750 and I scored 745, right? They wanted me to take it again, but I said to hell with it." He thought next of Penn State, but Maryland had to play Penn State the next few seasons and didn't want to face Namath.

Maryland's coaches promptly called Bear Bryant at Alabama, whom the Terps would not play, and Bear welcomed "the greatest athlete I've ever coached."

Despite his dismissal for the last two games of his junior season, Namath worships Alabama and his experiences and successes there. Bryant is the greatest man he has ever known, Joe even has the hint of a southern accent, his closest friends are from Alabama, and if there is anything that makes him mad today, it is the eastern press, which he calls "the northern press."

"There's only three things I'm touchy about," says Joe Willie, who naturally got that name down South. "No. 1, the northern press and how it ignores southern football when I'll guarantee you that a team like Louisiana Tech can beat about 80 of these lousy schools up here. Two is the publicity that Notre Dame gets. And three is a joke about a Hungarian."

One other tiny thing bothered him when he first went to the Jets after taking Alabama to three bowl games with seasons of 10–1, 9–2 and 10–1. He read a statement by a pro player who suggested that Joe might not want to "pay the price" with his big salary. "Can you believe that?" he said. "Why, you can't play for Bryant for four years and not know how to *pay the price* for what you get out of life."

Considering that the most money Joe ever had at one time before he signed the Jet contract was $600, which he got for peddling some Alabama game tickets, he might have been justified in blowing the whole stack on a car, a blonde and a diamond ring. He had a shrewd business consultant, however, in a Birmingham lawyer named Mike Bite. At Bite's bidding he learned to spread the money out as he would an evening on the town. He takes only $25,000 a year in salary, and will through 1968. He has $200,000 in bonuses working for him over the next 100 years or something like that. And he was generous enough to let members of his family in on the loot. Two brothers and a brother-in-law are on the Jets' scouting payroll at $10,000 a year.

Contrary to popular notion, Joe did give the St. Louis Cardinals, who drafted him in the NFL, some serious consideration. "And they weren't that far off in money," he says. "But they had it laid out wrong, like I had to do a radio show for part of my salary. I couldn't believe that. I said, man, I'm just a football player, and what I make will be for football only." He did guess that the Cardinals, who had an established passer in Charley Johnson, might be dealing for him in behalf of the New York Giants, who had nothing, and, one way or another, he wanted to "get to this town." Bear Bryant's only comment was that Ewbank had won a couple of championships at Baltimore and, if Joe was still interested in winning, he might give that some consideration.

He wasn't a winner right off, of course. The Jets' 5–8–1 record last season made New York the worst team Joe had ever played on. Admittedly, he didn't know the first thing about quarterbacking a pro team. He had the quickest delivery anyone had ever seen, and he got back into the Jets' exceedingly secure passing pocket, formed by Sherman Plunkett, Dave Herman, Sam DeLuca, and Winston Hill—his "bodyguards"—so fast that Kansas City's All-AFL lineman, Jerry Mays, said, "He makes the rush obsolete." But there was so much he had to learn.

At Alabama he had raced back only five yards and released the ball in approximately 1.3 seconds. Ewbank, however, demanded that he get eight yards deep and go 3.2 seconds before throwing. His firmly braced knee prevented him from using the threat of the run, which he had done so well for two and a half seasons in Tuscaloosa.

He had to learn how to read defenses, how to look for tips among the defensive backs, how to hit his receivers on the break, how to set up when he threw, how to call audibles and how to convince his Jet teammates that he could lead them.

"Last year," says defensive end Gerry Philbin, "there was an undercurrent of resentment—nothing you could pinpoint, but it was there—about Joe's money and his publicity. That was at first. It disappeared when everybody found out what a great guy he is."

Curley Johnson, the punter, says, "Mainly we wanted to see how good he was. He really didn't throw the ball that damn well for a long time. Now, we know how good he is—the best."

Says the ace receiver, Don Maynard, "At first he'd knock us over on short patterns. Now he's slacked off. His timing is great, and he adjusts to situations like a veteran." To this, George Sauer Jr., another top Jet receiver, adds, "He never knew how to throw on the break last season. The ball was always early or late. Now it's there."

Not according to Joe Willie, though. "I haven't thrown well since Alabama," he says. "Maybe it's my leg. I don't know. If I knew, I'd throw better. You hear a lot about getting the ball up here by your ear, but that's junk. It doesn't matter how you deliver as long as the ball goes where you aim it and gets there when it's supposed to. I don't know *how* I throw the ball, and I don't remember anybody ever teaching me to throw it. But there's a lot I *have* found out."

For one thing, Joe says, the quarterback who has to call a pile of audibles (changing plays at the line of scrimmage) is a dumb one. "You're supposed to know what the defense will be when you're in the huddle. I'll only call five or six audibles a game now. Last year it was more. That's funny, too, because the public thinks it's a big deal if a quarterback can switch plays a lot at the scrimmage line. They think it makes him brainy. Man, most of the time it means he's stupid."

A simple thing it took Joe all last season to learn was that backs key on the mannerisms of a quarterback and cover their areas accordingly.

"For example," he says, "about 80 percent of the time when the quarterback takes the snap, turns and races back to set up with his back to the defense, he'll throw to the right. That's because it's easier, more natural, to plant your feet when you start that way. On the other hand, it's easier to throw left when you drop straight back, without turning around. There are defensive backs who'll play you for this and, of course, you have to cross 'em up."

Among the defenders that have Namath's highest respect are Oakland's speedy Dave Grayson and Miami's Jim Warren, who was with San Diego a year ago. "All you can say about 'em is they play you tight and cover you. To beat 'em, you have to run what we call progressive patterns, you know, something that goes out, slant, down and in. The whole game is trying to get the defensive man's feet turned wrong."

Strangely enough, Joe finds that the ball has a tendency to turn wrong on his home turf of Shea Stadium. "It's my unfavorite place to play," says he. "Somehow, the wind swirls in there, and I don't like what it does to the balls I throw. It could be some kind of fixation, I don't know. Like I have about throwing a night football. It's different, man, I swear. The coaches and the sporting-goods salesmen say it's the same ball, but it isn't. It goes different. So does the ball in Shea."

It certainly went differently in Namath's first home game of 1966. He passed for five touchdowns as the Jets humiliated the Houston Oilers 52–13. Joe's hottest streak of all so far came in the fourth quarter of a game at Boston, where he had to hit 14 of 23 passes for 205 yards and two touchdowns so the Jets could salvage a 24–24 tie. This sent the Jets into pure ecstasy. "He brought us back from a bad day in a real clutch situation," said Ewbank. And publicity man Frank Ramos, with his usual sharp eye on statistics, pointed out, "The papers are raving about Terry Hanratty at Notre Dame, but do you realize Joe hit as many passes in *one quarter* as Hanratty hit against Northwestern all day long? I think that's interesting."

The supertest for both Namath and the Jets came Saturday night, however, and they were more than up to it. While Shea Stadium shook from the noise of 63,497 New Yorkers—an all-time AFL record crowd—who had come to cheer their town's only winning team against unbeaten San Diego, Joe Willie's arm was right when it had to be. He threw a touchdown pass to Matt Snell early that gave the Jets a 10–9 lead, which they carried into the last 10 minutes. Then, after San Diego pulled ahead 16–10, Namath rapidly fired three straight completions and whirled his team 66 yards to the winning touchdown and the final 17–16 score. He had shown once more that he could deliver in the clutch, and the Jets had the only defeatless record (4–0–1) in the AFL as proof.

If there is a single myth that Joe Willie would like to have destroyed about pro football, it is the widely held belief that the game's quarterbacks are pampered by opposing defensive linemen; that they are not "shot at," particularly himself because of his bad knee and what his drawing power means to the AFL.

"O.K.," he says. "How about the Houston exhibition in Birmingham in August? Don Floyd comes at me after the whistle, and I move to miss a shot and reinjure my knee. What's that? Of course, Don didn't mean to. He says he didn't hear the whistle, and I believe him. But he was comin' at me and I kind of think he'd of hit me if he could have. What about the Denver game? I still got a wrist bandage and a sore back from that one. Johnny Bramlett, one of their linebackers, is a buddy of mine —he played for Memphis State—and he had me over to dinner the night before the game. His wife cooked an Italian feast, plenty good, too. But the next day he was after me like a tiger, and he'd cuss me when he missed. He wanted to win, man. That's the way it is. I don't think any of our opponents are too interested in my health."

If he stays healthy, Joe Willie may achieve his deepest ambition, which is "to become known as a good quarterback, not a rich one." He may even become what Boston Owner Billy Sullivan says he is now: "The biggest thing in New York since Babe Ruth." Slowly, because trying to fathom youth is always a slow process, you get the impression that Joe is quite serious about it and, despite his hip ways, is working hard to make it. Beneath the gaudy surface there somehow beams through a genuine, considerate, sincere, wonderfully friendly and likeable young man. But he's going to be himself. He's going to do it his way, and nobody else's.

16 / BONUS

There Are No Coal Mines
in Beaver Falls

By Joe Namath

*During the year 1969, the year Joe Namath guaranteed and then
produced a Super Bowl victory, the year Joe and I collaborated
on his autobiography, we shared a lot of funny times. Like the
time he told me he was being investigated by the FBI and the
NFL and might have to quit playing football, a little bit of inside
information I never fed the publisher, for fear it might damage
his heart. Or like the time we flew from Miami to New York
together, so that I could talk to Joe for two hours away from
telephones and more shapely distractions, and I overheard a
passenger ask one of the stewardesses what's Namath like, and
I heard her reply, "He's nice, but I like the intellectual next to
him better." (Being called an intellectual next to Namath is like
being called a weight lifter next to Truman Capote, and, besides,
the stewardess who made the remark was the least attractive of
the crew.) Or like the time we went to Tom Jones's opening at
the Copa, and while we were sitting in the singer's dressing room,
a man who later matriculated at Atlanta Federal Penitentiary
walked in and gave Joe a warm, friendly hello, and I wondered
if Pete Rozelle might have a tap in the room. But for laughs,
nothing compared to the trip to Beaver Falls, Pennsylvania, for
"Joe Namath Day." It was a circus, a carnival, a nonstop party*

from top to bottom, and I hope the story that follows captures some of the spirit.

The story is a chapter in I Can't Wait Until Tomorrow . . . 'Cause I Get Better Looking Every Day, *Joe's modestly titled autobiography, and it was the easiest section of the book to write, the most fun. And, in all modesty, to match the title, I think it tells a lot about the forces that produced a Joe Namath.*

I was going home, back to Beaver Falls on May 24, 1969, to celebrate the first, and possibly last, "Joe Namath Day." I don't think it'll ever be a national holiday. I had just a small group with me—a lawyer, a public-relations man, a television crew, half a dozen photographers and writers, a couple of teammates, a few friends and two tension-easers, a tall one and a short one. You can't go home empty-handed.

The short one was wearing a completely transparent blouse. When our plane from New York landed in Pittsburgh, some guy from a local newspaper rushed up to the young lady and said, "Excuse me, miss, but is that a see-through blouse?"

I realize that most reporters are half-blind, anyway, but this guy was ridiculous. I mean, if he couldn't tell that was a see-through blouse, what did he think they were?

She answered his question very frankly, and after the guy recovered, we all piled into limousines for the twenty-eight-mile trip to Beaver Falls. I was a little nervous. Not for myself; I knew I'd survive. For Beaver Falls.

I arrived in Beaver Falls for the first time, May 31, 1943, a big disappointment to my parents, Rose and John Namath. They'd already had three sons—John Jr., who was then twelve; Robert, who was nine; and Franklin, who was six—and they'd waited a long time before they'd decided to try once more for a girl. They found out right away I was a boy. I wore my hair shorter then.

My father and my high school football coach, Larry Bruno,

who was the chairman of Joe Namath Day, shared the limousine I rode in. It was a nice limousine, and the boy who was driving, an end on the high school team in 1968, told me his father owned it. I was a little surprised. Beaver Falls isn't a very wealthy town, and not too many people own limousines. Then somebody told me the boy's father owns the local funeral parlor.

We drove northwest, a pretty, winding drive, past Ambridge and Aliquippa and Freedom and Monaca—great football country, the home of more All-Americans per square mile, I'll bet, than any other section of the country. Just a few miles before Beaver Falls, we cruised through Rochester, the hometown of Babe Parilli, my fellow quarterback on the New York Jets. I didn't know Babe back home. I never did hang around much with older people.

Every day, when I was in fourth grade at St. Mary's Grammar School, I used to pass an Army & Navy Store on my way to lunch. In the window of the store was a gold football helmet with the name Babe Parilli written across it. Babe was a pro football player then, and I was nine years old.

In New Brighton, the last town before Beaver Falls, we drove by the drugstore where my mother works as a saleslady. She works now because she wants to; she used to work because she had to.

When I was growing up, my mother was a maid up in Patterson Heights, the fancy section of Beaver Falls. At night, she'd stay up late, cutting down my brothers' old baseball and football uniforms to fit me. Now my mother lives up in Patterson Heights.

We crossed a bridge over the Beaver River, separating New Brighton and Beaver Falls. From the limousine we could see the railroad trestle connecting the two towns.

When I was a little kid, my best friend, a black kid named Linwood Alford, and I once walked across the trestle. A train came by, and we had to hang on to the railing, just about four feet clear of the train. A neighbor, riding on a bus, saw us and told my father. He beat the hell out of me. He really believed in discipline. So did my mother. Till I was thirteen, I thought my name was "Shut up."

The line of limousines turned into a place called Sahli Chevrolet, and most of us transferred into Chevy convertibles for a parade through the center of town. Weeb Ewbank—"Weeb who?" Don Maynard shouted—sat atop the back of one convertible. George Sauer trailed in another, Maynard in another, Johnny Sample in another. I followed them in a green convertible. Just to be safe, we put the two tension-easers in an enclosed car. I wasn't sure Beaver Falls was ready for them. Then, with a police escort, we pulled out of Sahli Chevrolet.

I still remember the last time I left Sahli Chevrolet with a police escort. I was a senior in high school, and our football team had just won the Western Pennsylvania championship, but they weren't honoring me. Sahli Chevrolet was on Seventh Avenue then, the main street of Beaver Falls, and there was a big helium balloon flying on its roof. Four of us—Wibby Glover, Whitey Harris, Red Christley and me—decided we'd climb up on the roof late one night, paint "Take 'em Tigers" in orange and black, the school colors, on the balloon, then take the balloon over to the high school. Someone must've spotted us sneaking up the fire escape to the roof because, the next thing we knew, we were surrounded by cops, waving guns. "Don't shoot," I said. They didn't shoot, but they did put us in jail, and Coach Bruno had to come and get us out.

From Sahli Chevrolet, we swung around to Sixth Street, in the Lower End, my old neighborhood. A lot of the houses in the neighborhood had been torn down, but outside of that, things hadn't changed too much. Most of the people along Sixth Street were black.

The Lower End was a black neighborhood during my child-

hood, and most of my friends were black. We ran in gangs and we had rock fights—maybe that's how I developed my arm—and we had a lot of fun. I didn't know anything about prejudice until, when I was nine years old, Linwood Alford and I walked into a pizzeria, and the lady who owned the pizzeria kicked him out. "We don't want your kind in here," she said. I really didn't know what she meant at first, but I left, too. I figured whatever Linwood was, I was the same kind.

We drove slowly past the house I grew up in, a narrow, two-story white frame house with a red brick base.

The thing I remember best about that house was that the bathroom was in the basement, and during the winter the basement was always freezing. I hated to get up in the morning to go to school, hated to get up and go down to that cold bathroom.

Right next door to my old house, we passed a 7-Up plant.

When I was a kid, I once got caught borrowing pop from the 7-Up place. We used to do a lot of borrowing, from the neighbors, from candy stores, just little things. Some of the kids used to borrow junk from the junkman. They'd borrow the junk from the back of the yard, then go around front and sell it to the junkman. He bought it, too. He wasn't the world's sharpest junkman.

From the car in front, Johnny Sample kept yelling back to me, "When are we gonna reach town? This the main street?" Johnny grew up in Philadelphia, and I guess he wasn't exactly awed by the size of Beaver Falls.

Beaver Falls is a steel-mill town. Newspapermen are always writing that I'm from a coal-mining town, which is about par for newspapermen. There are no coal mines in Beaver Falls. There are about 17,000 people, and more of them work in the steel mills than anywhere else.

The parade turned onto Seventh Avenue, and I could hardly believe the crowds, six and seven deep, lining both sides of the street. Somebody told me that there were at least 25,000 people watching the parade, which means that, even if everyone in Beaver Falls showed up, almost another 10,000 people had come in from the neighboring towns. Kids poured all over the street, running up to the car and shaking my hand and touching me and asking for my autograph, and I was really stunned. I'd expected a nice little parade, maybe 2,000 or 3,000 people, but this was fantastic. Damn, I enjoyed it. I must have recognized hundreds of people in the crowd. Wibby Glover, my old buddy, came off the sidewalk and I dragged him up on the car with me. The cop escorting the car was an old neighbor from Sixth Street. People I hadn't seen in eight or nine years kept popping out of the crowd, and after we'd gone four or five blocks along Seventh Avenue, I saw my mother standing on a corner. She came over and gave me a big kiss.

My mother and my father split up when I was twelve years old, and eventually each of them remarried. I stayed close to both of them. My mother—her name is Rose Szolnoki now—raised me, and she had her hands full. I think she did a helluva job. She taught me to be polite and to respect my elders. She's a great lady, and she loves to talk. She talks very slowly and very properly. We have a running gag among my friends that whenever my mother calls on the phone she uses up the first three minutes just saying hello. And she does some of the funniest things in the world. When she watches the Jets play on television, she prays to two saints, one when we've got the ball and one when the other team's got the ball. She's the only person I know who has an offensive saint and a defensive saint.

Kids were handing me scraps of paper to autograph, caps to autograph, baseball gloves to autograph, footballs to autograph, even a black wallet to autograph. Somebody kept tugging on my sleeve, saying, "Oh, please let me have your autograph. You're my hero. You're the greatest man in the world. Please let me have your autograph." I turned around, finally, and there was the tension-easer, in her see-through blouse, shaking up the whole population of Beaver Falls. I told her to get back to her own car before she got arrested.

Farther along Seventh Avenue, we passed the Blue Room, the local pool hall. I knew the place pretty well. I probably should have gotten my high school diploma from the Blue Room.

When I was a high school senior, a coach from the University of Michigan came to talk to me about college. Somebody told him he could find me at the Blue Room. When he got there, I was out front, lying on the hood of a car. He didn't even bother to talk to me. I guess he decided I wasn't the University of Michigan type.

After we got past the center of town, the crowd thinned out, and their screams faded away. I was able to relax for a minute. I was still surprised by the size of the turnout. Sample must've drawn the people. We drove by the Geneva College stadium, where we used to play our high school games, and we drove by the Babcock & Wilcox steel mill, where my father works as a roller in the No. 2 hot mill.

My father was born in Hungary and came to the United States in 1921, when he was thirteen. He's a strong man. He played a lot of baseball during his younger years, and he always encouraged me to play sports. When I was a kid, he'd buy me a new baseball glove before he'd buy himself a new shirt. He figured he didn't need a new shirt to work all day in the steel mill. When he was like the business manager of our Little League baseball team, we had our one big fight. Some kid did something wrong, and Dad started yelling at him. "Don't yell at him," I said. "He's trying. You're not the coach." Dad said, "Don't you talk back to me." I said, "Well, leave him alone. You're not the coach." I put up my hand to protect myself, in case Dad hit me. He thought I was going to hit him. We didn't talk for a month or two after that. Dad was really hurt.

At the end of the parade, the whole party drove out to the

Holiday Inn to check in and freshen up before the banquet
planned by the Beaver Falls Area High School Booster Club.
I had to sit through a brief press conference, a typical session
of brilliant questions and brilliant answers. Someone asked me
if I thought my outside interests were hurting my football. I
didn't know whether he meant Bachelors III or Johnnie Walker
Red. I was tempted to tell him the tension-easers weren't for
me; they were for my friends. Instead, I played it straight, as
straight as I can. "Well," I said, "they didn't seem to hurt me
too much last year."

I needed a drink after the press conference. I went upstairs
and had one, or two, with Coach Bruno and a few of the
Boosters, and my brother Frank came up to visit me. Frank had
come down from Detroit for the banquet. He's in the insurance
business there.

*When I was a senior in high school, Frank once heard a
ridiculous rumor that I'd been in a bar. I mean, it really was
ridiculous. I didn't go into bars when I was in high school. Hell,
I knew better than that. You can meet a lot of undesirables in
bars.*

*But this rumor did have a little truth to it. I actually had gone
into a bar, but only for a minute and only to get another kid to
come out. I'd been hanging around with this kid—his sister was
my girl friend—and I wanted him to go someplace with me.*

*It was right before the football season began, and the word
spread through town pretty fast that I'd been seen in a bar. When
Frank heard it, he drove right to the house where I was living with
my mother. He was a little bit upset.*

*Frank practically ran into the house. "Hey, Joey," he said.
"C'mon out to the alley. Right now."*

"What do you want?" I said.

"I want to talk to you," Frank said.

*I took a good look at him and I saw that he didn't have his
teeth in. He must've thought I was some kind of a dope. Sure,
he wanted to talk to me in the alley without his teeth in.*

I went out to the alley anyway—my mother was in the house

—but I walked out holding my hands high, up near my mouth. You learn that when you grow up in in a good neighborhood. When you expect trouble, you keep your hands in front of your mouth. It's better for your teeth.

"Were you in that bar?" Frank said.

"Yeah," I said, "but . . ."

Frank didn't let me explain. My own brother tried to steal a punch on me, tried to sneak one in quick before I was ready. I caught the punch on my hands and fell back against the garage. He moved in on me. I bounced off the garage, hit him in the stomach and started to run. Frank was just about as tall as me and weighed a lot more; he'd been a lineman in high school and in college. I didn't want to mess with him.

I ran to the front of the house, jumped into a ten-year-old Ford I had and locked the doors.

"You better open that damn door," Frank shouted. He ran for the car.

For a change, my engine started without any trouble, and I pulled away from the house and headed uptown. Frank got into his car and chased me. I guess he really wanted to talk to me badly.

When I got uptown, I parked; Frank parked across the street from me. I hopped out of my car, he hopped out of his car and started walking toward me, but I didn't wait for him. I crossed over to the other side. Then he crossed back, and I ran away from him. Hell, on foot, he didn't have a chance.

Finally, after I shook him, I got back in my car and drove home. Frank showed up a few minutes later, still wanting to talk to me. Just to even up the conversation, I grabbed a butcher knife.

I waved the knife at Frank. "Listen, you sonovabitch," I screamed. "You better stay the hell away from me. You ain't no brother of mine. You don't even want to listen to me. You won't even hear what I got to say."

I wasn't going to use the knife. Well, I don't think I was going to use the knife.

Frank had no choice. He had to hear me out. I told him the

story about just going to get the other kid out of the bar, and he checked into it and found out I was telling the truth. He stopped being mad at me. He didn't want to hurt me in the first place; he wanted to help me. He just wanted to make sure I wasn't getting into bad habits.

All the time I was chatting with Frank and with friends of mine who dropped in, Coach Bruno and the Boosters were after me to start getting dressed. They were afraid I'd miss the banquet. I don't blame them. I'm pretty bad about being on time for anything. I miss planes. I miss appointments. I guess that's probably my only vice.

Finally, I slipped into a green suit—soft green, not Jet green, to match my eyes—and rode over to the Geneva College field house for the banquet. I was stunned again. There were more than 1,300 people jammed into the field house. They'd paid ten dollars each to come to the dinner, which is a lot of money, especially considering that Geneva College is a dry campus. I don't think I'd pay ten dollars to go to any dinner where you can't drink, no matter who was the guest of honor.

The decorations in the field house were fantastic. They had a big map of the United States, with a green light showing Beaver Falls and a sign saying, "Thanks for putting us on the map." Red and green lights kept flashing on and off behind the dais spelling out the word "Broadway." The aisles on either side of the floor were labeled Broadway and Seventh Avenue, for the main streets of New York and Beaver Falls. There were pictures of me all over the field house, with Coach Bruno, in my high school uniform, in my professional uniform. My mother was there, and my father, and my three brothers. My oldest brother, John, really looked sharp. He was wearing his army dress uniform. He was the first quarterback in the family —all I remember about his football playing was that he wore No. 42—but as soon as he got out of high school, he joined the army. He's been in since 1950, in Korea and in Vietnam. He didn't like the idea of going into the mills any more than I did.

I really like my brothers. They're good people. Hell, I owe a lot to them. While I was still a little kid, they'd already made Namath a sort of magic name in Beaver Falls.

The day I started junior high school, I sat down in my first class, and the teacher said, "Joe Namath? Are you related to Frank Namath?"

"Yes, ma'am," I said.

"And Bob Namath?"

"Yes, ma'am."

"And John Namath?"

"Yes, ma'am, they're my brothers."

"Well, then," the teacher said, "you come right down here in the front row where I can keep an eye on you, and you'd better keep quiet."

After the meal was served, with dinner music by Henry Garcia and the Tijuana Trumpets, a big group in Beaver Falls, the program opened with a film of highlights from the Super Bowl game. I didn't particularly like the movie—I thought it was slanted in favor of the National Football League—but I did like the way it turned out. Then Butch Newton, the president of the Booster Club, gave a short welcoming speech, the only really short speech of the night.

The Beaver Falls Area High School Boosters do a lot for the football team, and one of the best things they do is send forty or fifty of the most promising players to a pre-season training camp. When I was a sophomore in high school, trying out for the varsity for the first time, I wasn't invited to training camp. I wasn't considered promising enough.

I guess I wasn't really surprised. I'd played quarterback in junior high, but I was only five feet tall and 115 pounds then, and I could barely see over the line of scrimmage to where I was throwing. The only reason I got to play at all was that the first-string quarterback, a kid named Jake Lotz, got hurt.

Then George Sauer, Johnny Sample and Don Maynard got

up and gave speeches. George just talked for a couple of minutes, Johnny just talked for a little longer and then Don talked
for a couple of hours. I mean, you give Don a free meal, and
he feels he's got to give you your money's worth.

Clive Rush, who was our offensive coach in 1968 and is now
the head coach of the Boston Patriots, presented a plaque to my
mother, and she thanked him and Beaver Falls in a few thousand well-chosen words. I'd been pretty embarrassed by what
the players had to say, but once my mother started talking I
thought I was going to slide right under the head table. (My
posture, I'll admit, always is a little weak.) But, damn, I've got
to say she was pretty good. She must've rehearsed that speech
for days.

Then Weeb Ewbank presented a plaque to my father, and
Dad said, "Thanks." He isn't usually that quiet, but it was
starting to get late.

After Phil Iselin, the president of the Jets, and State Senator
Ernest Kline, the master of ceremonies, made a few remarks,
Joe Tronzo, the sports editor of the *Beaver Falls News-Tribune*,
got up and talked. Joe's known me a long time, back to the days
when I was playing baseball for the Elks in the Little League.

*Baseball was my best game for a long time, and my favorite.
I pitched a little, but mostly I played the outfield—my hero then
was Roberto Clemente of the Pirates—and even when I was
struggling to learn to play football, I could hit a baseball. I
played first-string varsity for three years in high school and my
last year, when our team won the Western Pennsylvania championship, I hit about .450. Half a dozen major-league teams were
interested in me. I got bonus offers of $20,000 and $25,000, and
I heard rumors that I could have gotten as much as $50,000 if
I'd turned pro. The scouts talked to my father, but he didn't want
to be the one to decide whether I'd play baseball or go to college.
About six years earlier, my brother Frank could have gotten a
$20,000 bonus to play baseball, but my father didn't tell him
about the offer. My father had made up his mind that Frank was*

going to college. Frank stayed only a couple of years at the University of Kentucky; when he found out he could have had a baseball bonus, he was pretty angry. Dad told me to make up my own mind. I talked it over with my mother and my brothers, and my mother said she wanted to see me go to college. I did what she said, and I'm damn glad. Hell, if I hadn't gone to college, I never would have got to meet Pete Rozelle.

Weeb Ewbank and Phil Iselin excused themselves in the middle of the dinner and left to go catch a plane home. Weeb probably had some movies he wanted to study. They missed the speech by the mayor of Beaver Falls, Howard Marshall. Mayor Marshall presented me with the keys to the city. It was nice of him to do that but, by then, I would have preferred a glass of Scotch.

I wish the mayor had given me a key several years earlier, a key to the high school gymnasium. I always loved to play basket-ball. I played guard, and I could really jump. I could stuff a ball into the basket. In my senior year, I was the only white guy in the Beaver Falls starting lineup. The rest of the team was black kids from the Lower End, kids I'd been playing with for years. We had no place to play on Sundays, so one Sunday a few of us climbed through a window into the high school gym. We just wanted to play ball. We didn't hurt anything. But we got caught, and we were arrested and charged with breaking and entering, and we were expelled from school for three days. The basketball coach was pretty unhappy with us. I never did get along with him. He was from the old school, the conservative style of play, and we liked razzle-dazzle, fast break, passing behind the back, all that jazz. I fooled around a lot. I remember once some guy was guarding me awful tight, sticking his hand in my face all the time, so, finally, I took the ball and wound up and followed through just like I was going to throw the ball right in his face. Except, I held on to the ball. The coach took me out for that. In the middle of the season, we were getting beat in one game, and the coach decided to take me out for some reason. I was

*disgusted. I didn't even stop at the bench. I just walked straight
down the stairs to the locker room. I heard footsteps behind me,
and there came Benny Singleton, with a big grin on his face.
Benny and I were the co-captains and the leading scorers on the
team. "If you're quitting, Joe," Benny said, "I'm quitting, too."
We just did it on impulse. I mean, I wasn't even in the restaurant
business then, or anything.*

After a man from Mayer China presented me with a souvenir
plate, rimmed in gold and inscribed, "Joe Namath Testimonial
Dinner," and mentioned that I used to break windows at his
company's plant—I broke a lot of windows as a kid, with
baseballs, with footballs and with golf balls—the athletic director of Beaver Falls Area High School, Bill Ross, got his turn
to speak. He announced that the school was retiring my old
jersey—No. 19, Johnny U's number, from the days when people
used to call me "Joey U"—and he reminded everyone that he
had been the coach of the football team during my sophomore
year, when I wasn't invited to the pre-season training camp. "I
was a great judge of talent," Mr. Ross said, "and the next year
I wasn't coaching."

*Early in my sophomore season, I tried to quit the football
team. I just felt I was never going to make it in football and I
wanted to concentrate on getting ready for the basketball season.
"I don't think it's a good idea," Mr. Ross said. "I want you to
stay on the team."*

"But I don't have any future in football," I told him.

"I think you should stick with it," Mr. Ross said.

*Mr. Ross gave me the idea that he thought someday I might
develop into a pretty good football player. I don't know whether
he really believed that or not. He didn't believe it enough to use
me at quarterback in a single game. The one chance I got to play
all year, I played defensive halfback.*

I gave a little speech, thanking Bill Ross for persuading me
to keep playing football and thanking him, too, for giving me
my old No. 19 jersey.

*I had gotten the same jersey once before. During my senior
season, Coach Bruno told us that if we won the Western Pennsylvania championship, he would give us our orange-and-black jerseys to keep. We won the championship, but Coach Bruno had
to go back on his word. He said that the school board wouldn't
let him give away the jerseys, that the school couldn't afford it.
So a couple of other guys and I broke into the locker room and
borrowed our jerseys. Eventually, the word of our little adventure
spread around, and we had to give back the jerseys.*

Then I told a story about my days at the University of
Alabama, how I didn't have much money there and I applied
for a job working as a chauffeur for a very attractive lady who
lived by herself in a big house. "There were a lot of candidates
for the job," I told the people in Beaver Falls, "but, for some
reason, I was picked. I was the lucky one. I drove the lady
around, did chores for her and one day, when I was putting
away some groceries, she called to me from upstairs and said,
'Joseph, come up to my room.'

"I was very polite. I always did what I was told. I went up
to her room. I walked in, and she said, 'Joseph, take off my
dress.' I was very obedient."

The audience in Beaver Falls began to stir a little nervously.

"Then she said, 'Joseph, take off my slip.' "

I could see my mother turning colors. "Don't worry, Mom,"
I said, interrupting my own story.

"Then the lady said, 'Joseph, take off my bra.' I obeyed.

"Then she said, 'Joseph, take off my panties.' "

My mother looked like she was trying to disappear. I thought
she was going to cover her ears.

"Finally, the lady looked at me and said, 'Now, Joseph, don't
let me ever catch you wearing my clothes again.' "

Even my mother laughed.

I was laughing, too, yet the whole evening had given me a
new feeling for Beaver Falls. I really felt at home, comfortable,
like I was with the people I cared about and the people who
cared about me. I hadn't planned to say much about Beaver

Falls, but I couldn't help myself. "Eventually," I said, "I hope to come back here someday and settle down. I don't like the things there are to do here because there aren't any. But when I do finally get married, and I hope it's sometime in the near future, and I want to get married and have a family, I want to live here."

Damn, I hope Suzie didn't hear that line about the near future.

I'm glad I grew up in Beaver Falls. It was a great place to grow up, with good people, real people, and a river and woods and athletic fields and swimming pools and rock fights and junkyards, everything a kid could want. I remember funny things, and sad times. I remember once, at the golf course where I caddied, a member turning to a young black kid and saying, "Caddie, give me my spoon." The kid never heard of a spoon—hell, even I didn't know it was the No. 3 wood—and he turned the golf bag upside down looking for a spoon. "There ain't no spoon in here," he said, finally, "but I'll go back to the dining room and get you one."

I remember hunting once with a BB gun, and I shot a little bird, and I went over and picked it up, and the bird was still alive and it looked right at me and then closed its eyes and died. I never hunted again.

Coach Bruno finally got his chance to talk. He presented me with a plaque, and coming from him, I really appreciated it. He's a helluva man, a helluva football coach, always thinking. He spent most of the dinner copying down plays that Clive Rush gave him.

Larry Bruno became football coach at Beaver Falls my junior year. I was second-string quarterback most of the season, up from playing fifth-string in my sophomore year, but Coach Bruno started me in the final game, against New Brighton. We won by about fifty points, and I guess that's when Coach Bruno and I and my teammates began thinking we might have a real good team the following year.

We had a great team, a team they still talk about up in that area. We were the first Beaver Falls team in thirty-five years to win the Western Pennsylvania Interscholastic Athletic League title. We won nine straight games. We won our first two easily. Then we played New Castle. We hadn't beaten New Castle in forty years. We hadn't scored a point against them in thirty years. We beat them, 39–0. Then we had our closest game, beating Ambridge, 25–13. I had my worst game statistically, only three completions in fifteen passes, but after the game a doctor told me that I'd played with a shoulder separation. He said I couldn't play any more football all year. I went to an orthopedic man, and I played the next week. We won our last five games without any trouble. We had two great ends, Tom Krzmienski and Tony Golmont, who later had pro tryouts. Eleven men on our team won college scholarships, and all eleven finished four years in college. We were fantastic.

At the end of the ceremonies, I awarded the first Joe Namath Scholarship to a Beaver Falls High School senior football player. I hope the scholarship doesn't mean that he has to follow in my scholastic tradition.

I wasn't exactly a fantastic student. I had close to a C average in high school, and I never worked very hard on my studies. Lots of times, my mother used to say to me, "Joey, why don't you stop playing sports, or just play one sport, and put in more time on your schoolwork." If I'd given up any sport, I'm sure I would have given up football.

After the banquet, most of my family and friends retreated to a party at the Blackhawk Golf Course. We needed something to drink after all those speeches. I guess we drank up all the booze in sight, and then a bunch of us went over to my father's house to play a bowling game he's got in his basement. My brothers and I lied and cheated and yelled at each other, just like always, just having fun. I admired the new rug in my father's house. I'd given it to him as a birthday present.

One of the best things about the success I've had is that I'm able to do little things for my family. Sometimes my mother and my father and my brothers try to stop me. They say, "No, you've done this and you've done that, don't do anything more," and they really feel badly. Well, hell, that's what it's all about. What's it all for if you can't help your own family?

And, shoot, what I've done for them is like nothing next to what they've done for me. They've all helped to get me where I am. My brothers John and Bob teaching me how to throw a football. My brother Frank saving his shoeshine money to buy me a basketball for Christmas. My mother cutting down old uniforms for me. My father encouraging me and cheering me. Hell, if they were in the position I'm in, they'd do the same things for me. I know that. I absolutely know that.

I got to sleep for a couple of hours early in the morning, and then I woke up around eight thirty and went over to my mother's house for breakfast. My brothers Frank and John were around, with their children, and I just relaxed a little, just enjoying the family.

Then my father picked me up to drive me to the Pittsburgh airport, and we gathered together the whole crew that was flying back to New York, my teammates, my friends, the photographers and the writers, the two tension-easers.

The short one had changed her outfit. She wasn't wearing a see-through blouse now. Hell, no. She was wearing see-through pants. She had come down to Sunday breakfast in the Holiday Inn in Beaver Falls, Pennsylvania, wearing her best bare-midriff harem suit.

I don't know if Beaver Falls'll ever be the same.

Jimmy Hart's No Gamble

By John Devaney

*The big surprise of the 1974 National Football League season
was the St. Louis Cardinals. After three straight seasons of
frustration, the Cardinals won their first 7 games of 1974—the
only NFL team to stay undefeated so long—and wound up
in the play-offs for the first time in 27 years. They didn't make
it to the Super Bowl, but that wasn't the fault of their quarterback, Jim Hart.*

*John Devaney, a talented free-lance writer, put together
the following portrait of Hart in 1971, the start of three years
of famine. Now, perhaps, Hart is ready for the feast—a Super
Bowl appearance in his tenth season as a Cardinal.*

Wayne Mulligan hopped crazily from one foot to the other,
cavorting in front of Jimmy Hart, trying to attract the attention of the young quarterback. "Harumph! Harumph!" the
Cardinal center croaked in a frog like voice. "Harumph!
Harumph! Our leader is up to something."

Hart grinned at Mulligan but did not reply. He walked on
toward the Cardinal clubhouse at Busch Stadium, talking in

his easy, casual way to a writer. Jimmy Hart is 26 and the
Cardinals' No. 1 quarterback. He looks more like 16 and a
choirboy: round-cheeked and shiny-faced. The Cardinal
players used to call him Peach Fuzz, and the face is still fuzzy,
but now the Cardinals call him Jimmy, and that's only one
small way things have changed between this team and its
quarterback.

Hart heard Mulligan's laughter floating behind him as we
strolled across the field. "I have this habit of clearing my
throat before I call a play," Hart explained, flushing with
embarrassment. "It's not very loud, only the center can hear
me. But Wayne kids me about it."

He laughed, accepting Mulligan's mimicry for what it was:
kidding done in fun. A year earlier, in the Cardinal clubhouse, Jimmy Hart heard words neither spoken nor accepted
in fun.

"There was nothing direct," Hart remembers. "There'd
be an indirect statement. You could tell by the tone of somebody's voice that what was said was . . ." He pauses.

"Critical?"

"Ummm. Yes. There were some guys for Charley, there
were some guys for me." The face is flushed deeply now. "It
was uncomfortable, a bad situation."

The younger players wanted Jimmy Hart at quarterback, the
older players wanted Charley Johnson. The team, ignited by
championship ambitions, seethed with arguments: We can
win with Charley, we can win with Jimmy. The team won with
neither and finally stopped trying. A team that had won nine
games in 1968 won only four in 1969 and near season's end
Charley Johnson said loudly that either he or coach Charley
Winner had to go.

Winner stayed—on a one-year contract, knowing he had
to win in '70 or be gone. Johnson went to Houston in a trade
and Winner made Hart his man. Near midseason the Cardinals
had forged out in front in the NFC's Eastern Division and
while Hart ranked only ninth among the league's passers, he

was guiding an offense that had averaged 24 points a game.

One Saturday this fall I sat with Charley Winner in his small office under Busch Stadium. Winner is a small, slender, sharp-featured man who reminds you more of a lawyer than a football coach. "You gambled with Jimmy Hart once in 1967 and now you're gambling with him again," I said, more a statement than a question.

Winner stared, hard-eyed, unsmiling. "I gambled with Jimmy Hart in 1967," he said. "I am not gambling with Jimmy Hart this time. Jimmy Hart is no gamble."

Winner's 1967 gamble with Hart led to the Cardinal troubles of 1969. The Cardinals of 1966 had come close to winning the Eastern title, fading only after Johnson was hurt late in the season. The 1967 Cardinals—most of them, like Johnson, in their mid-20s—were convinced they had the blend of youth and experience that could make them the Packers of the late '60s.

A few days before the start of the 1967 season, the Army called on Johnson to serve two years. "It seemed everyone but me knew about Charley going into the Army," Hart said. "He and I were walking home from practice and he told me he'd been called up. The next day it broke in the papers. I was stunned. People told me I was the No. 1 quarterback. I thought: You got to be kidding."

Jimmy Hart had good reason to be amazed. A year earlier every pro team had snubbed him in the college draft. The pros had selected the likes of Jim Leclair of C.W. Post, Dave Neilson of Albion, Ron Meyers of South Dakota State, Benjy Dial of East New Mexico. But not Jimmy Hart of Southern Illinois.

His college coach, Don Shroyer, once had been a Cardinal assistant. Shroyer phoned St. Louis and got someone at the right moment. The Cardinals needed a fifth quarterback at camp to throw to a multitude of receivers. Hart was signed as a free agent, then won a job as the taxi-squad quarterback. Late in 1966, with Johnson hurt, he played about eight minutes of a game. Now, at the start of the 1967 season, he was being thrown into the starting lineup. "I'm going to go all the way with you," Winner told him, emotionally, a few days before the first game. "I could try to make a trade for a veteran quarterback, but I'm not. You have the arm, the release, the potential, everything to be one of this league's greatest quarterbacks."

In his first game an unnerved Hart threw four interceptions and the Cardinals lost. But he showed he could rally the team to come from behind. The Cardinals finished third with a 6-7-1 record. Hart ranked tenth among the league's passers, completing 48 percent of his passes.

In that 1967 season Johnson flew to the games on weekend passes from an Army base in Oklahoma. He stood in his football uniform on the sideline. "I'd see him standing there alone and I knew it hurt him," Hart said, "not being on the field. This had been his team."

In 1968 Johnson, still in the Army, stood on the sideline as the Cardinals finished with a 9-4-1 record, only a half-game away from the first-place Browns, whom they beat twice.

That finish put new visions into the heads of the Cardinal veterans. If they could do that well with a kid quarterback, they could win in 1969 with Johnson. "But Charley," says one Cardinal official, "never had the hardest-throwing arm in the world. When he came out of the Army, whether it was because of rustiness or all the injuries to him over the years, he wasn't throwing the ball real hard at all."

"I knew at the start of training camp that I had to pick either Jimmy or Charley as the No. 1 quarterback," Winner said this October. "I knew there'd be trouble with two No. 1's. We kept statistics on every ball the two of them threw at camp." He jerked a sheaf of papers out of a bottom drawer and waved them at me. "We left nothing to guesswork. Near the end of camp I had made the decision: Jimmy would be the No. 1 quarterback."

But Hart jammed a finger on his throwing hand so Johnson

started the first two games, the Cardinals winning one and losing one. Hart started the next two and again the Cards split.

Johnson thought he should start and so did most of the veterans. Hart, grown confident during his two years as a starter, thought he had proven himself. Cliques formed, lines were drawn, and on the Cardinals you were either for Hart or against Hart, for Johnson or against Johnson.

Winner heard the rumblings. "I was hoping," he said, "that one or the other would take the bull by the horns, have a terrific couple of games, and so out-distance the other that there'd be no question in anyone's mind who was No. 1. But neither one could win the job and it became a bad situation." The Cardinals dropped their final three games, sometimes not seeming to care whether they won or lost.

The blame, said Cardinal players this fall, could be traced to the instabilities inherent in a two-headed offense. "On the pass block," veteran tackle Ernie McMillan said, "I had to protect my inside first with Charley, because he drops back only three yards. With Jimmy, who drops back nine yards, I could concern myself more with the outside rush. But the thing was, going from one quarterback to the other, we weren't reacting automatically."

The receivers also had to adjust to the two quarterbacks. "Say you were supposed to run a pattern to drive back a cornerman," said wide receiver Jon Gilliam. "With Charley you had to make sure to drive your man back ten yards, otherwise he had time to recover while the ball was getting to you. With Jimmy you have to drive him back only five yards. He can't recover in time because Jimmy throws the ball so much faster than Charley. You never got the chance to get down the timing you got to have between a passer and a receiver."

Finally there was the uncertainty in each quarterback's mind. "Both Jimmy and Charley had to wonder: If this play doesn't go, will he take me out and put the other guy in?" said linebacker Larry Stallings. "The uncertainty showed in

Jimmy's play-calling last season and it was reflected in his leadership and all through the offensive unit."

The overall results were a 4-9-1 record and the postseason trade that sent Johnson to Houston for a No. 2 quarterback, Pete Beathard, and defensive back Miller Farr. This summer Cardinal owner Stormy Bidwill was proclaiming a "New Cardinal Era." Probably by no coincidence, of the 40 players on the roster for the 1970 season, 27 were, like Jimmy Hart, with five or fewer years of pro experience.

The Cardinal coaches noticed a change in Hart the day after he heard the trade announced on the radio: "A year ago," says one coach, "you might have seen Jimmy come to the office during the offseason maybe once a week to pick up cans of film to take home. But now he was around here most every day to get film, to talk to the coaches, to keep in shape by playing handball, or to run."

In the opener against the veteran Rams, Hart completed only 12 of 41 as the Rams won easily, 34-14. Against Washington the next week he completed four of eight before someone's flying elbow knocked him out. Beathard came on to guide the team in the second half to a 27-17 victory.

The following week, recovered from the knockout, he sailed two touchdown passes, one to Gilliam covering 59 yards, and the Cardinals upset Dallas, the team that had been favored to win in the NFC East. As the Cardinals got ready to play their fourth game, against the Saints, Hart had completed only 39 percent of his passes but his average gain was a highly respectable 7.38 yards. His interception rate also was high: 5.6 percent.

When I went to Hart's ranch house in the hilly suburbs 25 miles beyond St. Louis, I rang the bell and was greeted by Mary Hart. She had one of their 14-month-old twins and told me Jimmy would be right along; he was changing the diaper of the other twin.

A little later we sat in the living room. Jimmy was dressed like a college senior of the Eisenhower years: a yellow cardigan, neat and conservative plaid slacks, brown loafers, a button-down shirt open at the neck. His close-cropped hair was neatly parted, a mild outgrowth of his college crewcut. He sat at one end of the couch holding little Suzanne, Mary at the other end holding Bradley. At their feet plopped their German shepherd, Sonchin, warily eyeing their two cats, who were preening in the doorway. Later that afternoon Jim would be speaking at a luncheon for the Fellowship of Christian Athletes, of which he is a member. But most afternoons, he says, he likes to flop around the house playing with the twins. His wife calls him a homebody and Jim does not deny it.

He was always shy. His stepfather, he says, "gave me the little shove I needed to get involved in sports when I was a kid." Hart was born in Evanston, Illinois, his father a chauffeur who died when Jim was seven. His mother married a business-man in Morton Grove, Illinois, where Jimmy grew up.

Jimmy played shortstop for the Niles West Township High School. He also played sandlot football, as a quarter-back for a team in a suburban league. "But baseball was the foremost thing in my mind up to my senior year in high school," he said. "I was led to believe by coaches that I had a chance for a career in baseball. I had done nothing in football."

During his junior year Jimmy tried out for the football team and won the passing job—"by default," he said—when the first-string quarterback broke his wrist. His senior year his team won the conference championship and Southern Illinois offered him a football scholarship. "I accepted it but I was hoping I could play baseball down there, too," he said. "I was still hoping at spring practice of my sophomore year. Our quarterback was a terrific thrower and he was like me, he wanted to play baseball.

"He told the football coach that spring that he was going out for baseball. 'Okay,' the coach said. 'But you have no assurance that you will have the quarterback job when you come back.'

"I got the job. That cured me of going out for baseball.

I didn't want anyone to take my job the way I had taken it
from that quarterback."

Southern Illinois won only eight games in Jimmy's three
years at quarterback. "In Jim's senior year," Don Shroyer says,
"I played ten sophs and Jim. I can't count how many passes
were dropped." Jimmy, nevertheless, set most every school
passing record and the Rams wrote to tell him they were
interested. But no one drafted him."

If it hadn't been for Shroyer and his connection with the
Cardinals, it's likely that Jimmy Hart never would have seen
the inside of a pro football camp. (Only two players signed as
free agents are now pro quarterbacks. One is Jimmy, the
other Johnny Unitas.)

Jimmy came to camp with Charley Johnson, Terry Nof-
singer, Buddy Humphrey and Iowa All-America Gary Snook:
all were in front of him. In the 1966 NFL Yearbook Jimmy
Hart's name wasn't even listed on the Cardinal rookie roster.
Snook got hurt, Humphrey cut. "Suddenly I was No. 3,"
Jim said. "I was on the taxi squad and real happy to be there."

A question rose in my mind and I had to ask it: How had a
nice guy like Jim Hart, who once described himself as "always
feeling like the little fellow among the big guys," made himself into the authoritarian pro quarterback?

"I'm not by nature a person who bawls out people . . ."
He stopped and began again. "Some quarterbacks raise hell
for missing a block. But it's hard to see what's happening out
there, especially when it's my job to concentrate on what's
happening downfield, not on what's happening around me.

"I say things to the team in general. 'Hey,' I might say,
'give me a little more time to throw, you guys,' or I'll point
a finger at someone in the huddle and say, 'This play is going
your way, let's give a little extra.' Something like that."

The next afternoon at Busch Stadium, Jimmy Hart handed
off to MacArthur Lane on the second play from scrimmage
and the big halfback tore up the middle for 74 yards and a

touchdown. A little later, the Cardinals still ahead, 7-0, tight end Jackie Smith pulled Hart aside. "On that cut zone they're using," Smith said, "that weak safety can't get over fast enough to cover me."

A few plays later Hart looked for Smith. He saw the weak safety hanging down the middle, too close to Smith, Hart thought. Hart looked away.

Midway through the fourth period the two teams were tied, 17-17. Hart was on his way to his best day passing so far in 1970—18 of 34 for 255 yards. But two interceptions and a lapse in the St. Louis secondary had helped the Saints to stay close.

With 6:40 remaining in the game the Cardinal offense took over with the ball on its own 19. During a TV timeout Smith said to Hart for what he figured was the sixth time that day, "It's there whenever you need it." Again Hart nodded.

Jimmy threw a pass to the left side to Dave Williams, hitting the wide receiver in the chest for a first down on the Cardinal 32. On the next play he threw to Mack Lane cutting over the middle, the big back tumbling to the ground with the ball at the Cardinal 49 for another first down.

The Cardinals huddled. Hart called for the same play—another pass over the middle to Lane. He stepped back nine yards, looked down the middle and saw Lane pressed between two defenders.

He looked elsewhere. *It's there whenever you need it.* He looked for Smith and saw him running all alone at the Saint 30. He threw. The ball arrowed on a shallow arc some 35 yards, dropping into Smith's cupped hands as he ran in full stride, the ball getting there in less time than it took you to read this sentence. Smith ran into the end zone for the touchdown that won the game, 24-17. The first one to arrive in the end zone to shake his hand was Hart.

In the clubhouse later Jimmy Hart tried to hide the pride with a cool, businesslike look on his face as he talked about the game. But sometimes joy clutched at his throat and made him gulp as he answered the writers' questions. He could have made himself a bigger hero; instead he stressed how often Smith had told him he was open. "It sure took me long enough to see Jackie, didn't it?" he said, grinning.

That night he and Mary went to a party at punter Chuck Latourette's house. All the Cardinal players were there, black and white, as well as players who had been pro-Johnson a year earlier. This is a team that had been split along racial lines in 1966, along quarterback lines in 1969. "Now everyone's together," Mary Hart said later to someone. She glanced at her husband, who was in another corner of the room answering the telephone. "It wasn't always like that around here," she said.

18/ PLIMPTON

"Hut-Two-Three ... Ugh!"

By George Plimpton

The history of American sports, like the history of American politics, is filled with men who never rose above the mediocre. But very few athletes, and almost as few politicians, brazenly admitted that their mediocrity was their main strength. George Plimpton is an exception. He is the master of mediocrity; he has elevated his lack of skill to an art form. For the sake of his art, Plimpton has been a mediocre pitcher, a mediocre basketball player, a mediocre fighter, a mediocre comedian, a mediocre musician, a mediocre circus performer, a mediocre golfer and, to justify his place in this book, a mediocre quarterback.

All of this unskilled labor would have been wasted, except for the fact that Plimpton as a journalist and writer is anything but mediocre. He has a keen eye, a keen ear and an abiding sense of his own frailties. He also maintains a reasonable degree of awe for the people who are able to do with flair the things he does with flaws. Plimpton has turned out a number of books, starting with his memorable series of Paris Review *interviews with writers. His most notable book has been* Paper Lion, *a literary and commercial success but a celluloid failure (the movie version featured Alan Alda as George Plimpton, a lapse in his past that Alda, through* M.A.S.H., *has been able to overcome). The following*

article, excerpted and adapted from Paper Lion, *appeared in*
Sports Illustrated. *It is included here for several reasons: In the
first place, it reads good; second, it's different and interesting (to
fit my original definition of a quarterback). Most important,
Plimpton's here because he makes the editor's job easier. It's still
tough to decide who's the best quarterback in the book, but it's
a snap to name the worst. George doesn't mind the abuse. He's
suffering all the way to the bank, presumably the Dry Dock
Savings Bank in New York, for which he does commercials.*

    *Incidentally, of the 17 quarterbacks profiled within these
pages, Plimpton is the only one who went to an Eastern college
(Harvard). That tells you all you need to know about the relative
quality of Eastern football.*

The Detroit Lion players were all interested in what my first
reactions would be quarterbacking in the intra-squad scrimmage in Pontiac, Mich.—how my amateur's eyes would take in
the world they knew so well. Wayne Walker, the big linebacker,
thinking back on his first days as a professional, had an idea that
the light seems to dim, that on the first two or three plays one's
concentration is such that general observation is difficult.

    "Everything gets dark," he had told me, "like seeing every-
thing from a dark tunnel."

    "You mean that the peripheral vision goes?" I had asked
mournfully. "That's about the only physical attribute that
. . . well, that I might possess."

    The night before the game I had dropped in on Milt Plum
and Earl Morrall, the Detroit quarterbacks, in their dormitory
rooms at the Cranbrook training camp, hoping they might have
some advice to offer.

    "Wayne Walker tells me everything's going to go black," I
said.

    They grinned and looked at each other. "Well, he's blunt
enough about it," Morrall said.

"He didn't mean I was going to get hit," I said hastily. I explained what he had said about the field of vision seeming to diminish. The two quarterbacks said that was new to them, but they both spoke of the advantages of peripheral vision—"a type of split vision," was how Morrall described it. "Tomorrow night," he said to me, "suppose you run your pass play 93 [one of the five plays I was going to call]. Once you're back in the pocket here's what you *should* see: you spot your short receiver, the No. 3 man, and you see how he is going. Then you pick up the long man, the No. 9, to see if the defensive safety's got him covered, then back to the 3 man, and you throw to him"— Morrall slapped his fist into his palm—"unless the linebackers are in his zone, in which case you throw out into the right flat to your swing man, the safety valve. Then you have, in addition, the 8 man going down 10 yards on the left and buttonhooking, so that actually you have four possible receivers in an arc of 180° —and since you've only got two or three seconds, once you're in the pocket, to pick one of those people out, you can see how helpful a wide angle of vision can be."

"Of course, the angle seems to widen with experience," Plum said. "When you start out and don't know quite where to look, it's as thin as a flashlight beam, which is what Walker is saying."

"Pass patterns are set up to help you see your receivers fast," said Morrall. "Both your primary receivers are usually on a direct line of sight from you. For example, tomorrow night"— every time he said "tomorrow" I could feel my stomach tighten —"if your short man is covered, all you've got to do is raise your eyes, like clicking the sight up on a rifle, and there's the long man on the same line."

The two quarterbacks began talking about the other mandatory attributes of their position.

Morrall said: "If you could put a quarterback together with all the skills he ought to have, you'd give him, first, speed— speed going back those seven yards into the pocket, which a quarterback like Van Brocklin had. This gave him time to see

the action and the pass patterns develop. Then you'd give him
the ability to fake well, which Y. A. Tittle and Eddie LeBaron
have: good dramatics and action, good enough to make the
defense lean the wrong way. And then, of course, an arm, a
good arm, and strong."

"I'd put that first," Plum said. "The coaches look for someone who can throw the ball 50 yards, and almost on a line. In
college there's not much emphasis on pass defense—it takes too
long to develop a good one. With your receivers getting 10 yards
clear of the defense, you can loft the ball without danger. But
any pass which gets up in the air in this league will have four
defenders crowding around waiting for it to come down—like
an infield pop in baseball."

They could see from my fidgeting that I was uncomfortable
as they put together their composite superquarterback. On the
training field both of them had seen my passing efforts, which
over the length of 20 yards began to develop the high trajectory
of a howitzer shell. "Look," said Morrall. "You don't need to
worry tomorrow. Call plays that get the ball to the running
backs. Make those people pick up the yardage for you."

I was ready to follow this advice when Coach George Wilson
sent me in as his starting quarterback the next evening. As I ran
out across the sidelines the teams were waiting on the offensive
unit's 20-yard line. The kickoff was dispensed with. In the
controlled scrimmage the defense would get one point for keeping the offense from getting a first down, two points for an
interception or a fumble recovery. The scoring for the offense
was regular.

Bud Erickson, the Lions' publicity man, was on the public
address system telling the crowd how the scoring would work.
It was a sellout crowd, packing the high stands that flanked the
field, out to see the season's first appearance of the Lions. The
rookies would be of particular interest to them. They had settled in their seats, watching me trot along the sidelines, my
number, which was zero, staring up at them like an eye. They
listened to Erickson explain that "number zero," coming out,

was not actually a rookie but an amateur, a writer, who had been training with the team for three weeks and had learned five plays, which he was now going to run against the first-string Detroit defense. It was a nightmare come true, he told them, as if one of them, rocking a beer around in a paper cup, with a pretty girl leaning past him to pay the hot-dog vendor in the aisle, had been suddenly carried down underneath the stands by a sinister clutch of ushers and encased in the accouterments (the tape, the supporter, the wraparound girdle, the thigh pads, the arm pads, the shoulder pads, the sweat shirt, the jersey, the silver helmet with the two protruding bars of the cage jammed down over his ears) and sent out to take over the team. The crowd was interested, and I was conscious, though just vaguely, of a steady roar of encouragement.

My team, the first-string Lion offense, was waiting for me, grouped in the huddle, watching me come, their faces unrecognizable, lost in the shadows of their helmets. For the first call the running play I had available for them—following Plum's and Morrall's advice—was the 26 near o pinch. In it the quarterback receives the snap, turns and takes two steps straight back and hands the ball off to his 2 back coming laterally across from right to left. The ballcarrier then cuts into the No. 6 hole (the holes are numbered 9-7-5-3-1 from the right, and 0-2-4-6-8 leading out to the left). That is what is designated by 26—the 2 back into the 6 hole. The mysterious code words "near o pinch" referred to blocking assignments in the line, and I was never sure exactly what was meant by them.

I went into the huddle and called out, "Twenty-six!" forcefully, to inspire them, and a voice from one of the helmets said, "Down. Down. The whole stadium can hear you."

"Twenty-six," I now hissed at them. "Twenty-six near O pinch, on three! Break!" Their hands cracked as one, and they streamed past me out of the huddle, moving up to the line of scrimmage fast as I wheeled and started for the line behind them.

I kept my eye on Bob Whitlow, my center, as he trotted up

over the ball, and I followed in his tracks. Earl Morrall had told me that sometimes a quarterback, distracted, will stray off center as he walks up to the line of scrimmage, concentrating on the alignment of the defensive backs, perhaps considering the advisability of calling a checkoff play, and he will step up not behind the center but behind a guard, whose eyes widen inside his helmet as he feels the unfamiliar pressure of a hand under his backside, and more often than not he bolts across the line and causes an off-side penalty. On one occasion Jug Girard, playing quarterback then, stepped up behind a guard by error, but his count was so quick that the play was under way before the guard could demur, and the center beside him popped the ball back. It shot straight up in the air as the two lines came together, as if squeezed up like a peach pit by the pressure.

So I kept an eye on Whitlow, who was poised over the ball, and I ambled up behind him and rested a hand at the base of his spine, as if on a windowsill, a nonchalant gesture I had admired in certain quarterbacks, and I looked out over the length of his back to fix in my mind what I saw.

I had the sense of a portcullis down. On the other side of the imaginary bars the linemen were poised, the light glistening off their helmets; behind them the linebackers were drawn in close. Joe Schmidt was just opposite me, the big number 56 shining on his white jersey, jumping back and forth in quick, choppy steps, his hands poised in front of him, and he was calling out the defensive code words—colors they happened to be, "blue! blue! blue!" which indicated a variety of zone coverage or "red! red! red!" which designated man-on-man coverage. The defensive code words varied. When Jim Ninowski, a former Lion quarterback, was traded from Detroit to Cleveland, the defensive signals, which Ninowski knew, of course, had to be changed when the two teams met—from colors to girl's names, it was decided. One of them was Ninowski's young wife's name —Judy, I think it was. He would call a play in the huddle and come up behind his center to hear the linebackers across the line all hollering "Judy! Judy! Judy!" The Lions hoped that this would jar him somewhat. I had only the vaguest idea what these code words meant and could not have used such knowledge to advantage, since I knew no checkoff plays. "Jumbo!" was the only cry I had an ear cocked for—the linebackers' signal that the quarterback rush was on, the red dog.

I cleared my throat and began the signals. The count begins with three meaningless numbers. I have a sort of New England cosmopolitan accent, often mistaken for an English accent, and the Lions delighted in imitating my signal calls—"fawty-fowah! fawty-tew!" I'd hear them yelling in the shower after practice —so I avoided such numbers. I had a harmless non-accent number ready at hand to start the series: 16.

"Set!" I called out, my voice loud and astonishing to hear, as if it belonged to someone shouting into the ear holes of my helmet, "16, 66, 55, *hut* one, *hut* two, *hut* three," and at "three" the ball slapped back into my palm. The lines cracked together with a yawp and smack of pads and gear, and I had the sense of quick, heavy movement as I turned for the backfield. Not having taken more than a step, I was hit hard from the side, and as I gasped, the ball was jarred loose.

My first thought was that at the snap of the ball the right side of the line had been engulfed as I turned and stepped back for the hand-off. Someone, I assumed, had messed up on the assignments designated by the mysterious code words "near O pinch." In fact, my own man had bowled me over—John Gordy, whose assignment as offensive guard was to pull from his position and join the interference on the far side of the center. He was required to pull back and travel at a great clip parallel to the line of scrimmage to get out in front of the runner, his route theoretically passing between me and the center. But the creaking execution of my turn put me in his path, a rare sight for Gordy to see, his own quarterback blocking the way, like coming around a corner in a high-speed car to find a moose ambling across the center line. He careened off me, jarring the ball loose, and I stumbled after it, hauling it under me five yards back of the line of scrimmage, hearing the rush of feet and the heavy jarring and wheezing of the blockers fending off the defense, a great roar coming up from the crowd and, above it, a relief to hear, the shrilling of the referee's whistle.

It was not new for me to be hit down by my own people. At Cranbrook I was knocked down all the time by players on the offense—the play patterns run with such speed along routes so carefully defined that each player had to do everything right and at the proper speed for the play not to break down in its making. I was often reminded of movie film clips in which the process of a porcelain vase, say, being dropped by a butler and smashed, is shown in reverse, so that the pieces pick up off the floor and soar up to the butler's hand, each piece on a predestined route, sudden perfection out of chaos. Often it did not take more than an inch or so off line to throw a play out of kilter. On one occasion, while practicing hand-off plays to the fullback, I had my chin hanging out just a bit too far, something wrong with my posture, and Pietrosante's shoulder pad caught it like a punch as he went by, and I spun slowly to the ground, grabbing at my jaw. Carl Brettschneider, one of the linebackers, said that afternoon: "The defense is going to rack you up one of these days—that is, if your own team would let you stand long enough for us defense guys to get at you. It's aggravating to bust through and find that you've already been laid flat by your own guys."

The referee took the ball from me and set it down. Whitlow was calling the huddle together. My confidence had not gone. Next on my list was the 93 pass, a play that I had worked successfully in the Cranbrook scrimmages. In the huddle I called with considerable enthusiasm, "All right! All *right!* Here we *go!*"

"Keep your voice down," said a voice. "You'll tip the play."

I leaned in on them and said, "Green right ["green" designated a pass play, "right" put the flanker to the right side], three right [which put the three back to the right], 93 [indicating the two primary receivers: 9 the right end, and 3 the 3 back] on three! Break!" The clap of hands again in unison, then the team hurried past me up to the line, and I walked briskly up behind Whitlow.

I knew exactly how the play was going to develop—back those seven yards into the defensive pocket for the couple of seconds it was supposed to hold, and Pietrosante, the 3 back, would go down in his pattern, 10 yards straight, then cut over the middle, and I would hit him.

"Set! 16!—88!—55!"

All quarterbacks have different moves getting back to the pocket, some of them turning away from the line at the snap and scampering for the pocket, wasting as few of the allotted seconds as possible to get there, then turning again to look downfield, but most backpedal, moving back with near disdain, watching downfield. This has the advantage of letting the quarterback observe the play unfold from the start and the patterns develop. My own style was to get to the pocket as quickly as I could, turning and racing for it.

"Hut one, *hut* two, *hut* three."

The ball slapped into my palm at "three." I turned and started back. I could feel my balance going, and two yards behind the line of scrimmage I fell down—absolutely flat, as if my feet had been pinned under a trip wire stretched across the field—not a hand laid on me. I heard a great roar go up from the crowd. Suffused as I had been with confidence, I could scarcely believe what had happened. Cleats catching in the grass? Slipped in the dew? I felt my jaw go ajar in my helmet. "Wha'? Wha'?" —the mortification beginning to come fast. I rose hurriedly to my knees, the referee's whistle bleating, and I could see my teammates' big silver helmets with the blue Lion decals turn toward me, some of the players rising from blocks they'd thrown to protect me, their faces masked, automatons, prognathous with the helmet bars protruding toward me, characterless, yet the dismay was in the set of their bodies as they loped back for the huddle.

I joined them, there being no alternative. "Sorry, sorry," I said.

"Call the play, man," came a voice from one of the helmets.

The third play on my list was the 42, another running play, one of the simplest in football, in which the quarterback receives the snap, makes a full spin and shoves the ball into the 4 back's stomach. He has come straight forward from his fullback position as if off starting blocks, his knees high, and he disappears with the ball into the No. 2 hole just to the left of the center—a straight power play and one which seen from the stands seems to offer no difficulty.

I got into an awful jam with it. Once again the jackrabbit speed of the professional backfield was too much for me. The fullback, Danny Lewis, was past me and into the line before I could complete my spin and set the ball in his belly. The fullback can't pause in his drive for the hole, which is what he must keep his eye on, and it is the quarterback's responsibility to get the ball to him. The procedure in the forlorn instance of missing the connection and holding the ball out to the seat of the fullback's pants as he tears by is for the quarterback to tuck the ball under his arm and try to follow the fullback into the line, hoping that he may have budged open a small hole.

I tried to follow Lewis, grimacing, and waiting for the impact, which came before I'd taken two steps. I was grabbed up by Roger Brown, a 300-pound tackle. For his girth he is called Rhinofoot by his teammates, or Haystack, and while an amiable citizen off the field, with idle pursuits—learning very slowly to play the saxophone, a sharp dresser, affecting a narrow-brimmed porkpie hat with an Alpine brush—on the field he is the anchor of the Lions' front line, an All-League player, and anybody is glad not to have to play against him.

He had tackled me high and straightened me up with his power, so that I churned against him like a comic bicyclist. Still upright, to my surprise, I began to be shaken around and flayed back and forth, and I realized that he was struggling for the ball. The bars of our helmets were nearly locked, and I could look through and see him inside—the first helmeted face I recognized that evening—the small, brown eyes surprisingly peaceful, but he was grunting hard, the sweat shining, and I had time to think, "It's Brown, it's *Brown!*" before I lost the ball to him. Flung to one knee, I watched him lumber into the end zone behind us for a touchdown.

The referee wouldn't allow it. He said he'd blown the ball dead while we were struggling for it. Brown was furious. "You taking that away from me," he said, his voice high and squeaky. "Man, I took that ball in there good."

The referee turned and put the ball on the 10-yard line. I had lost 10 yards in three attempts, and I had yet, in fact, to run off a complete play. Preliminaries had undone me—handling the ball from center, the spin, then being frustrated by being knocked over by my own men or missing the hand-off, or taking a pratfall, so that the play had yet to be developed fully. It was vaguely like turning the ignition key without the dignity of hearing the motor turn over, perhaps having it fall out of the bottom of the car instead.

The veterans walked back very slowly to the next huddle. They had wanted me to succeed. The first time George Wilson had sent me in to run a play in the training camp at Cranbrook the rookies happened to be in the offensive lineup, and the veterans, in a block, came hurrying after me onto the field of their own volition, wanting to see that I got the best protection, and there were quickly 20 men in the huddle, a lot of pushing and murmuring as the rookies were replaced, and I could hear George Wilson calling out: "What's going on there?"

But now they were dispirited, and when I called my fourth play—a slant pass to the 9 man, the strong-side end, Jim Gibbons—that crack of the hands as we left the huddle was missing, possibly because I had forgotten to give them the signal on which the ball was to be snapped. "Two!" I called in a stage whisper as we headed for the line, holding my fingers spread in a V and showing it around furtively, trying to hide it from the defense and hoping my people would see.

The pass was incomplete. I took two steps back (the play was a quick pass), and I saw Gibbons, who is tall, break, then stop, buttonhooking. His hand came up, but I threw the ball over his head. It was my first play of the evening, however, which functioned as a play should, and so did the next one, a pitchout play to Pietrosante, the last of my series. But the defense was keyed for it. One of my linemen told me later that the defensive man opposite him in the line, Floyd Peters, had said, "Well, here comes the 48 Pitchout" (they knew my repertoire), and it *had* come, and they were able to throw Pietrosante on the one-yard line, just a yard away from the complete humiliation of having moved a team backward from the 20-yard line to a safety.

I left quickly, as soon as I saw Pietrosante go down, heading for the bench on the sidelines at midfield. It was a long run, and I felt utterly weary, shuffling along through the grass. I heard applause, and I looked up and saw some people standing, and the hands going. I thought about the applause afterward—some of it, perhaps, in appreciation of the lunacy of my participation, but it occurred to me that most of it, even subconsciously, was in relief that I had done as badly as I had. It verified the assumption that the ordinary citizen could not survive in the brutal world of professional football. If by some chance I had uncorked a touchdown pass, there would have been wild acknowledgment—because I heard the groans go up at each successive disaster—but afterward the spectators would have felt uncomfortable. The proper order of things would have been upset. The outsider did not belong, and there was satisfaction in that being proved.

Some of the applause, as it turned out, came from people who had enjoyed the humorous aspects of my stint, and more than a few thought they were being entertained by a professional comic in the tradition of baseball's Al Schacht or bullfight clowns. Bud Erickson, who had been announcing on the public address system, told me that a friend of his had come up to him later. "Bud, that's one of the funniest damn—I mean that guy's *got* it," this man had said, barely able to control himself.

I did not take my helmet off when I reached the bench. It was

painful to do—wrenching it past my ears—and there was
security in having it on. I was conscious of the big zero on my
back facing the crowd when I sat down. I heard someone
yelling my name. I turned around and saw a girl leaning over
the rail of the grandstand. I recognized her from a dance place
in Dearborn where I'd gone with some of the team. She was
wearing an Italian mohair sweater, the color of pink spun sugar,
tight pants, and she was holding a thick folding wallet in one
hand along with a pair of dark glasses, and in the other a Lion
banner which she waved, her face alive with excitement, very
pretty in a perishable, childlike way, and she was calling,
"Beautiful! It was beautiful!"

I looked at her out of my helmet, lifting a hand just tenta-
tively to acknowledge her enthusiasm, and I turned back to
watch the field, where the true scrimmage was getting under
way.

After the scrimmage the disappointment stuck, and it was
hard to ease. It was quiet in the bus going back, everyone tired,
thinking back on the game. We were a long time blocked in
traffic outside Pontiac, but no one complained. It was dark
inside. I was sitting alone. George Wilson came down the aisle.
I was feeling low, and he knew it. He sat down, and looked, and
began talking easily—not a word about the scrimmage but
about football in general. He talked about the character of the
football player—Bobby Layne, the Detroit quarterback, whose
teams would take anything from him because he performed,
and at the base of it was the urge, if you wanted to play football,
to knock someone down; that was what the sport was all about,
the will to win closely linked with contact. He talked about
coaching, too, about its complexities, speaking almost with
regret, as if the pleasures of the game, with its fundamental
simplicity of physical contact, were unavailable if you were
watching from the sidelines, as if it were a frustration and a
nuisance to find self-expression in the action of others. No
matter, he said. It was a tough and absorbing job, marshaling
a host of minutiae within seconds and applying knowledge or

intuition to make a decision whose circumstances—since only
14 games were played a season—could cost him his job, even
though often something would happen, like a fumble, a penalty
or an injury, that removed the reins and made the coach as
much of a bystander as the fellow ripping tickets in half at the
gate or the hot-dog vendor in the aisles. And yet the disaster
on the field was his doing and his responsibility.

All of this made my own disaster seem far less important—
which Wilson had calculated, I'm sure, and it was easy to sense
why his men had such respect for him. "He's a players' coach,"
they said of him, as opposed to such Procrustean coaches as
Tom Landry at Dallas, who, or so players' gossip had it, pulled
the main switch at 10:30 to darken the training-camp dormito-
ries—the big deer-hunting lamps came out, the beams criss-
crossing the walls—or Vince Lombardi of the Green Bay Packers, the archrivals, who thought of players as "kids" and whom
the Lions referred to as the Jap.

The players themselves were concerned about my well-being.
A group of them took me out that night, a long, tearing night
through the Dearborn dance halls, celebrating, all of them
shouting, "Fawty-fowah, fawty-tew!" from time to time, fuss-
ing, and making me feel as though I had really done something
more than play the fool, until I began to say, "No, no, it was
nothing at all, really."

I lost my car somewhere, and by the time I'd recovered it and
got back to Cranbrook the sun was up. It was going to be a hot
day. I knew the heat would begin to build up in my room, but
the bed looked inviting. I hadn't been asleep for more than what
seemed a minute when I heard a voice sing out: "Up you get
there, rook'. No time for lying around."

I looked, and it was Harley Sewell standing in the door, one
of the finest offensive guards. He had been 11 years in the National Football League. He had pale, thinning hair, a rolling
gait like a sailor's, and was small in stature for a lineman (his
weight was in the record books as 230, though he looked much

lighter), but when he put his mind to something he was very insistent, and this determination was obviously a major part of his equipment. A Texan, born in a place called St. Jo, he kept after me to come down to his part of the world in the off season and try my hand at riding broncos. He was absolutely determined about it.

He'd say, "Now, when you coming down to ride them broncos?"

"Well, Harley, I don't know. . . ."

"I'd sure like for you to have that experience."

"Well, Harley. . . ."

"No trouble 'tall to set it up for you."

"Harley. . . ."

"When you think you can come?"

"Sometime in the off season," I'd say.

After the Pontiac scrimmage—I was told later—he had come looking for me in the dormitory. I would be downcast after my sorry performance and in need of company. He thought I would like a pizza pie, for some reason, so he had gone off in his car and gotten one somewhere, which he put on the back seat. Only two or three players were in the dormitory when he got there, chatting in one of the rooms about the scrimmage, and Harley appeared in the door, holding the big pizza in front of him. "Where's the rook' at?" he had asked.

They told him they thought I was off at the Club Gay Haven, a sort of twist palace, with some of the others. He waited around for a while, and they shared the pizza, though Harley kept a big piece of it in case I turned up. He left finally, and now here he was at 8 in the morning.

I had a sudden premonition that he had some broncos ready for me, waiting, outside on the lawn. "Wha'? Wha'?" I said. I sat up in bed. His two children were with him, staring around from behind him.

"Time to be up," Harley said.

"What time is it?" I asked.

"Eight," he said.

"God, Harley, I only just got in. I only had two hours' sleep."

"Time's awasting," he said. "We'll go for a drive."

"Harley, I've been in a police station, and I've. . . ."

He disappeared with his children, but they were back after a minute or so with coffee and rolls from the dining room. "These'll fix you up," Harley said.

I groaned and got up to dress.

"It's best to keep your mind occupied," Harley said.

"Harley, I was asleep."

"You would've waked up wrong," Harley said.

We went riding through the country in his station wagon. His children sat quietly in the back seat, flanking a lawnmower Harley had borrowed and had been meaning to return. When I closed my eyes I could feel sleep rock toward me, so I kept the window down to let the warm air hit, and I tried to keep my mind on what Harley was saying. He was talking about the tough people he had played against, the enormous defensive tackles and guards he had tried to clear out for the offensive backs, and the humiliations he had been forced to suffer. He was trying to make me feel better about my own humiliations the night before. He talked about Big Daddy Lipscomb. Harley said that he had played against him a number of times and that while he was one of the best, and he'd been humiliated by him for sure, he was not as good as Henry Jordan of the Green Bay Packers, who was faster and trickier and much harder on a good day than Big Daddy on an average day. Occasionally Big Daddy would put his mind to it, and then he was invincible. Harley's worst day against him was in the 1963 Pro Bowl Game, when he just couldn't handle him, so he came out and someone else went in to try, and couldn't and Forrest Gregg tried and couldn't, so finally they double-teamed him, two men driving at him, and that helped, but not much.

I asked Harley why Baltimore had traded such a valuable property, even if he did have a bad day or so, to the Pittsburgh Steelers. Well, they'd had problems with him, Harley told me: he was not an easy man, being prideful and quick-tempered, and on one occasion, the year before he was traded, one of the Colts gave a party to which Big Daddy was not invited. He prowled around until the idea that he was being snubbed got the better of him. He turned up at the party and threw the host through a window. There was a big ruckus, of course, particularly since the host, who was a very fleet scatback, cut a tendon in his ankle going through the glass. After that they didn't think they could keep Big Daddy.

"The vision I have of him," I said dreamily, "is him sitting in a dentist's chair."

"What's that?" asked Harley sharply.

"I've read somewhere he couldn't stand pain," I explained. "He wouldn't get in a destist's chair unless he had his wife with him, sitting on his lap, to calm him down at the slightest twinge. I never can think of him without seeing that dentist trying to get his job done with those two people sitting in his chair, and having to work around the girl to get at Big Daddy wearing one of those little bibs."

"I don' see Big Daddy like that 't'll," said Harley. "Regretfully, I see him down across the line from me, maybe that shirt out and hanging down behind him like a tail, and then trying to move that boy—like running up agin a barn."

Big Daddy had died earlier in the year of an overdose of drugs, but his presence had been such that Harley spoke of him as if he were still around.

"I'll tell you something, though—he could be humiliated," said Harley, and went on to explain that Lipscomb had a flaw Detroit was able to take advantage of, which was that he liked to pursue and tackle in the open field, preferably by the sidelines, where he could knock his man down in full view of the great crowds who had come to watch him do such things. He would reach down and pick his victim up by the shoulder pads, set him on his feet and whack his rear with a big hand.

The Detroit ruse was to get Big Daddy to range off toward the sidelines looking to make such a play, and then run the ball through his vacated position. The play was called 47 o cross-

buck takeoff, and it required the guard opposite Big Daddy—
Harley, say—to pull from his position, indicating that he was
leading the interference in a move toward the end, sucking out
Big Daddy with him, and then the back—usually Pietrosante
—would light out through the 7 hole with the ball. Of course,
if Big Daddy didn't fall for it and stayed there in the 7 hole,
refusing to trail out after the guard, it suddenly became very
unpleasant for Pietrosante, and humiliating for him. But he was
a showboat sort, Big Daddy, and the chances were—at least, at
the beginning of his career—that he'd move off laterally after
the guard, the long jersey shirttail, which always came out
toward the end of a game, trailing behind him.

"He had his bad days, I'll tell you," said Harley, looking over
at me.

"Like mine?" I said, grinning at him.

"Sure," he said, quite seriously.

Harley turned off the road, and we drove up a short driveway
to a house on a wooded ridge. Friends of his were waiting on
a screened-in porch. He hadn't told me we were going there, but
it was like him not to. I was introduced around. Coffee was
brought out. They'd heard about the game, and they were eager
to get the details of my participation.

I sat down and took some coffee. I rather looked forward to
telling them. "Well, it was a disaster," I said. "Just awful."

Harley was out in the kitchen overseeing something or other,
the cutting of coffee cake, and he came hurrying in. He said,
"Well, hold on now, I don't know about that."

"Come on, Harley," I said, grinning at him. "I lost 20 yards
in five tries, fell down without anyone laying a hand on me, then
had the ball stolen by Roger Brown, then threw the ball at least
10 feet over Jim Gibbons' head—that's pretty awful. . . ."

Harley said, "You didn't do too bad . . . considering." He was
very serious, really trying, consciously, to keep me from
remembering and being humiliated.

"Harley," I said, "you're just a poor judge of disasters."

The others on the porch kept after me for details, but Harley wouldn't let me discuss the subject. "It don't do any good dwelling on such things," he said.

"Aw, come on, Harley," they said.

"No sir!" he said.

So we humored him and talked about other things, and eventually I managed to tell them just enough about the game to satisfy them, though we waited until Harley was off the porch, out on the lawn with his children.

He drove me back to Cranbrook after a while. It had been a pleasant morning, and I told him so, standing in the driveway, hands on the car door, though Harley, inside behind the wheel, continued to look preoccupied. He was still worried about my state of mind. "The thing is not to fret on it," he said. "Your luck wasn't running too good. Just forget it, and get yourself going again."

"Listen, Harley," I said, "I really am grateful to you."

"When you wake up it'll be all right."

"Sure," I said.

19/GILLIAM

The Trials of a
Rookie Quarterback
(Who Happens to Be Black)

By Phil Musick

Funny thing about those black guys. They make terrific tackles, great running backs, fantastic pass defenders. They sure know how to get into the rhythm of the game. But you can't put them at linebacker, or at quarterback. Oh, no. Those positions require too much intelligence, too much decision making and too much leadership. Besides, they've got weak ankles.

That's more or less how the party line in pro football used to go in the days when Jimmy Brown was eating up yardage, Big Daddy Lipscomb was eating up ballcarriers and Em Tunnell and Night Train Lane were eating up errant passes. Then along came Dave Robinson, and then Willie Lanier, to rip the linebacker myth, and many ballcarriers, to shreds. The myth about black quarterbacks is dying, too.

Until recently, gifted black quarterbacks who turned professional could generally count on getting a fair chance—at a different job, like defensive back or wide receiver. Willie Wood of the Packers, for instance, was a black quarterback transformed into an All-Pro safety; Marlin Briscoe of the Dolphins was advised to stop throwing passes and to start catching them. One of the most amusing developments in college football was the arrival several years ago of a white quarterback at Grambling College, the predominantly black school that turns out all-pros with startling regularity. What did Grambling do with its white signal-caller? Converted him to defensive back. He probably had weak ankles, anyway.

Joe Gilliam is not the first black man to start a National Football League game at quarterback, but he could, in time, be the best. He got his chance in 1973, when Terry Bradshaw and Terry Hanratty of the Steelers both fell victim to physiology, and although he didn't threaten any records, Gilliam demonstrated he could throw bullets, often straight at the target. What's more, playing on a team that lists Louisiana Terry Bradshaw as its regular quarterback and blacks Franco Harris, Mean Joe Greene and Dwight White as its stars, it would be a terrible thing to say that Gilliam is not bright enough or light enough to lead those men.

Phil Musick, a top-notch Pittsburgh newspaperman, wrote this profile of Gilliam in 1972, when the black quarterback was a rookie, trying only to match the modest success of an earlier black quarterback, James Harris. Gilliam's goals are higher now.

On July 12, Joe Gilliam, rookie quarterback, reported to the Pittsburgh Steelers training camp. Joe Gilliam, *black* rookie quarterback. An anomaly, as it were. A surfer in the Sahara; Dayan at an Arab League picnic; Woody Allen at Muscle Beach; a poker player with a facial tic. You get the message.

There are, of course, no such things as black quarterbacks; only figments of the liberal imagination. Somewhere on their way to the pocket—poof!—they become defensive backs, flankers, pulling guards, automobile mechanics, insurance salesmen. The prototype black quarterback was Choo-Choo Charlie Brackins, who is best remembered for not having played the position for Green Bay in 1955. There have been several since, all converted to their rightful place in the natural scheme of things,

among them Eldridge Dickey. This year there are four, none of
them competing for a No. 1 spot. James Harris made it at
Buffalo—does anyone ever really make it in Buffalo? John Wal-
ton is with Los Angeles, Karl Douglas is with Baltimore and
then there's Gilliam. Joe Gilliam knows all about Dickey, his
predecessor at Tennessee State. He shakes his head when he
thinks about Dickey getting only a cursory look at Oakland as
a quarterback.

"Dickey was the best I ever saw. He had as much talent as
Terry Bradshaw," he says. "I can't understand why he didn't
make it. Dickey is so talented. So. . . ."

So black he could not survive the National Football League
stereotype that has resulted in only a rare black playing quarterback or center or middle linebacker, the "thinking" positions?
So it is that Gilliam often thinks about his buddy, Eldridge
Dickey, the noted pass receiver.

But, despite history, the color of his skin is the least of
Gilliam's worries as training camp opens. The competition he
faces is established and experienced. Behind the Steeler regular
Bradshaw, the man with the golden arm, are Terry Hanratty,
the ex-Notre Dame All-American, and Bob Leahy, a steady cab
squad veteran. Two quarterbacks will make the roster, one will
make the taxi squad, one will make the unemployment office.
Gilliam tries to forget about the color of his skin.

"They're all the same . . . lazy," I remember hearing a Steeler
assistant coach blurt in a moment of bitter frustration. "No,
damn, I don't mean that . . . but some of them are." Can you
dig what that line of reasoning can mean to the making, or
unmaking, of Joe Gilliam? Gilliam can dig it. Humorously:
"I'm not going to wake up tomorrow white." Emotionally: "I
don't know how the players feel, man!" Intellectually: "If I go
around thinking 'I'm a black quarterback,' I will misinterpret
people, attitudes, occurrences." Rationally: "What can I do
about it?" Hopefully: "I hope they accept me."

Yeah, Joe Gilliam can dig it, but he correctly senses he will
not be judged by his color. Not because he purposely stumbled

to a slow 5.0 clocking for 40 yards—to prevent being switched to another position, nor because he is too light to play another position, but because of two men, Art Rooney and Chuck Noll. Rooney owns the Steelers and for 39 years he has treated them as he would have an affectionate but not-quite-bright child.

Held together by a common bond, suffering, the franchise has become one of benevolent paternalism, and therefore, an excellent site for a black rookie quarterback. Art Rooney grew up on the mean streets of Pittsburgh's North Side at a time when people spit on Irishmen. Without hesitation he refers to Gilliam as "a nice boy." Yeah, the location is fatherly and right.

The Steeler coach, Noll, is a man of single purpose and is honest enough to say, "I'm not aware of the color of his skin, or I don't think I am." Gilliam nods: "He wants to win too bad to let anything interfere." So the coach is right. All of this is to say that in his attempt to become pro football's first outstanding black quarterback, Joe Gilliam is surrounded by reasonable people. His blackness will not weigh heavily against him. A ten-year white veteran, Ray Mansfield, says, "I think the older white guys are really pulling for him. In this age of awareness most of us feel it is time for a black quarterback and then, selfishly, we'd like to see it happen for the sake of team unity." The black veterans watch the situation closely to see, as one says, "if they give him the shaft." But offensive captain John Brown, a black and perhaps the most widely respected player on the team, says simply: "The time is right."

And on this sultry July day—the mugginess almost visible as it drifts across the Alleghenies to the Steeler training camp 40 miles east of Pittsburgh—Joe Gilliam hopes it is. It is his first day as a pro. The sun hammers down on the Steeler practice field at St. Vincent College just outside Latrobe, a small town that boasts of Arnold Palmer as a resident and very little else. In the middle of the field Gilliam flees swiftly from an imaginary pass rush, sets up on dancing feet and flicks the ball on a line to a receiver 40 yards away. One flashing, coppery arrow of a pass and questions about his arm disappear. He, in the NFL vernacular, can zing it.

"The thing I like about him is his release; he gets it away very quickly," says Noll, a pleasant, bright man of 40. "He's much further advanced—reading defenses, finding primary receivers —than most young quarterbacks because they use a pro offense at Tennessee State." That potential is evident as another Gilliam pass, delivered with a wicked snap of the wrist, screams into the hands of a receiver only to leap free and ricochet to the ground. "He has the tools," Noll says.

A question hangs in my mind. Gilliam had sneered when I asked his reaction to being drafted in the 11th round. "I got over it," he had said. "I thought I was a winner. But I can play with any quarterback that graduated last year . . . any quarterback." So I ask Noll why the Steelers hesitated in choosing a passer who had thrown 65 touchdown passes in college, lost only one game in his last two years. "We didn't need a quarterback," he says, irritation on his square, agreeable face. "In the 11th round, he stood out like a sore thumb."

"Only two of our five scouts questioned whether he'd make it, and then only because they wondered if he could stand up under the punishment," says Art Rooney Jr., a Steeler vice president. "Hell, some people thought he was the best quarterback in the country."

In the dining hall following the morning workout, Gilliam eats sparingly. He is rail thin, 6-2 and 179 pounds. Already he has attracted the curiosity of the news media, come here to this sylvan glade hard by Arnie Palmer's farmhouse to see the latest Eldridge Dickey. Gilliam is well aware of his uniqueness. "Couldn't I just be a rookie quarterback instead of a black rookie quarterback?" he sighs after the day's fourth interview is arranged.

For all the mundane questions he has already formulated the pat answers which he hopes will hide his fears and feelings. "I've got a lot to learn, I'm hungry to be a pro quarterback; I can't change my color; I try not to think about it; Bradshaw is a fine leader." They drone on, his voice consciously pitched low and even as if to claim that here, reporter, is a little cool, a little self-assurance. I expect to hear that tone often in the days ahead. But, as I later discover, a natural gregariousness prevents Gilliam from bringing off that pose. He is too driven to self-expression to suffer his own sham, tolerate his own armor. For a few moments he maintains the mask, only to suddenly whirl about and confront me with fierce, flashing black eyes and questions without answers. "If I do get a raw deal, what can I do about it?" he demands in a voice that rises like smoke. "It won't come from the coaches, I know that." Realizing he has fingered his teammates as a possible subversive force, he lets prudence claim his passion. "The players don't have to accept me. . . . I hope they do," he says quietly.

In the first two weeks of camp, Gilliam knows both the agony and the ecstasy of rookiedom. He is fined $25 for missing a weigh-in when, incidentally or otherwise, his weight has dropped to 170.

In his first camp scrimmage, despite ignoring running plays and forcing many of his passes to receivers who are covered, he completes seven of 11, including a 59-yard touchdown pass that brings a low whistle of respect from his teammates. When he overthrows he beats his hands together, then catches himself, and it is almost possible to see his brain throw ice water on his heart. "I've got my hero," chortles the Steeler publicist as he rushes off to inform the wire services of Gilliam's success. But seven days later, his father and college coach on the sidelines, Gilliam's timing is erratic and in his second scrimmage he knows no success, completing only one of 11 passes.

"Young quarterbacks always throw a lot," Noll smiles later. "They make an impression quicker that way. He's looking fine. We gave him a big, fast dose of info to see if he would stagger under it and he didn't. We can't wait for young quarterbacks to develop in camp, but he is staying right there for the No. 2 job because he is keeping up. Sometimes he hurries his throws, makes up his mind too soon. When a quarterback comes up here, his accuracy is about as good as it'll ever get. What hurts him is indecision—who to throw to. Joe's learning that now."

A question I had been putting off demands an answer, so I

finally ask it: "Are the Steelers ready to accept a black quarter-back?"

"The color of his skin's got nothing to do with it," growls Noll, obviously insulted. "We're not doing any favors for anyone. The No. 2 job is open because there is competition for it now. Gilliam has a quicker arm than Hanratty and more potential than Leahy, if he can reach that potential. He's working like hell and so far he's stood out. He's got an opportunity to make the team."

Standing out becomes more difficult for Gilliam after he has bombed out in the scrimmage. His stomach is bothering him and he seems to get skinnier, bonier, day by day. "Gawd, he isn't as big around as one of Bradshaw's legs," a veteran laughs one afternoon during lunch.

Even Joe Gilliam Sr., in camp for a few days, is worried. "Joey's always been intense, even as a little child," says the father, assistant head coach at Tennessee State. "He always tries to follow a thing through to its conclusion, even if it's detrimental to him. His sophomore year, he was fighting for a regular position and struggling with himself so hard he wasn't playing well. As soon as he was assured the job was his, he changed overnight. We lost one game in two years after he got straightened out."

The Gilliams have lived a quiet, slightly nomadic life focused on an academic environment. Joe Sr., an articulate, compact six-footer, prides himself on being a teacher and his wife Ruth also teaches. But the Gilliams are among the first families of American sport. Joe Sr. was a fine all-around college athlete. His eldest son, Craig, had a tryout as a defensive back with the Steelers in 1967. Junior Gilliam, the former Los Angeles Dodger star and now a coach, is a distant cousin. As are John Gilliam, a brilliant wide receiver for Minnesota, and Herm Gilliam, an NBA player.

"Joey's pressing. . . . He's not eating," says the elder Gilliam. "He's been sick a major part of the day." Joe Sr. is confident his youngest son can make it as a pro and he is delighted the opportunity has come with the Steelers. "Joe and Noll have great rapport," he says. "Basically Noll is a teacher—I have 45 hours toward a doctorate in education and I know teachers. I don't think that overall pro management is ready for a black quarterback, but the Steelers are."

The son is not certain he is ready for the Steelers several nights later. He is thinking about Saturday's intrasquad game, and the major squad cut that will follow it.

"I think I'm still holding my own," he says softly, studying a milk shake, one of the many he is supposed to drink each week as part of a weight-gaining regimen. Often his speech—soft, clipped and generally articulate—leaves an inescapable impression of melodramatics. A studied effect. Pseudo-cool. He strokes a wispy goatee which fails to rob his lean face of the strength brought to it by the burning eyes, a Romanesque nose and a cocky, challenging tilt of the head. In toto, he looks like a young riverboat rake.

"I'm learning, oh, so much," he says, quietly but knowingly parading his dedication. But, as it always does, the pose quickly disappears, and for the very first time Joe Gilliam allows a degree of uncertainty to spill into his voice.

"I'm going pretty good . . . I guess," he says, as pensive as a poet at a secluded pond. "You have good days and bad days. I think I'm holding my own. It was heavy at first, the volume, so much to learn." So much to learn: Don't drill it, don't loft it. . . . "A full pivot on that hand-off, Joe." . . . On the AQ pattern, always look for the tight end first. . . . Is that a reverse zone? . . . "Follow through on the pitch, Joe." So much to learn. I think of Steeler quarterback coach Babe Parilli huddling with Gilliam that afternoon and later saying, "He's got a long way to go, but so did Bradshaw when he came here." And Noll admitting, "We may be forced into a decision by the time factor, before any decision is clear-cut."

Later that night Gilliam pores over the old Steeler game films that almost consume him. Down the hall two Steeler quarterbacks are sleeping, a third is playing poker. Gilliam's eyes are red-rimmed. "I want to be prepared as well as it is possible to be prepared," he says, yawning. "You study a defensive back. How does he play the game? Does he come up quick on the sweep? What will he do under such-and-such conditions? What about underneath coverage—where are their linebackers going to be? You look at film from our practices. What could I have done to get the ball there—step up, quicker release? When an idea comes to me, I've got to see about it right then, no matter what time it is. Now, not later. Learning. That's what being a pro quarterback is all about."

When Gilliam enters the intrasquad contest between the offense and the defense, he completes a 49-yard pass on his very first play. But obviously nervous, he then overthrows three straight times, the last one a bullet that goes five feet over the head of a receiver wide-open in the end zone. Still he finishes eight-for-15, moves the offense, and outshines the competition.

The Turk, that mythical figure of gloom who notifies the players they've been dropped from the roster, stalks the dorm the following night. He does not visit Gilliam, who was listening for his footsteps. "Man, I'm glad I'm going," sighs a relieved rookie. "A guy has to be crazy to live with the pressure." Gilliam, agrees: "You can feel it." But he is an uneasy survivor. "My passing wasn't on," he moans about the most recent scrimmage. "When I missed that one in the end zone I was mad, screaming mad. Hell, if I would've gotten it down, I still threw the thing so damn hard he wouldn't have caught it. I was pressing."

He is pressing a week later as Leahy, replacing an injured Bradshaw in the second quarter, surgically guides the Steelers to a 22–3 dissection of the Giants in their exhibition opener. Noll has decided Gilliam's debut will come the following Saturday in Seattle against the New York Jets.

"I wanted to play, badly," Gilliam says in a Seattle hotel room less than 24 hours before his NFL baptism. He knows the questions about his future remain unanswered. If he is a prospect, he is also a suspect. His passing has been both impressive and imprudent, his play selection undisciplined, his ballhandling adequate but inartistic, his ability to survive physically debatable. For all of his work, and for all of the Steelers' thinly disguised eagerness to make his trial impeccably fair, Joe Gilliam is an unknown quantity. And on this night again his intrinsic honesty destroys his attempt to cloak himself in protective rhetoric.

"I'm not having any difficulties; I'm ready," he says. No difficulties. Other than fear and uncertainty. "Yeah, I have doubts," he admits. "Not about my abilities, about my future. I feel a lot of things I can't explain. Nothing detrimental to anyone. Bad vibrations. I wonder if I can truly be accepted."

"You having trouble, a racial thing?" I ask him.

"I feel I can deal with complex personalities, but I don't think that me being a black quarterback will ever leave anyone's mind. And that's what I am. A black quarterback."

"Are you getting a fair shake here?"

"I can't evaluate that because it's not over yet. I don't think the players feel I'm a novelty now, and that's a good feeling. I can instill confidence in these guys, and I know they have confidence in me. But I have to have the good games. This is my first one. I'm excited, scared, a little anxious. I *like* to do well. . . . I *hope* I do well. . . . I *think* I can."

But liking, thinking, hoping don't get it done, and after the Steelers score on passes by Bradshaw on the first three plays and go on to zap the Jets, 22–3, the jury is still out on Joe Gilliam. Playing the second half, he has good moments. Despite two completions nullified by penalties, he is six-for-16 for 66 yards. Fumbling on his first series, he recovers to handle the ball well. He sets up quickly in the pocket and stands rooted against a Jet blitz that puts marks on him. But there are not-so-good moments. He is called for intentional grounding and, forcing the ball to covered receivers, he is intercepted once. In eight series, he does not once move the Steelers with consistency. It is an inconclusive test and when it is over he crosses the hall to talk briefly with the quarterback he most admires, Joe Namath, perhaps looking for encouragement, which Namath gives him.

As the Steeler charter slips silently through the night sky enroute to Pittsburgh, Gilliam is animated. "I wasn't too nervous," he begins, but he is snatched by his omnipresent conscious. "The truth of the matter is I was too anxious to prove myself. But, yeah, I think I can play. I always knew what coverage they were in. If there was a good thing about the game, it was my reading. I could've been better. Next time I will."

At the front of the airplane, Noll is understanding of a rookie's nervousness, his inadequacies. "He settled down and threw well," Noll says. "The thing I liked was that he knew what the hell was going on out there. That's a good sign for a young quarterback. He needs more work and he'll get it."

But the time for a rookie's opportunity to prove himself is rapidly disappearing and Noll has other concerns. Bradshaw reinjures his knee slightly the following week in a 31–17 romp over Atlanta and Hanratty plays excellently, increasing the pressure on Gilliam and Leahy. "Bradshaw needs more work to get ready and he gets priority," Noll says. "We'll probably get to the final exhibition game before we decide about our quarterbacks."

Parilli, who will have a voice in the decision, is blunt but encouraging. "Gilliam is a prospect, but I don't think he is ready to be a No. 2 quarterback yet. There is a lot to learn."

So Gilliam waits and learns and wonders. "I used to think about what I would do if I had to go home," he says, with Noll's decision only days away. "Now I don't think about it. I can perform as well as anyone if I know what to do. And I'm learning that. I think that I can make this team."

Six days, one short burst of excellence and two missteps by Leahy later, he does make the team. In the lone series he played against Baltimore in Tampa, Gilliam "put it all together." For the first time he seemed self-assured and exuded that air of majesty that successful quarterbacks almost always have, and he coolly guided the Steelers 80 yards in nine plays for their only touchdown in a 16–13 loss. Eluding Colt linemen by thrusting himself forward into the pocket and throwing point blank over the shoulder of a rampaging Bubba Smith, Gilliam fired a 49-yard strike that buried itself in the midriff of tight end Larry Brown at the Baltimore 16. After completing his third straight pass of the drive, Gilliam skipped lightly around the right side on a nine-yard bootleg to score.

But it wasn't just Gilliam's success that assured him of a place on the team. It was also Leahy's failure in a key situation. Quarterbacking the Steelers late in the game, Leahy threw two intercepted passes, which handed Baltimore a final-second win.

Leahy was put on the waiver list. And that meant Gilliam had, at worst, a berth on the taxi squad. No unemployment lines for Gilliam this season.

"I was confident I could move the team," Gilliam said later. "Maybe it's the universal feeling all quarterbacks have. We have our aces and we believe. Maybe that's not all of the battle, but it sure is part of it."

The first trial of a black rookie quarterback, seeking success where there had been little but failure, was over.

POSTSCRIPT

Quarterbacks Are Overrated

By Fran Tarkenton

At the end of the 1974 Super Bowl game, while I sat in front of my locker and nursed a cut on the back of my hand, a major injury by my standards, reporters kept trying to get me to say, in effect, that the defeat was the worst thing that had ever happened to me in my life. I wouldn't. I refused to accept the idea that a defeat in a football game was a crippling psychological blow—and I refused to accept the implication that the quarterback had to take most of the blame for the defeat.

Not that I didn't do my share. I did. But a quarterback's share in defeat, or in victory, isn't quite the gigantic thing some reporters seem to think it is. I told the press then that the quarterback isn't all-important, that he can't by himself make the difference between victory and defeat, that if he were so important, Joe Namath would never lose a game.

I meant what I said in Houston, and I mean it now. Quarterbacks aren't gods, not even with a small g. They aren't as important now as they were a decade or two ago, and in the future, they'll probably be even less important. The game keeps getting more complex, in the sense that coaches keep discovering new techniques and new responsibilities for each position. Once a coach figured that if his quarterback was well prepared, his team was well prepared, but that's not true any longer. An offensive guard has a variety of blocking responsibilities; if he forgets those responsibilities, or mishandles them, he can play a major part in offensive failure. An outside linebacker has a variety of coverage responsibilities; if he forgets, or fails to perform, he can play a major part in defensive failure.

The key to the 1974 Super Bowl was not any quarterback wizardry—Bob Griese played very well, but he was hardly the dominant force even in his offense—but *defensive theory,* the Miami defensive theory developed, I presume, by Bill Arnsparger, their defensive coordinator. They didn't stop men; they stopped penetration. They were willing to give us the line of scrimmage every play, and maybe even an extra yard or two. But they wouldn't give us good gains; they wouldn't give us the kind of yardage that would enable us to open up our offense and endanger their defense. Bill Arnsparger, I suspect, had a lot more to do with the outcome of Super Bowl VIII than I did, or than Bob Griese did.

Still, it's very unlikely that anyone in the near future will put together a collection of stories about defensive coordinators. The stories probably wouldn't even fill a leaflet.

For a while, at least, I guess quarterbacks are going to remain the glamour players of professional football, the ones who get the most money, the most publicity, the most credit and the most blame. I'm not complaining. As a matter of fact, I'm happy to be included here among the overrated; it certainly beats the opposite extreme.

ABOUT THE AUTHOR

Dick Schaap is younger than Johnny Unitas, slimmer than Sonny Jurgensen, taller than Fran Tarkenton and has better knees than Joe Namath. But, somehow, very few people are surprised that instead of playing quarterback in the National Football League, he has been senior editor of *Newsweek*, city editor of *The New York Herald Tribune*, a syndicated newspaper columnist and the author of more than a dozen books and several hundred magazine articles. He is currently a sportscaster for WNBC-TV, the editor of *Sport* magazine and, with his wife, Madeleine, and their two children, a resident of New York City.

PLAYBOY'S INVESTMENT GUIDE
Michael Laurence
Written by *Playboy*'s award-winning business and finance editor, this is the widely acclaimed guidebook to stock and bond markets, mutual funds, commodities and collector's items—every area where adventurous investors can reasonably expect profits.
$1.50

INSTANT MILLIONAIRES
Max Gunther
Exciting and provocative stories of 36 business geniuses who wanted to get rich quick—and succeeded. Plus 14 "uninvented inventions" that can lead to a fast fortune.
$1.50

CHIODO—UNDERCOVER COP
Charles Whited
The extraordinary but true story of a New York City undercover cop—more revealing than *Serpico* and more explosive than *Super Cops*.
$1.50

KEN PURDY'S BOOK OF AUTOMOBILES
The number-one book on cars and drivers by the number-one writer on motoring.
$1.95

HOW TO TALK DIRTY AND INFLUENCE PEOPLE
Lenny Bruce
The controversial comedian's own story, told in the style that made him famous.
$1.50

THE SUPER CROOKS
Roger M. Williams, ed.
The most flamboyant and clever hustlers, swindlers and thieves of England and America are captured here, including Moll Cutpurse, John Dillinger, Jesse James, Billie Sol Estes, the Brinks Robbers and Britain's Great Train Robbers.
$1.50

Order directly from:

Playboy Press
The Playboy Building
919 North Michigan Avenue
Chicago, Illinois 60611

No. of copies	Title	Price
_____ C16259	How I Would Pitch to Babe Ruth	$1.50
_____ B16222	Super Detective	$1.25
_____ C16188	Men of Courage	$1.50
_____ C16246	Solo	$1.50
_____ C16233	Great Courtroom Battles	$1.50
_____ C16254	Playboy's Investment Guide	$1.50
_____ C16243	Instant Millionaires	$1.50
_____ C16235	Chiodo—Undercover Cop	$1.50
_____ E16216	Ken Purdy's Book of Automobiles	$1.95
_____ C16241	How to Talk Dirty and Influence People	$1.50
_____ C16242	The Super Crooks	$1.50

Please enclose 50¢ for postage and handling.

Total amount enclosed: $

Name _____

Address _____

City _____ State _____ Zip _____